AF321596

witness

Jurgen Schadeberg

witness

52 years of Pointing Lenses at Life

Witness – 52 Years of Pointing Lenses at Life

Jurgen Schadeberg
First edition, first impression 2004

Protea Book House
PO Box 35110, Menlo Park, 0102
1067 Burnett Street, Hatfield, 0083
protea@intekom.co.za

Typography and design by PrePress Images
Cover page by PrePress
Reproduction by PrePress Images
Printed and bound by ABC Press

ISBN 1-86919-067-X

This book is dedicated to Claudia, my wife and partner,
who continuously encourages me in my work.

A special thanks to Nicol Stassen of Protea Book House for making this book possible;
Andrew Meintjies for producing outstanding scans from my photos;
Gabriel Muj for invaluable assistance in all aspects of the book.

THE INVISIBLE PRESENCE

WHEN A YOUNG, NAIVELY CONFIDENT Jurgen Schadeberg first arrived at *The Star* news offices in Johannesburg with a Leica strung over his shoulder, he was informed by the paper's chief photographer that he wouldn't last long in the industry with such a tiny camera. Never before was the voice of professional prophecy proven so wrong.

In a career spanning over half a century, Schadeberg has come to represent much more than the prototype of the visual storyteller. He epitomises the very best in photojournalism – a photographer with an uncanny sense of timing – momentarily and historically. He possesses an instinctive, idiosyncratic way of seeing, coupled with a rigorous sense of organisation. These attributes are combined with an astute insight into the human condition. He occupies nothing less than legendary status among contemporary photojournalists.

In many respects the twentieth century was the time of the photojournalist. It is through the eyes of the visual storyteller that the impact of the century was most profoundly felt. It is, after all, the visual storyteller who, with the help of the 35 mm camera, went beyond "the decisive moment", illuminating the lives of the century's horrors and hopes.

A lexicon of legendary photojournalists will include Alfred Eisenstadt. As a news photographer in Berlin in the late 1920s Eisenstadt instinctively understood that with a new small camera invented by Dr Erich Salomon, the Ermanox, it would be possible to work unobtrusively, recording people as they really are.

Then of course there was Henri Cartier-Bresson. This French-born photographer coined the phrase "the decisive moment" – the recognition, in a fraction of a second, of the significance of an event as well as the precise organisation of forms which gives that event its proper expression.

And there is Jurgen Schadeberg.

He was born in 1931, in Berlin. In that year the 22-year-old Cartier-Bresson purchased a Leica, discovering a new kind of seeing, spontaneous and unpredictable, through the 35 mm viewfinder.

For Schadeberg, the 35 mm camera was also to become an "extension of the eye".

After leaving school at the age of 15, he trained as a photographer in Berlin before becoming apprenticed to a German Press Agency in Hamburg. By then, the 35 mm camera had begun to revolutionise documentary photography. It was small, handy and mobile, offering the photojournalist an unprecedented opportunity to poetically register the moment. This "art of the snapshot" also heralded a burgeoning culture of illustrated magazines such as *Life*, *Picture Post* and *Paris Match*.

When the Nazis came to power, progressive picture editors and photographers left Germany en masse. Many went to London, Paris and New York, nurturing a new generation of photo-journalistic excellence. For Schadeberg, Nazism was a mental, creative nightmare. He longed for personal liberation, but after the Second World War it was not easy to leave Germany. Fortunately a friend organised him a permit for South Africa.

In 1950 he arrived in Johannesburg.

Besides lagging behind the rest of the world in photography, South Africa had no professionally recognised black photographers. The title of "press photographer" was yet another exclusively white domain. Black professionals were merely "street photographers".

Schadeberg joined *Drum* magazine's staff of three as a freelance photographer in 1951, aged 20. Although he was never formally appointed a full-time post, he soon became chief photographer, picture editor and art director. At the time *Drum* modeled itself on publications such as *Life* and *Picture Post*, attempting to document, expose and entertain its predominantly black readership through pictures and writing.

As *Drum* grew into Africa's leading lifestyle magazine during the 1950s and early 1960s, Schadeberg's role included building up a photographic department of black photographers. To this end he cast his eye on young 17-year-old switchboard operator Bob Gosani and started training him in cutting negatives and doing "mug shots". Eighteen months later, Gosani was already acquiring legendary status. Schadeberg's tutelage helped nurture a new generation of outstanding South African photographers, some of whom acquired world-class status, including the late Ernest Cole and Peter Magubane.

He worked closely with literary icons such as Henry Nxumalo – subsequently dubbed *Mr Drum* due to his acerbic social insights and lyrical prose. Nat Nakasa was also a close colleague, as was Bloke Modisane. Even today, Schadeberg's mental database brims over with anecdotes of navigating the gauntlet of Homburg-hatted apartheid bureaucrats together with his intrepid black colleagues.

He was once on assignment at the Department of Home Affairs with Nxumalo. Although Nxumalo was the journalist firing the questions, the minister in question directed his answers to Schadeberg. In the halcyon era of "baasskap", responding to a "bantu" or addressing him in anything but the third person was deemed politically incorrect.

Schadeberg's photographic contribution and opposition to one of the most oppressive periods in South African history is well documented. His fearless images recorded vibrant, urban, black culture of the 1950s and its growing resistance to racial discrimination and apartheid laws. His themes evoked powerful parallels to the African-American experience. This affirmation of black experience threatened the apartheid regime. In fact, the bookends of his career have bracketed both apartheid and early post-apartheid South Africa.

He photographed the new generation of ANC leaders, among them a young Nelson Mandela several years before his incarceration for treason. Schadeberg's iconic images of forced removals, particularly the destruction of Sophiatown, are still regarded as among the most definitive documents of the effects of apartheid on South Africa's majority.

But his photographs of that period are principally images of affirmation and celebration: they capture the vitality of a community that was optimistic of a new day dawning. And by affirming their humanity as survivors rather than victims, Schadeberg achieved a denunciation of oppression that made his work more subversive than graphic images of violence and horror. In this respect he encapsulates the eloquent observation of Roland Barthes that "ultimately photography is subversive, not only when it frightens, repels or even stigmatizes, but when it is pensive".

The pensive elements were not always overt in Schadeberg's *Drum* photos. But their subversion of the black stereotype made them antithetical to apartheid's apologists. His documents of a separate world of suburbia occupied by affluent white South Africans were free of shock or schlock elements. They were images of ordinariness that served effectively to highlight the chasm between South Africa's black and white communities. The latter were clearly oblivious to or dismissive of the cultural and intellectual vitality of South Africa's oppressed majority.

Particularly memorable are his sessions with jazz musicians such as Kippie Moeketsi, Vi Nkosi and the Harlem Swingsters, to mention but a smattering of the formidable talent blossoming in the townships. He photographed them in dingy and dilapidated makeshift dancehalls in Sophiatown, the Bantu Men's Social Centre and in the industrial areas on the outskirts of Johannesburg. With spats and their Florsheims, their sharp threads and swanky hairdos, many of these musicians modelled their images on American counterparts, emulating icons like Sammy Davis Jr. Many bought into the myth that America truly was the land of racial freedom. And American jazz seemed to say it most eloquently.

Having taken an interest, in his youth, in the American New Orleans jazz scene with the likes of Louis Armstrong and Charlie Parker, Schadeberg found township jazz invigorating. In South Africa the American jazz sound was adapted and africanised giving it a unique South African township flavour. Much of the music driving the fifties became a form of defiance, a means of survival and a symbol of freedom.

"In those days we saw apartheid as an absurdity promulgated by a bunch of buffoons," recalls Schadeberg. "Draconian racist laws were already being introduced but were not yet being enforced with the religious fervor of the Verwoerd era. We all felt that liberation was round the corner. After all, this was the era of decolonisation and stories reflected this. They incorporated a sort of gallows humour with an unadulterated sense of irreverence."

Consequently the German-born photographer was frequently the victim of police harassment. "The pay was low, the risks were great, but I did it in the belief that it was worth it because I was capturing an essential slice of history," he recalls. But South Africa's schizophrenic society brought back the nightmare recollections of Nazi Germany. In 1965 *Drum* was banned. The previous year Schadeberg moved to London where he edited *Camera Owner* which became *Creative Camera*, and taught photography and filmmaking at the Central School of Art & Design. He also worked as a photojournalist for the *London Weekend Telegraph Magazine*. Milestone photographic projects co-ordinated by Schadeberg during this time included "The Quality of Life" exhibition in London – a group show resulting from a community project Schadeberg initiated for his students. Another exhibition resulted from a project documenting the old Jewish quarter of London's Whitechapel district.

During the sixties and seventies he freelanced as a photojournalist for various prestigious magazines in Europe and America. He also taught photography at the New School in New York, and the Hoch Kunst Schule in Hamburg. His imagery during this era encapsulates the cultural vibrancy of Europe: from the swinging sixties and seventies to the affluent 1980s. He photographed with equal alacrity celebrities and small-town communities and exhibited across Europe and America.

He studied painting in Spain to "understand colour, and to say something else about the world". His tutor was Joe Baumgarten, a Hungarian Jew who had learnt to paint in Paris during the era of the Cubists and Picasso.

In 1984 he returned to South Africa for a visit and to retrieve the vast number of negatives from *Drum* magazine lying neglected in the Bailey barn on his farm. It was a volatile time – detention without trial, torture and death had become the mainstay of South African society. Yet, simultaneously, secret talks were being held with exiled and imprisoned leaders. The final death rattles of apartheid were clearly audible.

Schadeberg decided to remain in South Africa with his filmmaker wife Claudia. He held several retrospective exhibitions and immersed himself in making documentaries about the 1950s, 1960s and the vibrant South African urban cultural history. In 1994 Schadeberg again photographed Mandela, this time as a free man gazing through the bars of his former cell on Robben Island.

Today Schadeberg is regarded as a principal figure in world photography. He is widely dubbed the Alfred Eisenstadt of South Africa. The amount of work he has produced throughout his lifetime – and continues to produce – is prodigious. His photography is constantly being rediscovered through cover stories, scores of exhibitions, books, films and a collection of some 100 000 negatives.

His pictures and pictorial essays have been published in most of the world's major magazines for over five decades. His work captures a wealth of timeless and iconic images, exercising a profound and far-reaching influence. He has the ability to eloquently articulate and translate visual theory into practice. Schadeberg's work still succeeds largely in telling it like it is, even in an era in which the image has become increasingly mediated and deconstructed. As far as possible he remains an invisible presence and lets the image talk for itself. He has immense respect for the discipline of press photography, of communicating a story crisply in one striking picture. His work is kept memorable through a journalistic grappling with the realities of people and events, his sense of news and history, and his belief in the social role of photography. Fifty-two years after embarking on his extraordinary photographic journey Schadeberg's invisible presence has become indelible.

Hazel Friedman
Cape Town, 2003

LIFE'S LITTLE LEITMOTIFS

EACH HUMAN EXPERIENCE has the potential to become a leitmotif – a melody, or a movement that remains long after the moment has lapsed. In many respects Schadeberg's photography is precisely that – a collection of leitmotifs. They are pockets of human experience: complete within themselves, yet pregnant with universal meaning and suggestion. His world of images is one where banalities – a reflection in a mud-puddle; graffiti on a wall; the slant of a silhouette against the mist – radiate significance at once familiar and "other". In a sense his aesthetic is an anti-romantic poetry of vision. It finds beauty in things as they truly are: in the reality of here and now. It is a beauty that might otherwise be overlooked with the blink of an unobservant eye.

Like Eisenstadt, Schadeberg displays the curiosity of a child. He never stops being amazed and delighted by observing and photographing the people around him.

Unlike the diminutive Eisenstadt – the undisputed master of "absent presence" – Schadeberg is not a physically unobtrusive figure. Elegantly handsome, his presence is striking. And his acerbic, droll sense of humour, punctuated by high-pitched, idiosyncratic guffaws of laughter, is impossible to ignore. Yet he has the uncanny ability to appear absent when photographing his subjects, much like an invisible presence evoking honesty, dignity and respect without intrusion.

When the gaze of his subjects directly meets the lens, as in "Spanish ladies in bar, Mijas" (1971), it is with an unselfconsciousness borne of ease and trust. The "Spanish men in bar, Mijas" (1971) evokes a similarly unselfconscious dignity amid the revelry. The "Lovers in London pub" (1982) are clearly oblivious to the lens. As is the case in "Gamblers in a smoky corner in Sophiatown" (1955). Here Schadeberg effectively evokes the gritty realism of the streets while bathing the characters in an almost incandescent glow. As with "A Glasgow pub" (1968), his subjects are sometimes reminiscent of paintings by Cézanne in the way that light and shadow frame their forms.

Despite the dramatic lighting in these images, the photographer has become the proverbial invisible presence. Although the subjects are depicted up close and personal, unlike celebrity photographer Helmut Newton, Schadeberg remains deliberately aloof from his visual leitmotifs. He is unambiguously out of the picture. A woman is caught stealing a glance at her reflection in a shop doorway in "Shopping in Covent Garden" (1978). A couple of well-heeled mothers prepare a picnic lunch on the bonnet of their convertible in "Picnic at Eaton College, England" (1981). Schadeberg has the knack of framing tableaux of elegance and ordinariness with humorous ease, and has a detached yet empathetic eye. In other images, such as "Lesotho tribesmen" (1961) and "The end of the line, London Docks" (1974), a wide-angle lens is utilised to reinforce the distance between cameraman and subject, thereby broadening and shifting the narrative before him.

"To document effectively, one has to be an outsider," he explains. "This inevitably affects one's personality. Responses become internalised, introverted. One becomes used to standing back."

Schadeberg refuses to manipulate a scene to make a point: visually, emotionally or ideologically. Some of his most evocative works are those in which he has simply gone with the momentary flow. Such is the case with his seminal series of images of the San in the throes of their trance dances (1959). The shamanistic evocations of these mystical rituals are enhanced by their grainy, slightly blurred outlines. His subjects were obviously not standing still. He would never have dreamed of requesting them to strike a pose, hence the ethereality of the series and ultimately its resonance. "Sometimes a situation arises where one is unconsciously involved with the moment both emotionally and visually, as with the images of the San. In such moments the technical challenges somehow solve themselves."

Although Schadeberg has never shied away from confrontational scenes, he does not engage in graphic records of overt violence. Like David Goldblatt, he is possessed of a "thinking" eye, rather than a "shooting from the hip" approach. But, whereas Goldblatt engages in "geological probes" – to quote artist Neville Dubow's eloquent essay on the veteran photographer – Schadeberg specialises in traversing vast human social-cultural landscapes. Ultimately he is a traveller, both literally and metaphorically, passing through multiple worlds without scraping sides.

He shies away from terms like "document", for that implies "an ownership of sorts". He also avoids the hunting, predatory terminology associated with photography like "shoot". For him the camera is neither a weapon nor an instrument of struggle. It is a tool of representation. "I'm trying to present a scene or a moment," he emphasises, "not capture it."

As in the case of the San trance dance series, Schadeberg sometimes subordinates technical concerns to the interests of narrative or nuance. But first and foremost he is a formalist – a technical perfectionist.

"Of course photography is about seeing, but it's about much more. It entails understanding the light and controlling it. It's also about controlling space and time. First, the eye decides the image, the composition and the space containing it. Second, is the decision when to release the shutter.

"Constant repetition is required in order to master the commands that need to be given to your body to make it operate automatically." He adds: "The eye decides, like the fingers when playing an instrument. You speed yourself up and slow yourself down in accordance with what takes place around you. It's about attuning oneself to the magic of the moment." He cautions that precision training means being aware of that moment in time: being able to control oneself to find the right movement within the moment.

For Schadeberg, the power of an image lies in both its sense of timelessness and the specifics of its history. This is partly why his photographs of the Sophiatown demolitions and forced removals (1959–1960) still resound with iconic force. He was commissioned to do the pictures by a London agency. After submitting four rolls of film, he received a lengthy letter detailing all the visual blunders he had made, accompanied by a polite rejection of his work. Today there are few images that encapsulate in quite such epic vocabulary the iniquities of apartheid and its consequences.

The power of these images also lies in the sense of familiarity they evoke of a not so distant past, and in their unsentimental depiction of suffering. They lay down routes of reference, even serving as totems of socio-political causes. They help construct – and revise – our sense of the past.

In a sense these works touch on the ongoing significance of the photograph in an era suffering from television and cinematic image-overload. Photographs that permit one to linger over a single image still impact more than violence on television and in movies. The still image is more direct and thus more powerful.

"Memory freeze-frames; its basic unit is the single image," writes Susan Sontag in her recent book *Regarding the pain of others*. "We tend to believe that photographs have a more innocent and accurate relationship with reality. They furnish concrete evidence, a way of verifying that such and such actually did happen. We rarely question what we are seeing."

What Sontag underscores is the apparent, yet arbitrary, truthfulness of the photographed image. Those photographs that everyone recognise have become a constituent part of what society chooses to think about, suggests Sontag. Society calls these ideas "memories". But strictly speaking, while there might exist such a concept as "collective instruction", the notion of collective memory is, to all intents and purposes, a fiction. What is called collective memory, Sontag says, is not a remembering but a stipulating that this is important, and that this is the story about how it happened. It is ultimately the pictures that lock the story in our minds. And this forms part of a collective instruction.

In this society comprised principally of consumers and spectators, the photographed image tends to mediate our experience of the real. It can become more real than the first-hand experience of reality itself. Paradoxically, an event known through photographs becomes less real after repeated exposure. Images create and simultaneously shrivel sympathy. This augments the arbitrariness of their status as "truth tellers". An excess of mediated realism tends to blur the spectator's visceral responses to the moment represented by the image.

In certain hands the camera can deaden conscience because it implies that we know about the world if we accept it as the camera records it. But as Sontag observes in *On Photography*, this is the opposite of understanding, which starts from not accepting the world the way it looks. Yet the photograph does not preclude the emotional experience of witnessing a moment of extreme joy or suffering. Nor are the photographer and the tool of representation conscienceless, amoral witnesses to the endless pantheon of suffering through history. There can be no real neutrality in observation. And Schadeberg is all too aware of the paradoxical role of the photojournalist – as visual storyteller and witness.

He embraces the surrealism of the causal relationship between a photographer, a subject and the camera. According to Sontag: "What renders a photograph surreal is its refutation of pathos as a message from time past, and the concreteness of its intimations about social class." Or, put somewhat differently: "What is surreal is the distance imposed, and bridged, by the photograph: the social distance and the distance of time."

And as Schadeberg acknowledges, we are all voyeurs whether we like or not. Photography serves to illuminate the life of each of us, albeit privately. Photographs preserve, however tenuously, the mark of individual experience in the undifferentiated mass of victims and heroes.

If there is a recurring refrain in his 52 years of photojournalism, it is in his ability to individualise experience, crystallising moments – both significant and insignificant – through sharp, clear images and an idiosyncratic way of seeing.

This is evident in the way that Schadeberg has positioned his images in the book, allowing for parallel readings. He arranges them two per page, not in terms of chronology, nor necessarily content, but in terms of mood, structure and composition. On the page they become universal vignettes. Although they are clearly rooted in the specifics of time, place and culture, there appears to be a blurring of spatial and temporal boundaries between the images. "Ditchworkers, Johannesburg" (1951) is placed adjacent to "Street cleaner, Glasgow" (1968), suggesting an unavoidable interface between the subjects. The toreador photographed during a Spanish village festival in 1971 is juxtaposed against a stylised image of Nathan "Dam-Dam" Mdledle in 1951. The contextual differences are self-evident, as are the ways in which each has been shot: exterior versus interior, natural light versus tungsten. Yet both images convey a similar sense of the theatrical.

His "Mannequins, London" (1972) also provide – possibly inadvertently – a quirky commentary on the adjacent "Disco lady, London" (1980). The latter was photographed, with her cavernous cleavage and a camera perched in her hand, while Schadeberg was snapping celebrities at a London club. She strikes a pose – mannequin-style – as shafts from the strobe light overhead appear to pass through her form. Yet the mannered pose is completely spontaneous. It exudes an unselfconsciousness that is the hallmark of much of Schadeberg's work.

Yet his narrative and technical style have shifted subtly over the decades. During his time at *Drum* the pictures had to be simple in design, clear and sharply lit. They were printed on coarse screens due to the worldwide shortage of newsprint. The tabloid press at SAAN was purchased second-hand from India.

The portraits "Piano fingers" (1952) and "Priscilla Mtimkulu" (1954), or "Dolly Rathebe, South African jazz and blues queen" (1952) suitably illustrate the techniques Schadeberg was employing during that time. Similarly "Measuring up for *Drum* cover, Johannesburg" (1955) demonstrates the stylised theatricality of the studio picture in the 1950s. In later works his composition is less controlled, his lighting softer and more diffuse. The 1968 Glasgow pictures, for example, are subtle, relying not on artificial highlights and shadows but on the soft, ambiguous, ephemeral light of nature. However, though his work in later years becomes more complex, the form and structure continues to be built from a simple grammar.

Many of these images inevitably beg the question as to how Schadeberg has positioned himself in relation to his subject or story, and the factors influencing his decisions to frame an event or scene in a certain way. The background to one of his most emotive series of inner-city portraits might provide some illumination. Schadeberg was commissioned by the *London Telegraph* to do a story on the childhood of an alleged murderer who was on the run after killing two policemen. The suspect had been born and raised in Gorbals, a crumbling neighbourhood in Glasgow, characterised by dilapidated tenement flats, potholed streets and other relics of urban decay.

Schadeberg's research revealed an achingly lonely, neglected youth spent navigating a gauntlet of gangs, drugs and domestic abuse. The resulting images, although generic in intention, provide a haunting insight into this ethos. They are much more than illustrations to a narrative. They become the narrative, telling a story not only of one man's descent into crime but of a city's deterioration. Most cities have their "Gorbals" – areas which were once respectable but, with industrial and population growth and the passage of time, have become cesspools of crime and grime.

In a way then, it is fitting that the most recent works in this collection are those taken of the community in Kliptown – the place where the ANC's historic Freedom Charter was signed in 1955.

Established in 1903, Kliptown is the oldest urban settlement in the Johannesburg area to accommodate people of all races. But, despite its distinguished political history, the town has suffered years of neglect and most of its historical buildings are dilapidated. There is no water-borne sewerage and some houses still use the bucket system. Despite the fact that it remains a community born of deprivation and neglect, poverty and unemployment, Kliptown exudes an inextinguishable energy. A thriving informal business sector exists among the sprawling collection of settlements.

In 2002 the Gauteng Provincial Government and City Of Johannesburg jointly committed themselves to providing more than R375 million towards the renovation of Kliptown. Schadeberg has been commissioned to photograph the community before the old edifices are torn down. He has been traveling there daily, doing what he does best: providing glimpses into the daily lives of the community as they perform daily chores, hang out on street corners, or congregate near the old bioscope.

In the gritty realism of a woman hanging her washing and the derelict walls of the cinema steeped in history, Schadeberg is not trying to show ugliness or beauty … just some of life's little leitmotifs, unadorned and unaltered.

Hazel Friedman
Cape Town, 2003

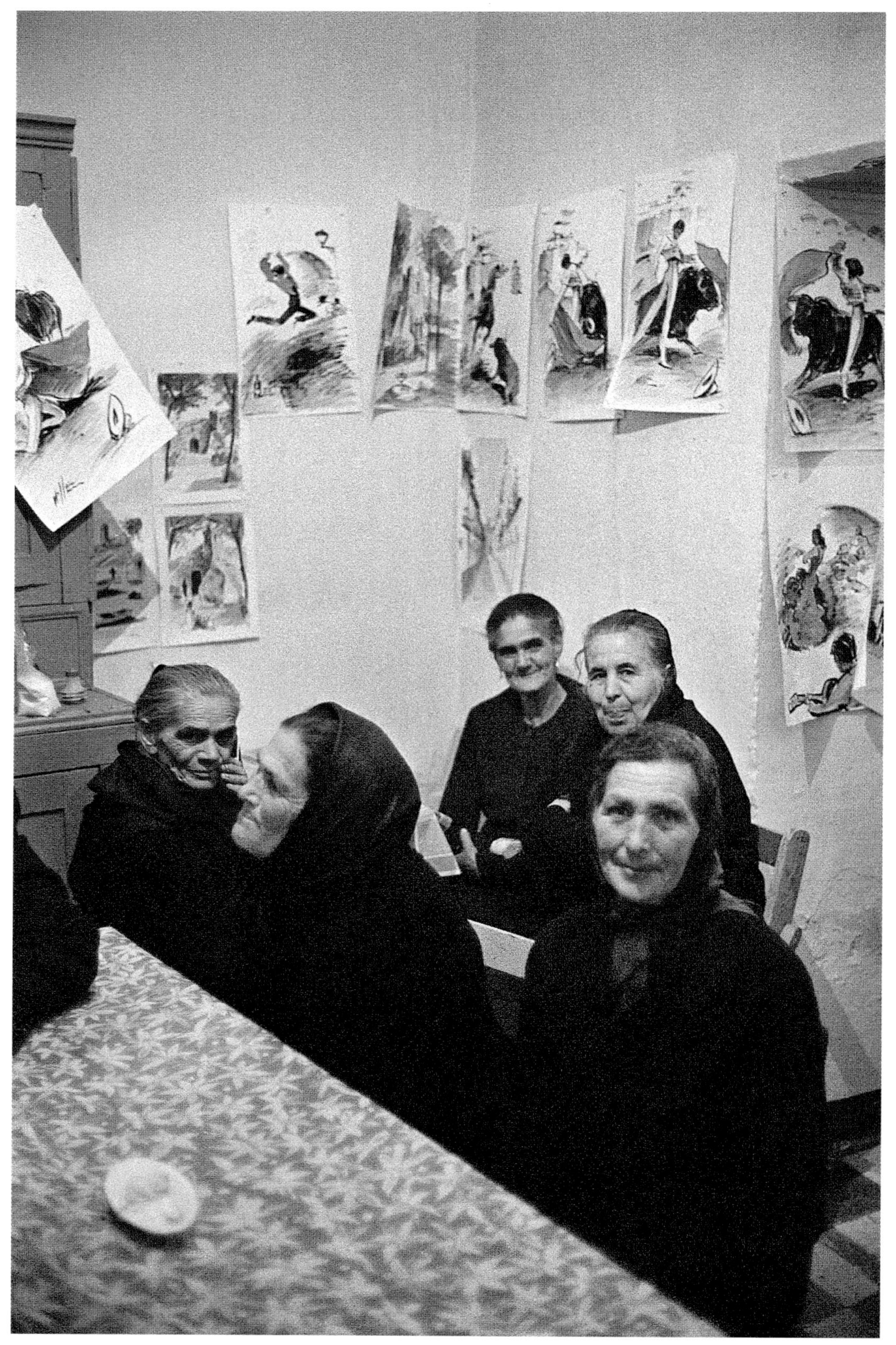

   SPANISH LADIES IN BAR, MIJAS 1971

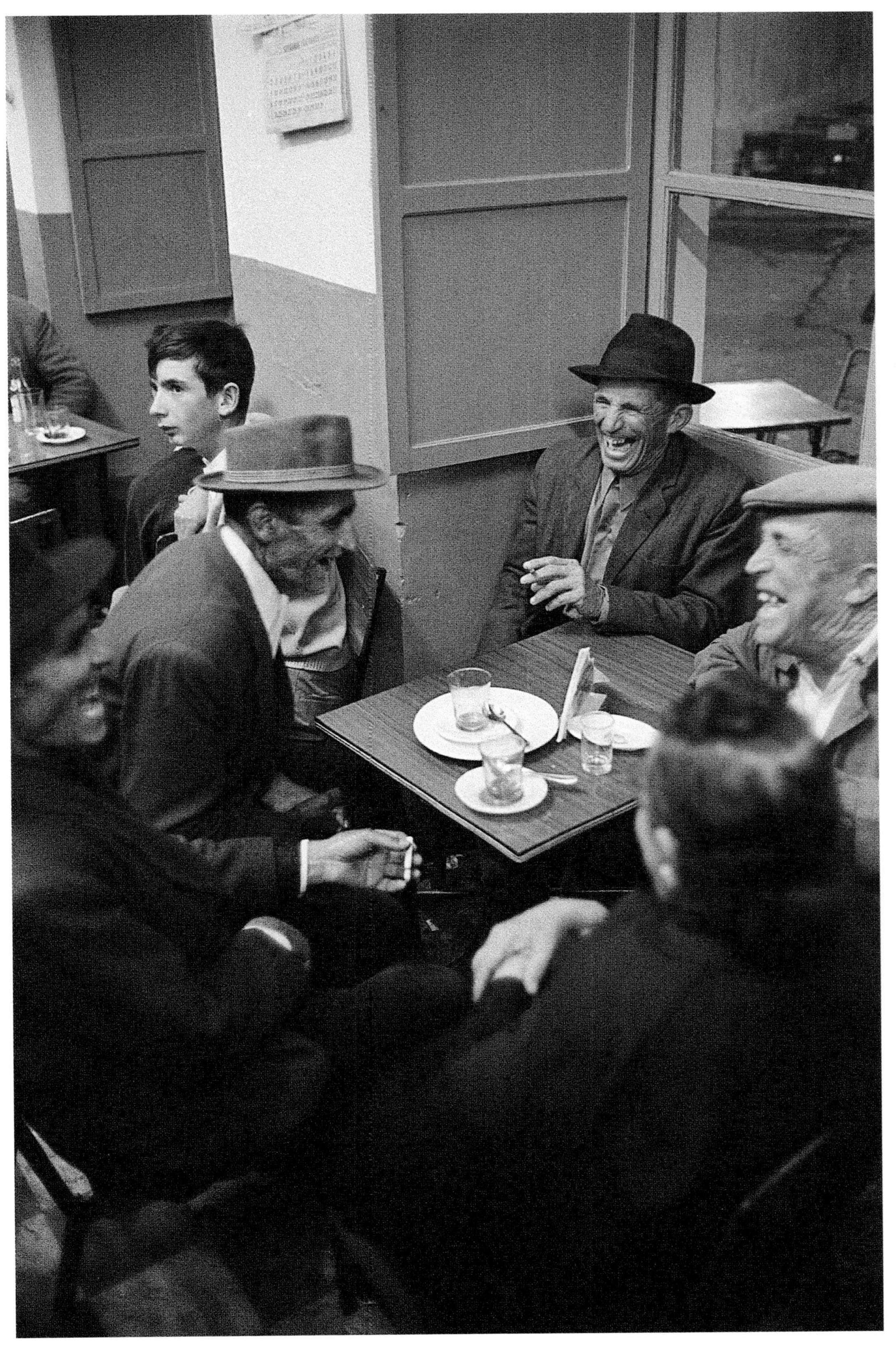

Spanish men in bar, Mijas 1971

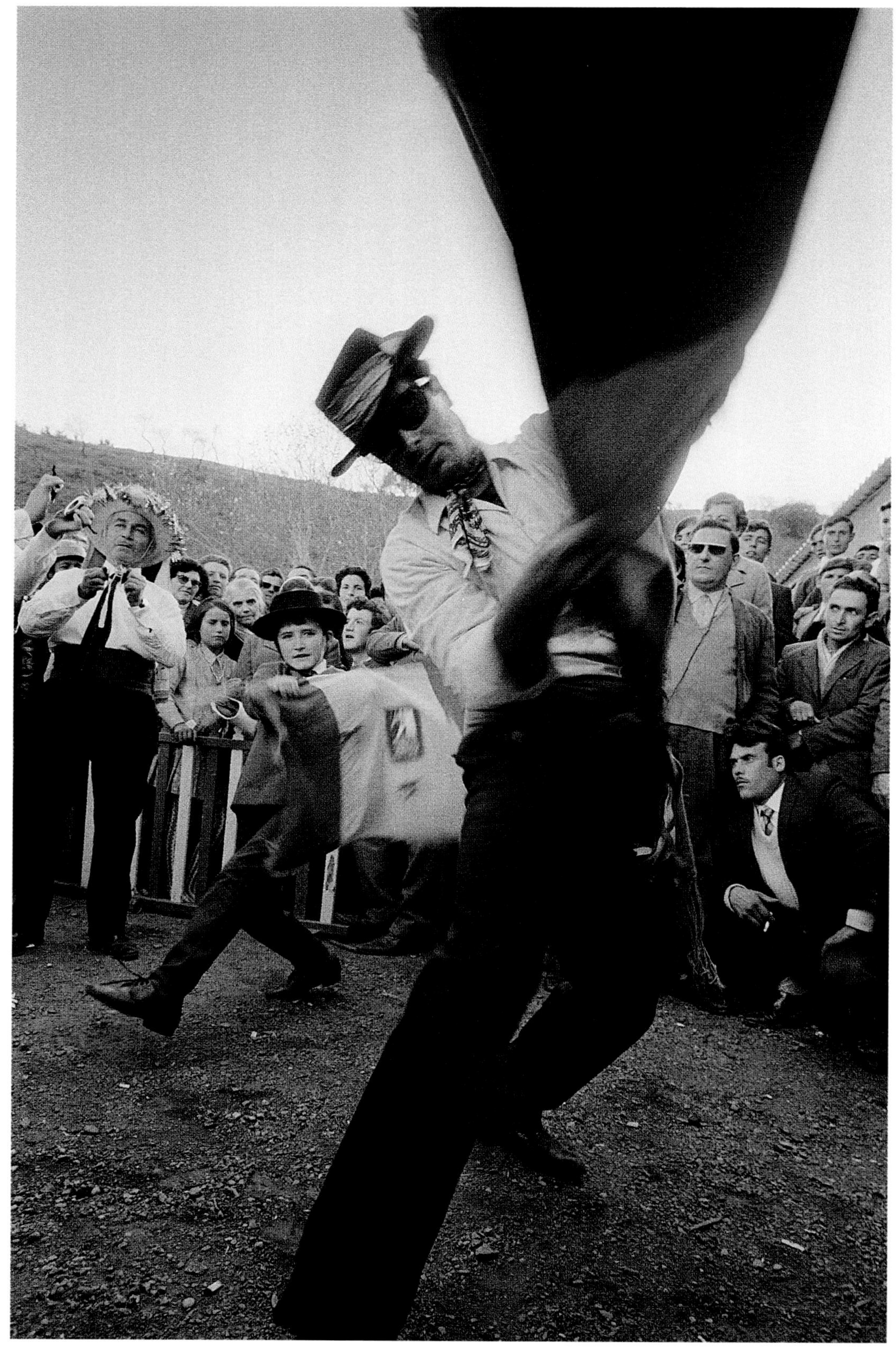

 SPANISH VILLAGE FESTIVAL 1971

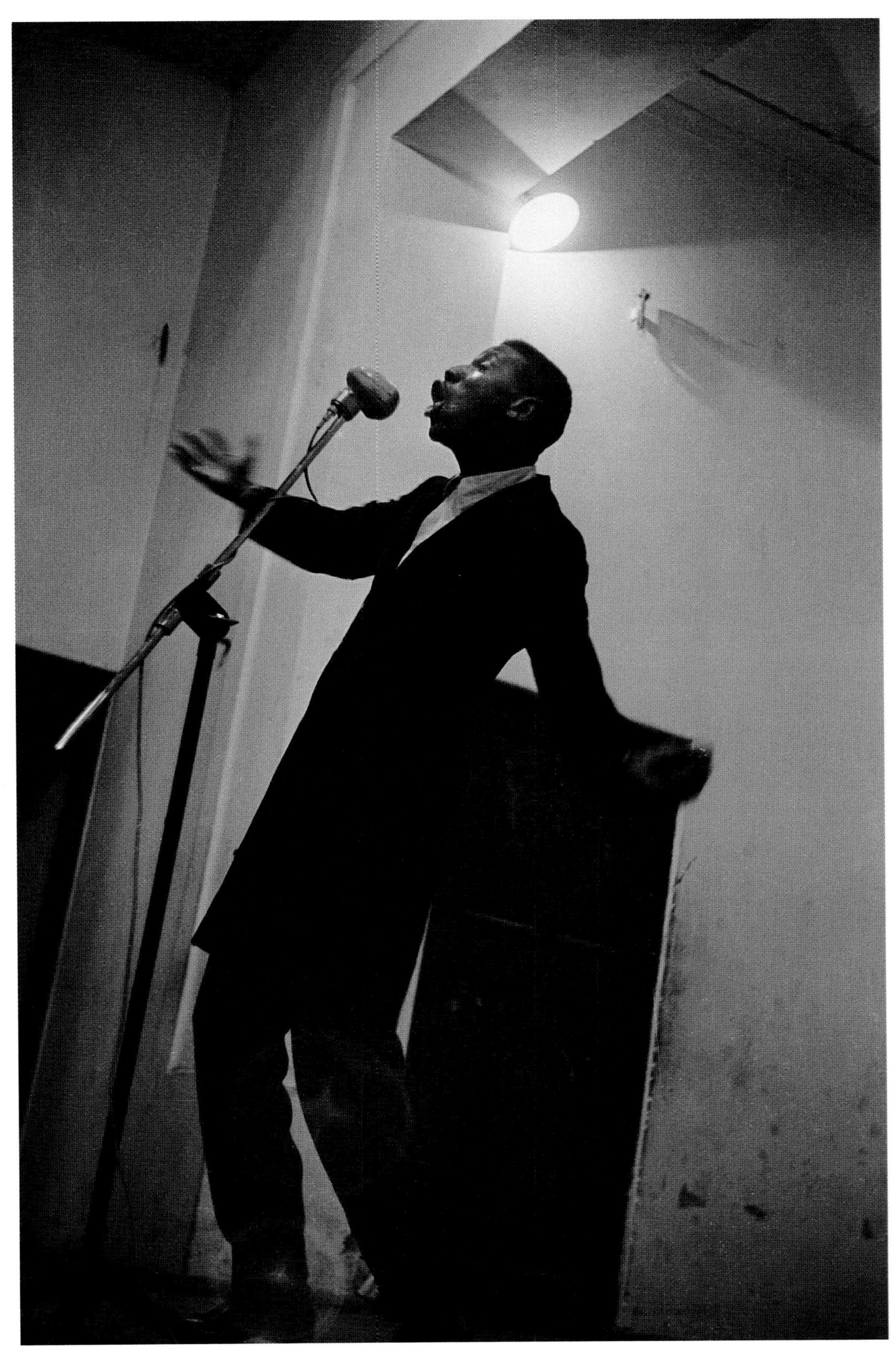

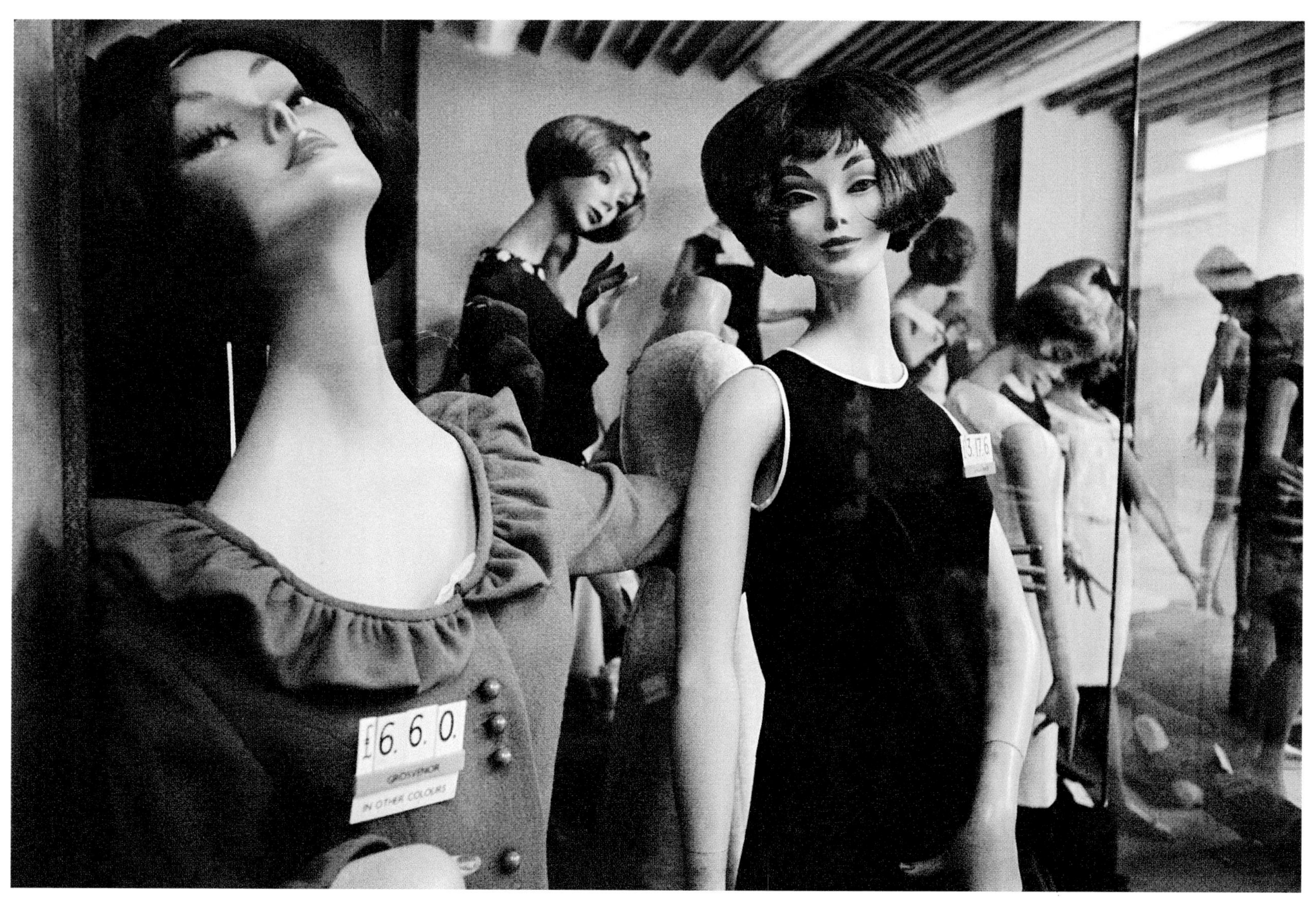

MANNEQUINS, LONDON 1972

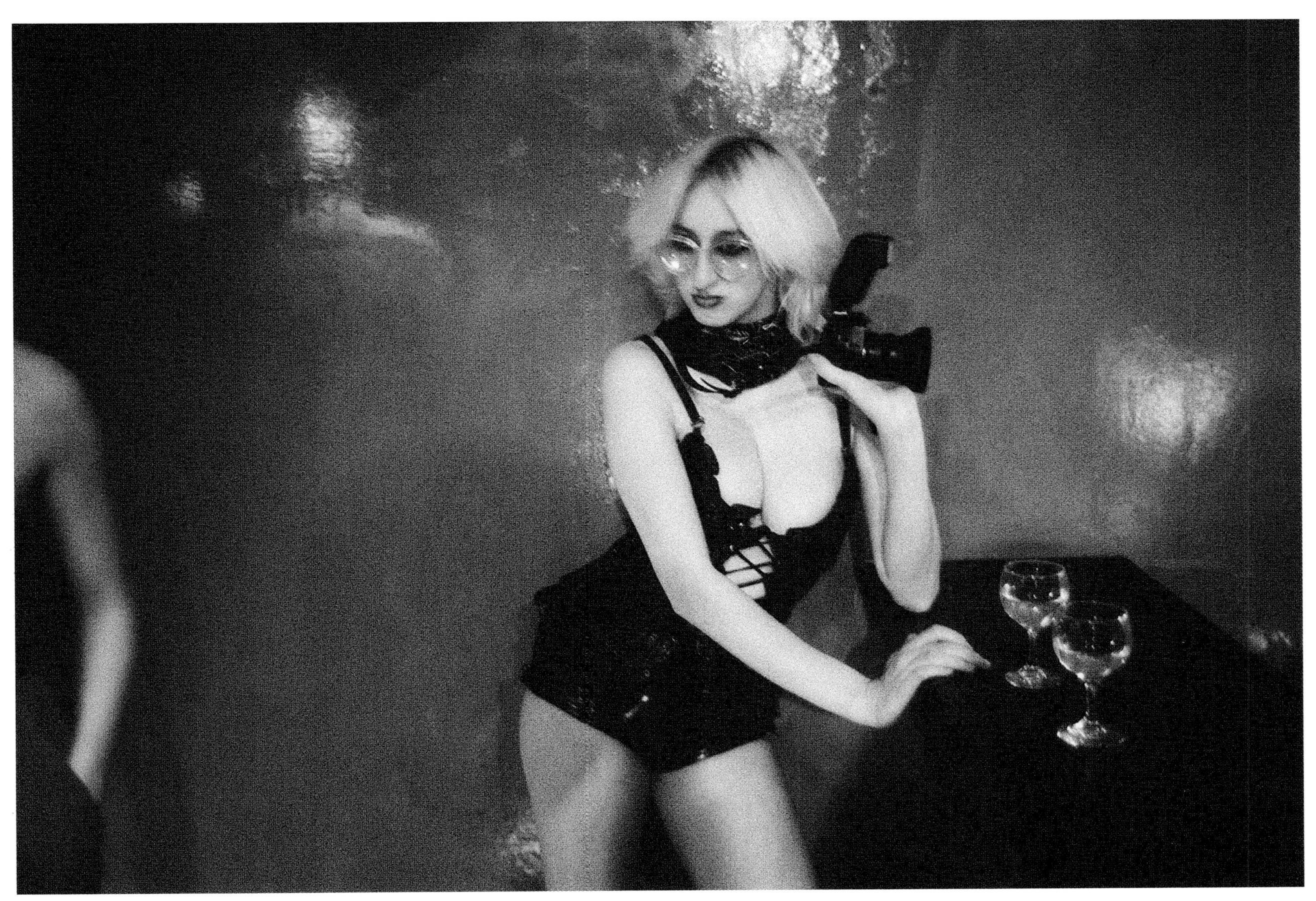

Disco lady, London 1980

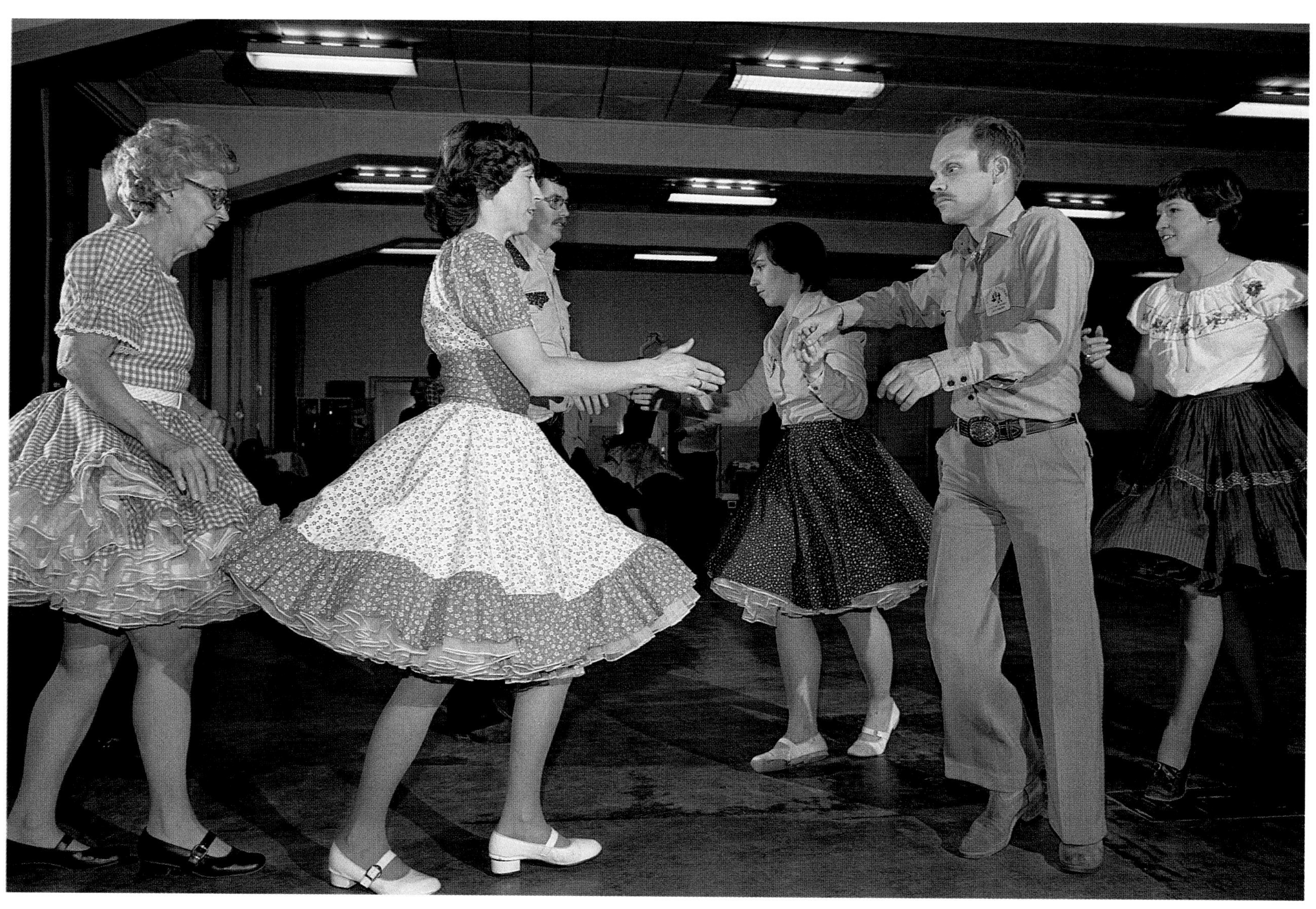

   Square dancing Americans, army base, Germany 1981

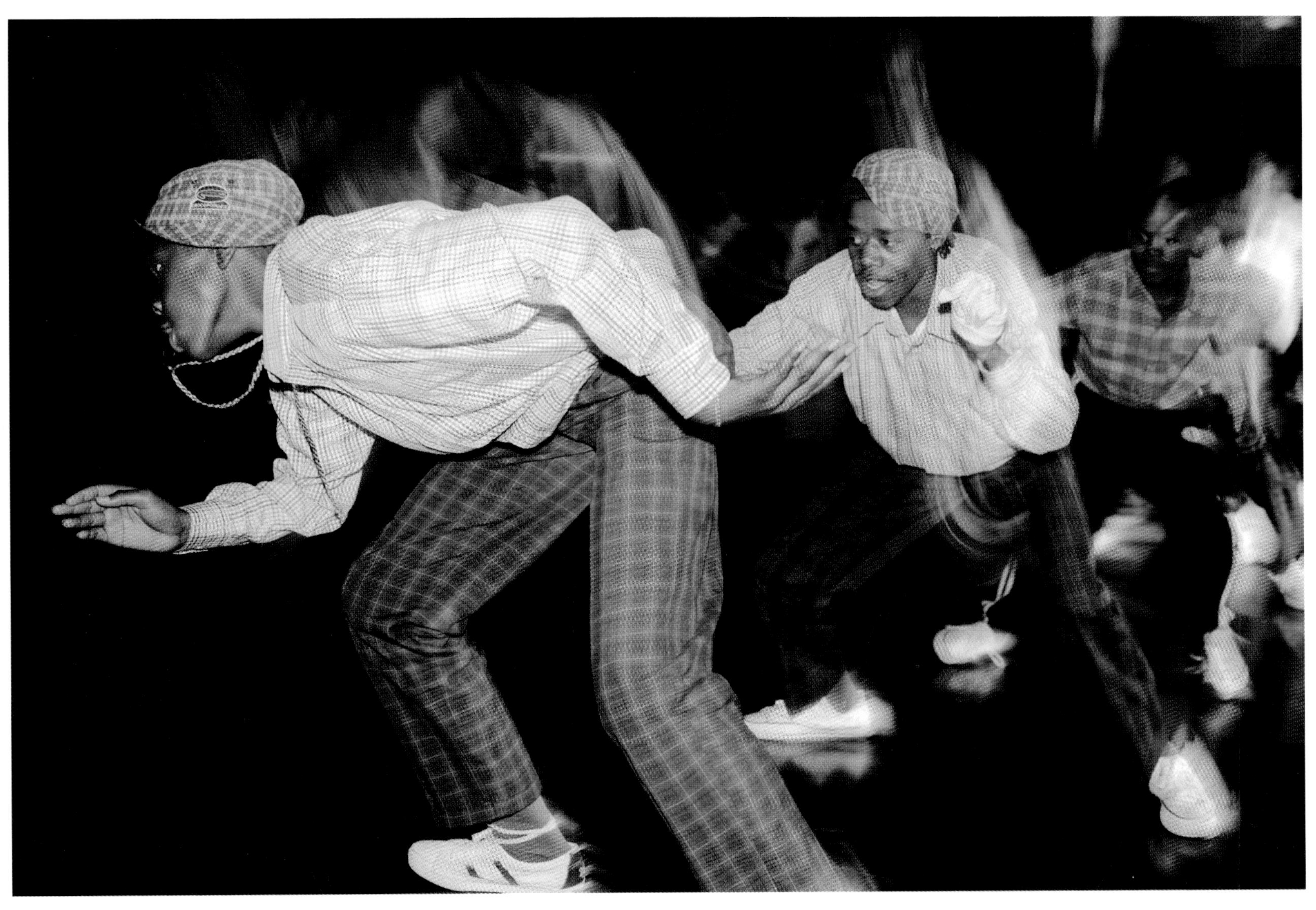

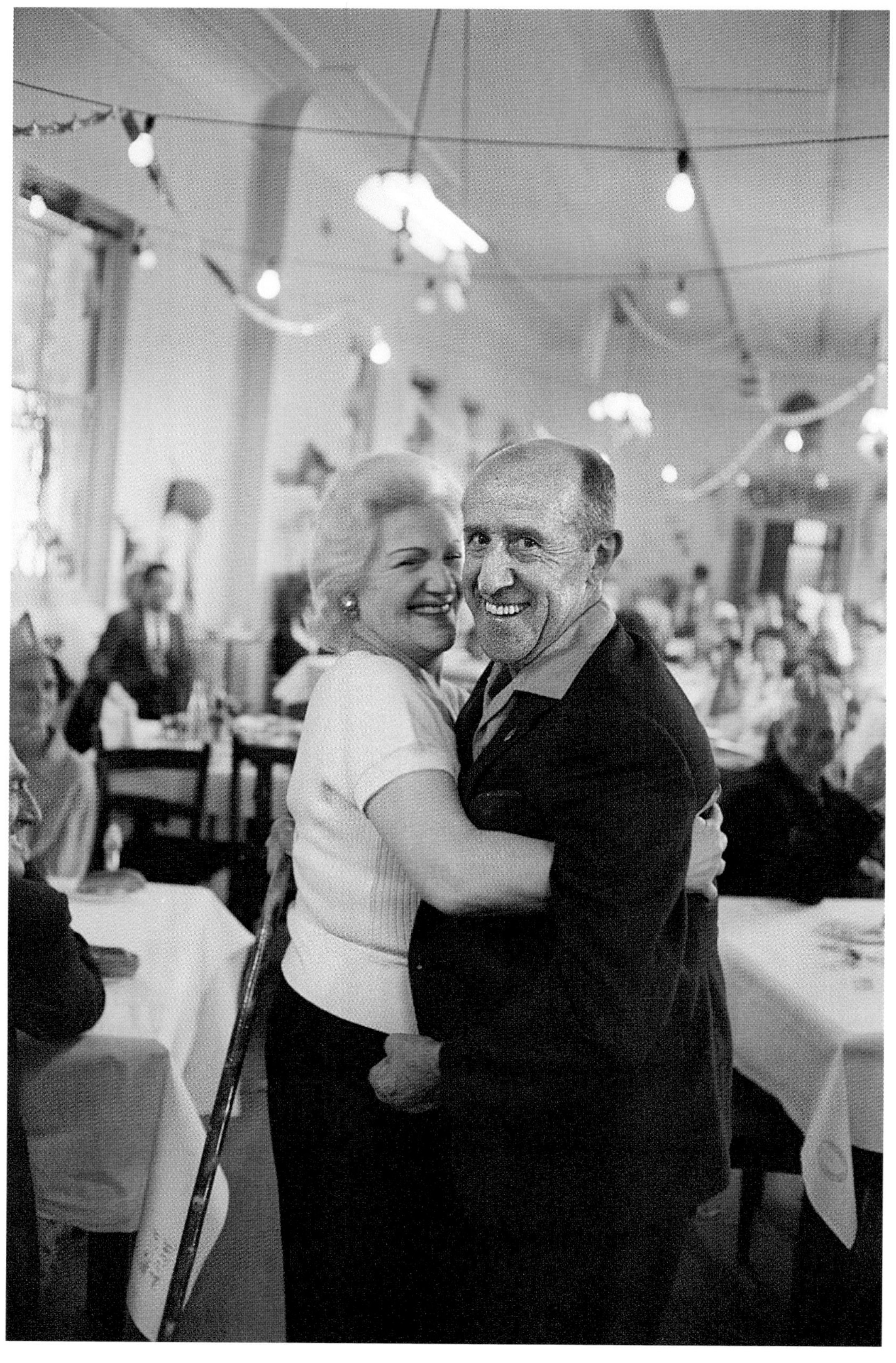

Christmas party, old age home, Johannesburg 1960

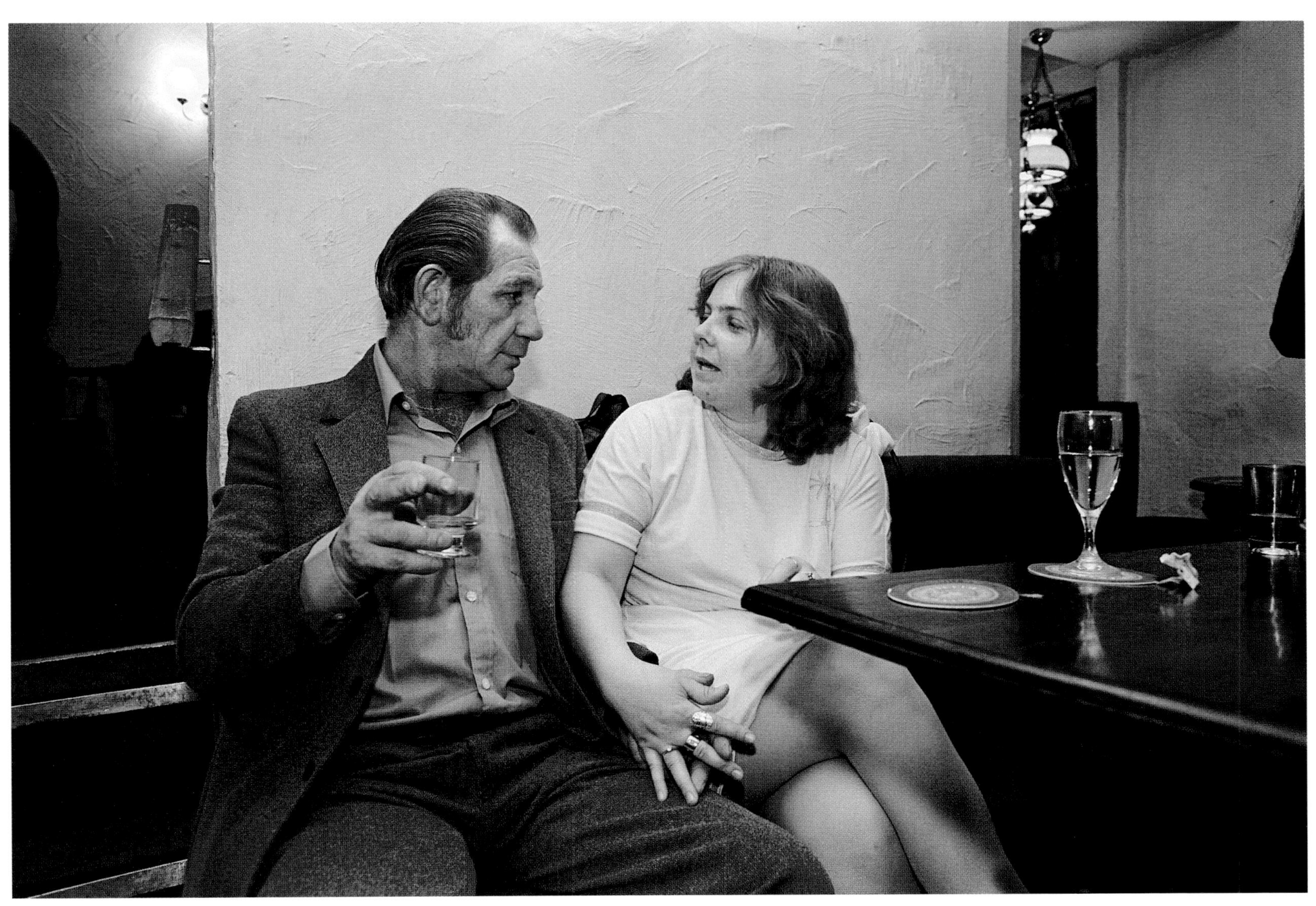

LOVERS IN LONDON PUB 1982

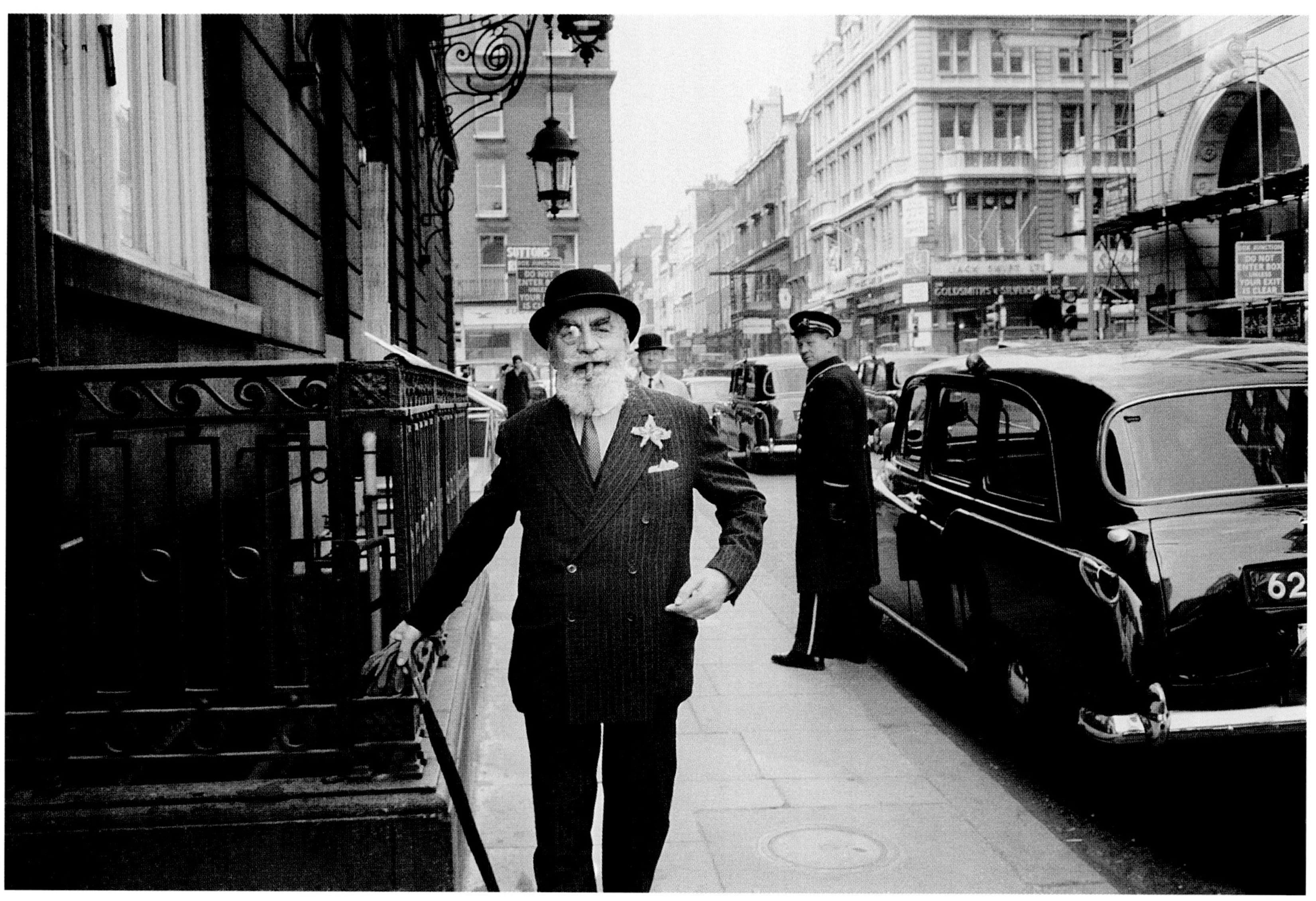

 Out for a stroll, Gulbenkin, London 1967

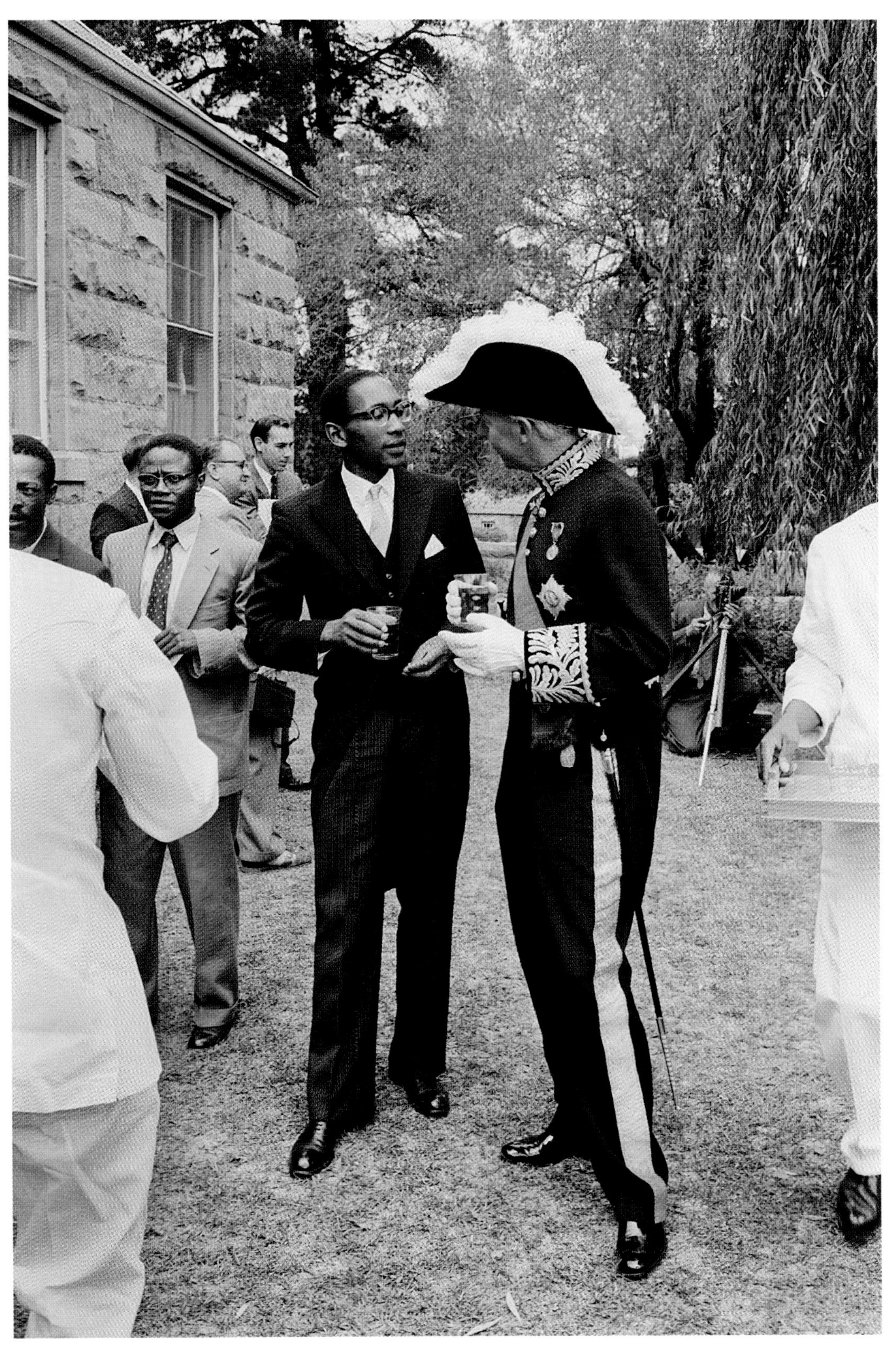

Sir Hugh Lloyd, British High Commissioner,
and King Moshoeshe of Lesotho at coronation ceremony 1960

29

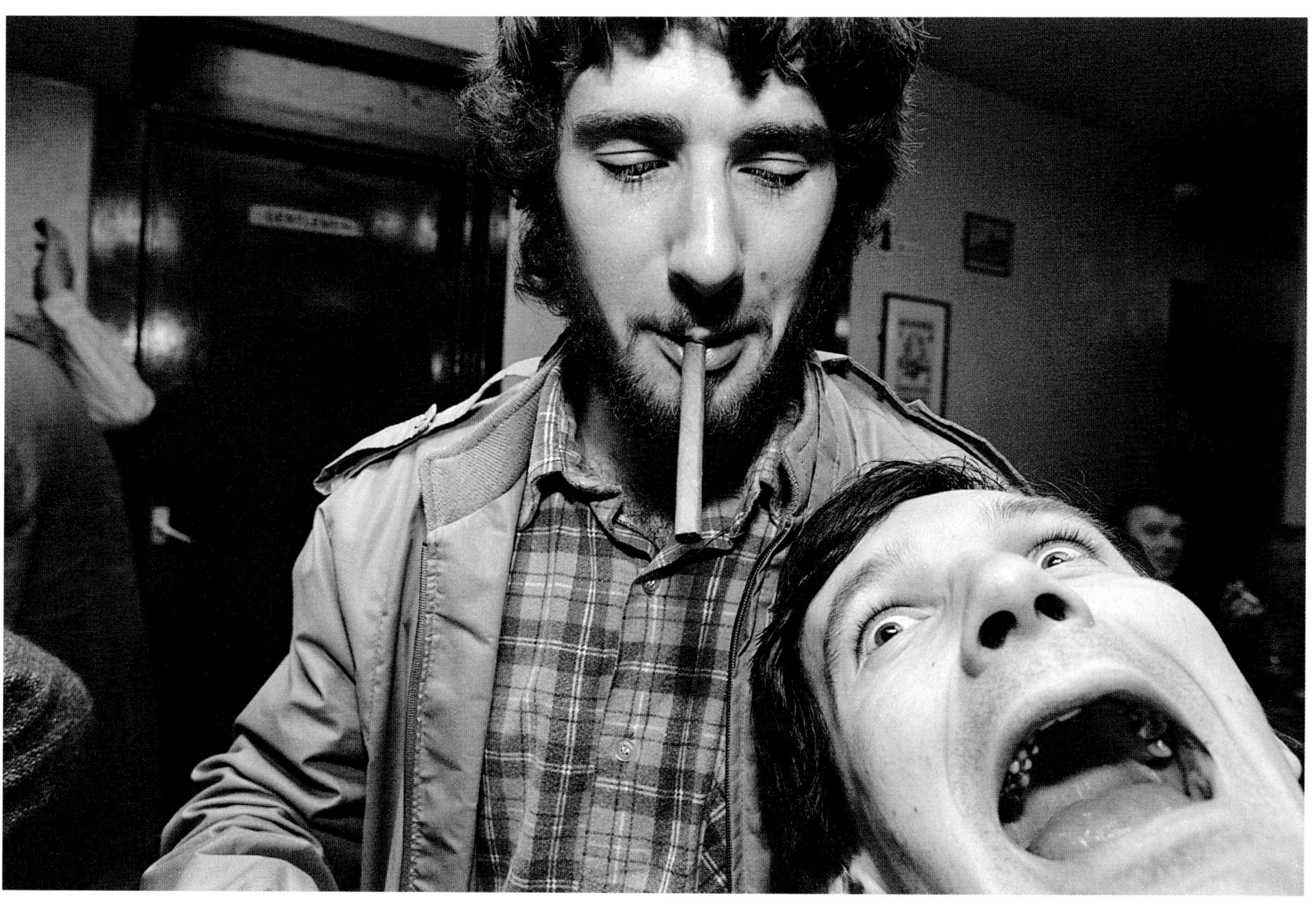

Pub face, Newport, Wales 1984

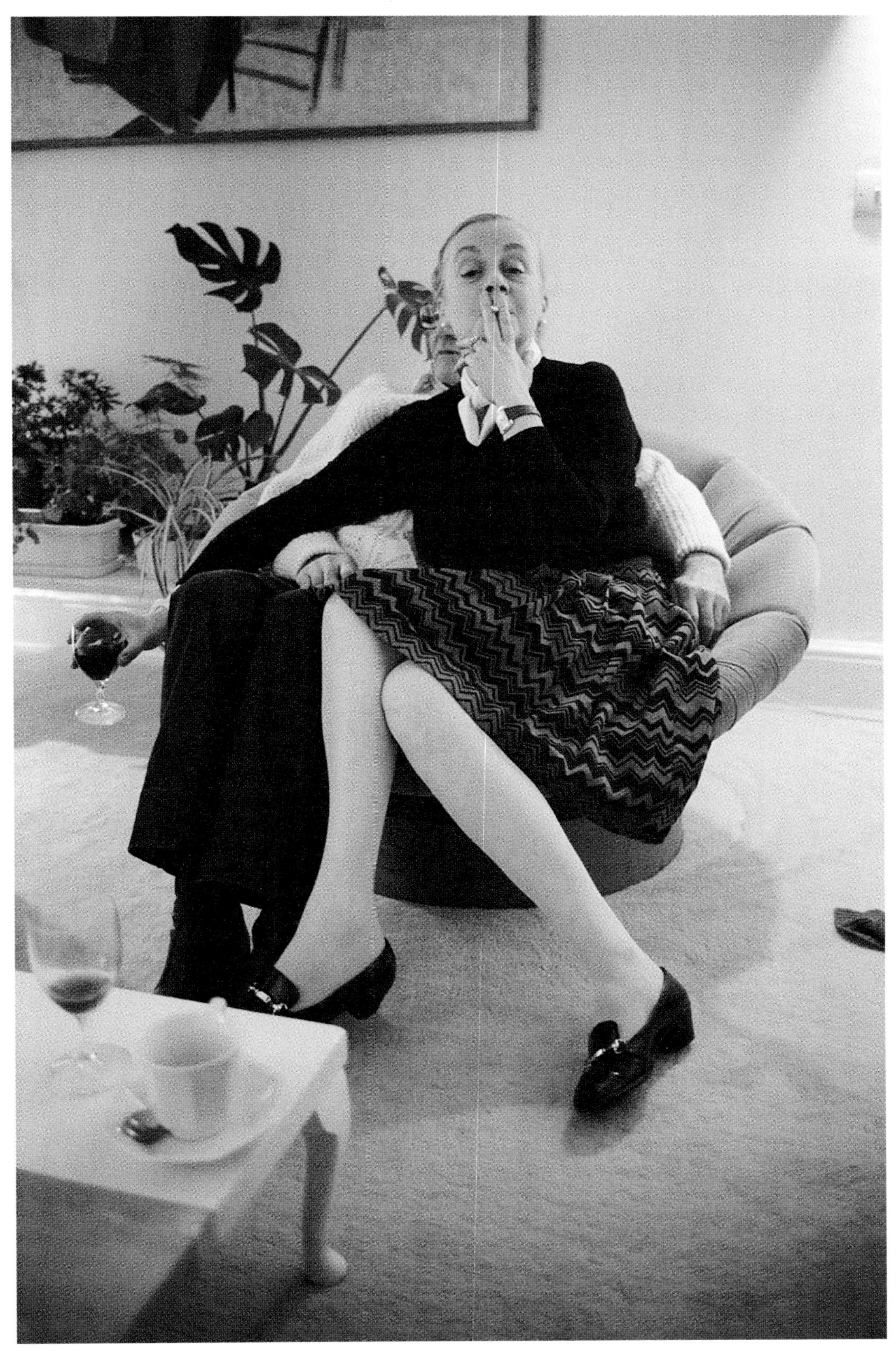

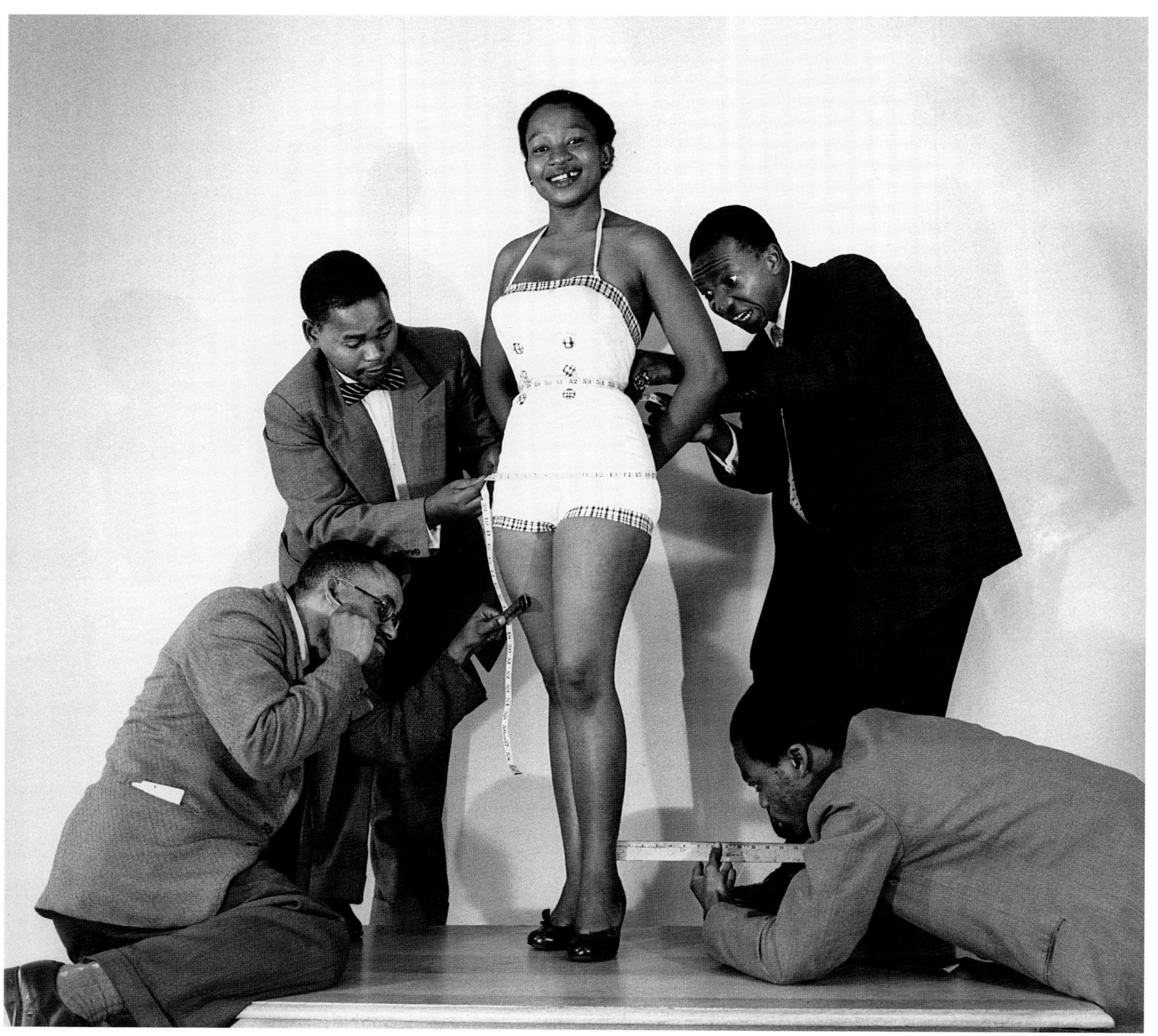

   MEASURING UP FOR DRUM COVER, JOHANNESBURG 1955

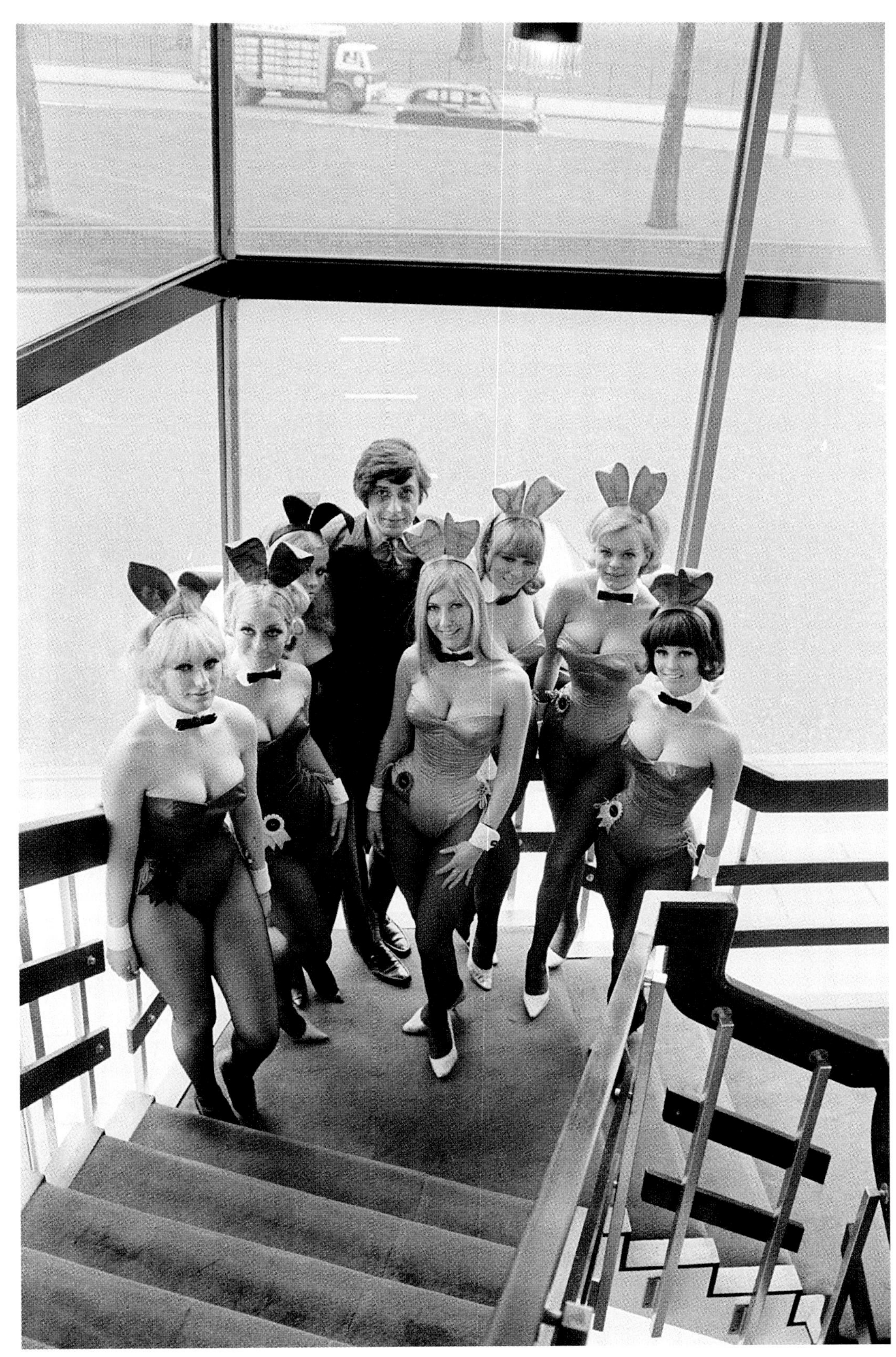

Victor Lowndes & bunny girls, Playboy Club, London 1967   33

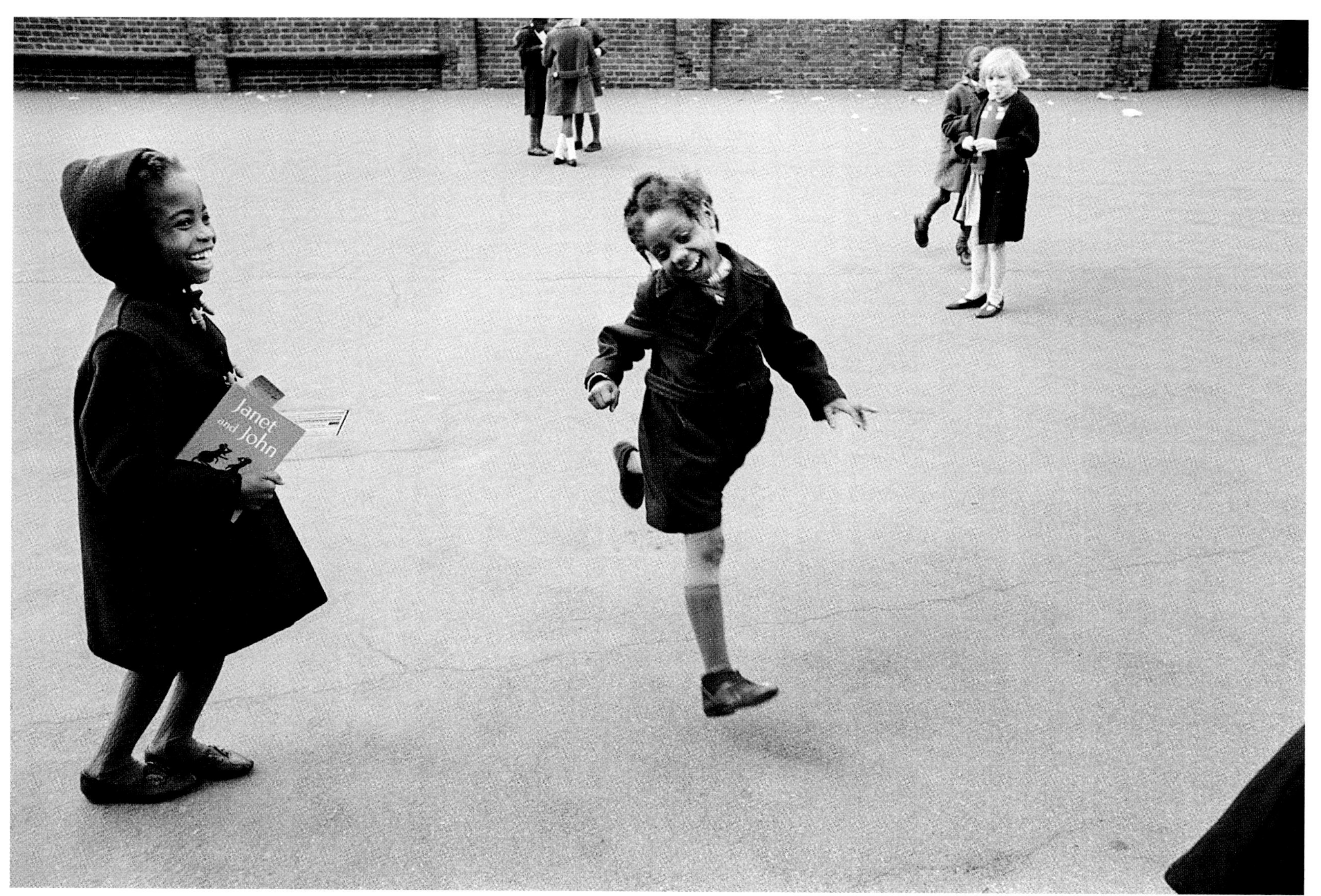

 SCHOOL PLAYGROUND, BRIXTON, LONDON 1968

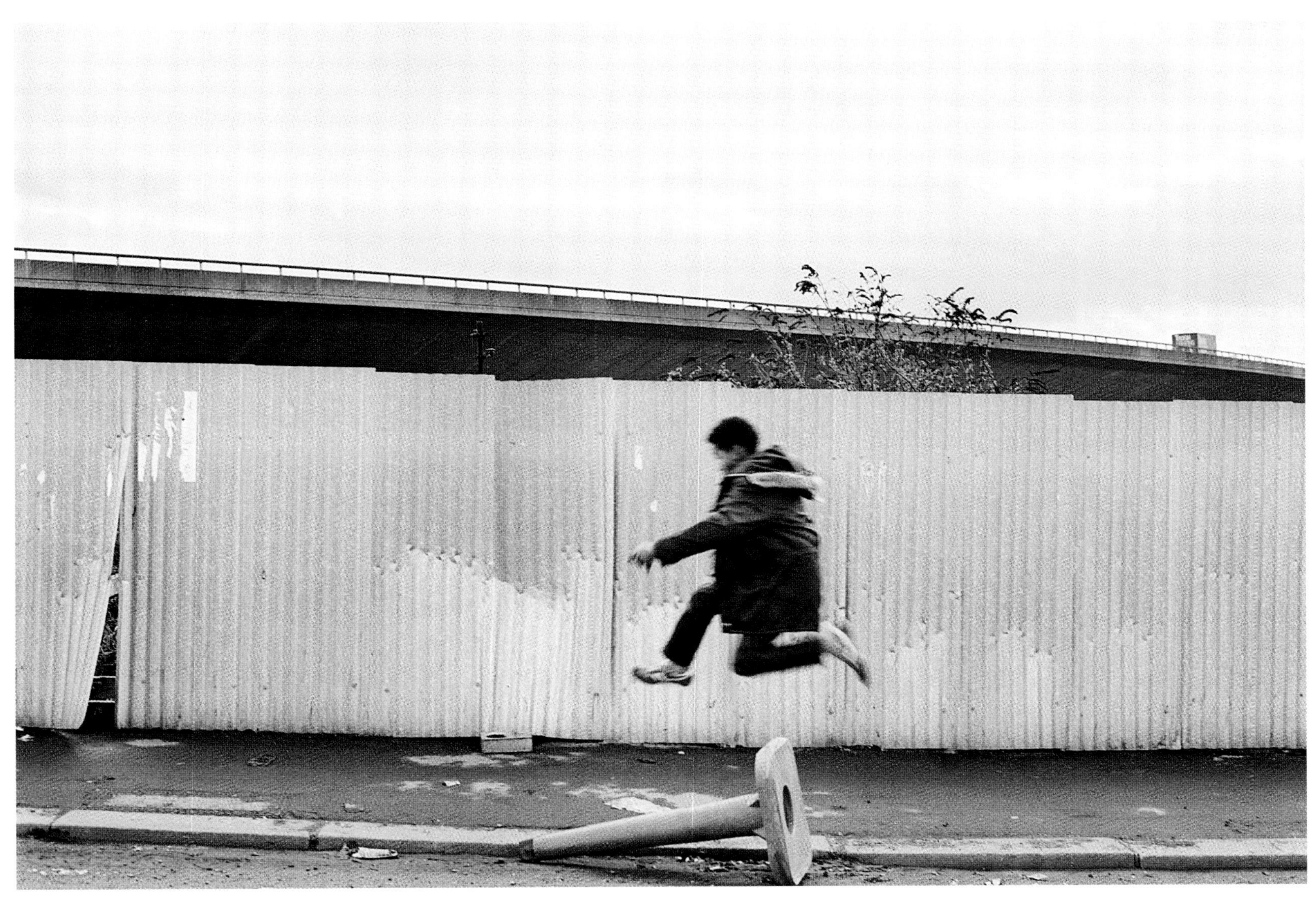

High jump, London 1979

35

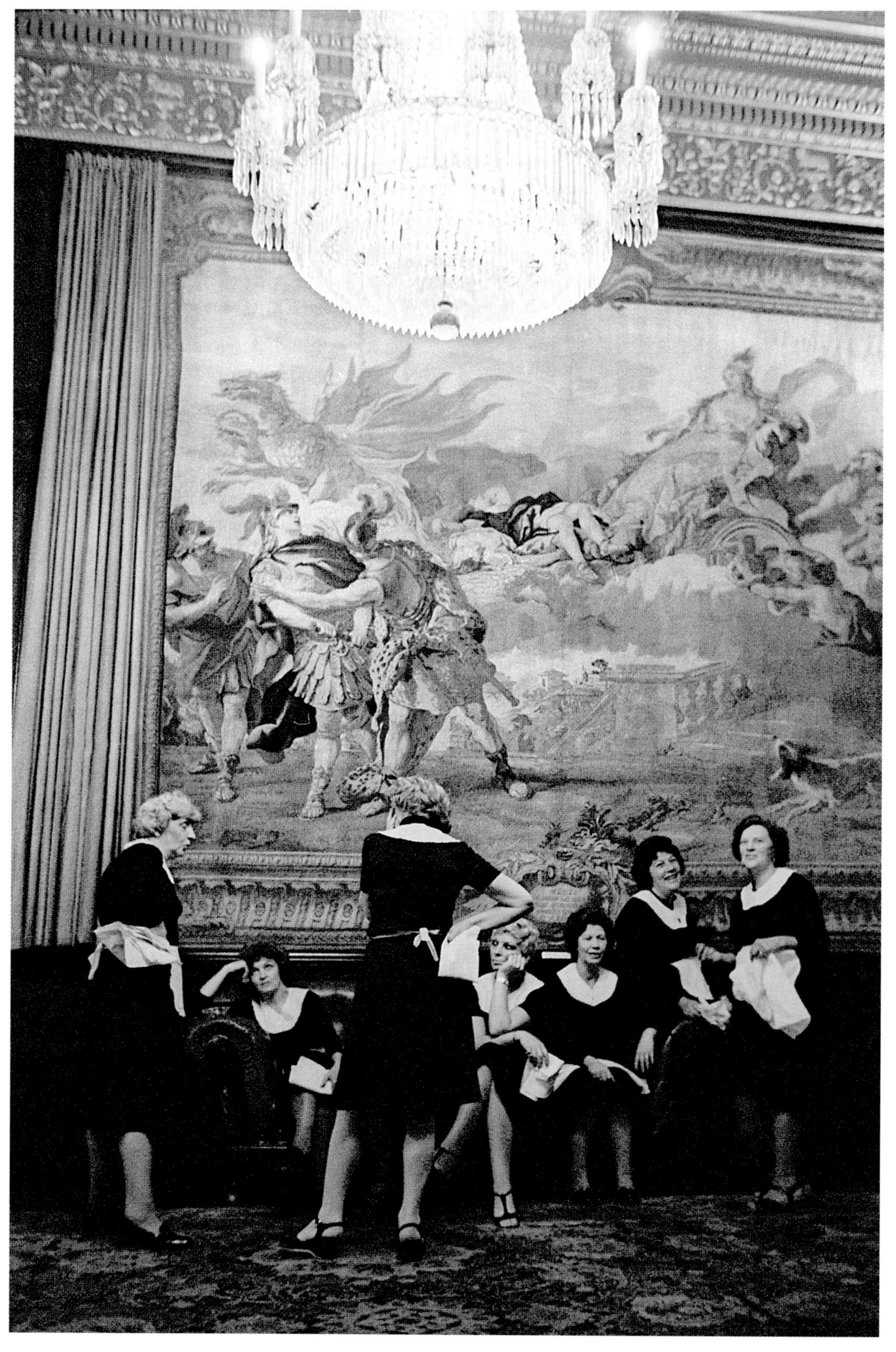

WAITRESS BREAK, LONDON CITY HALL 1979

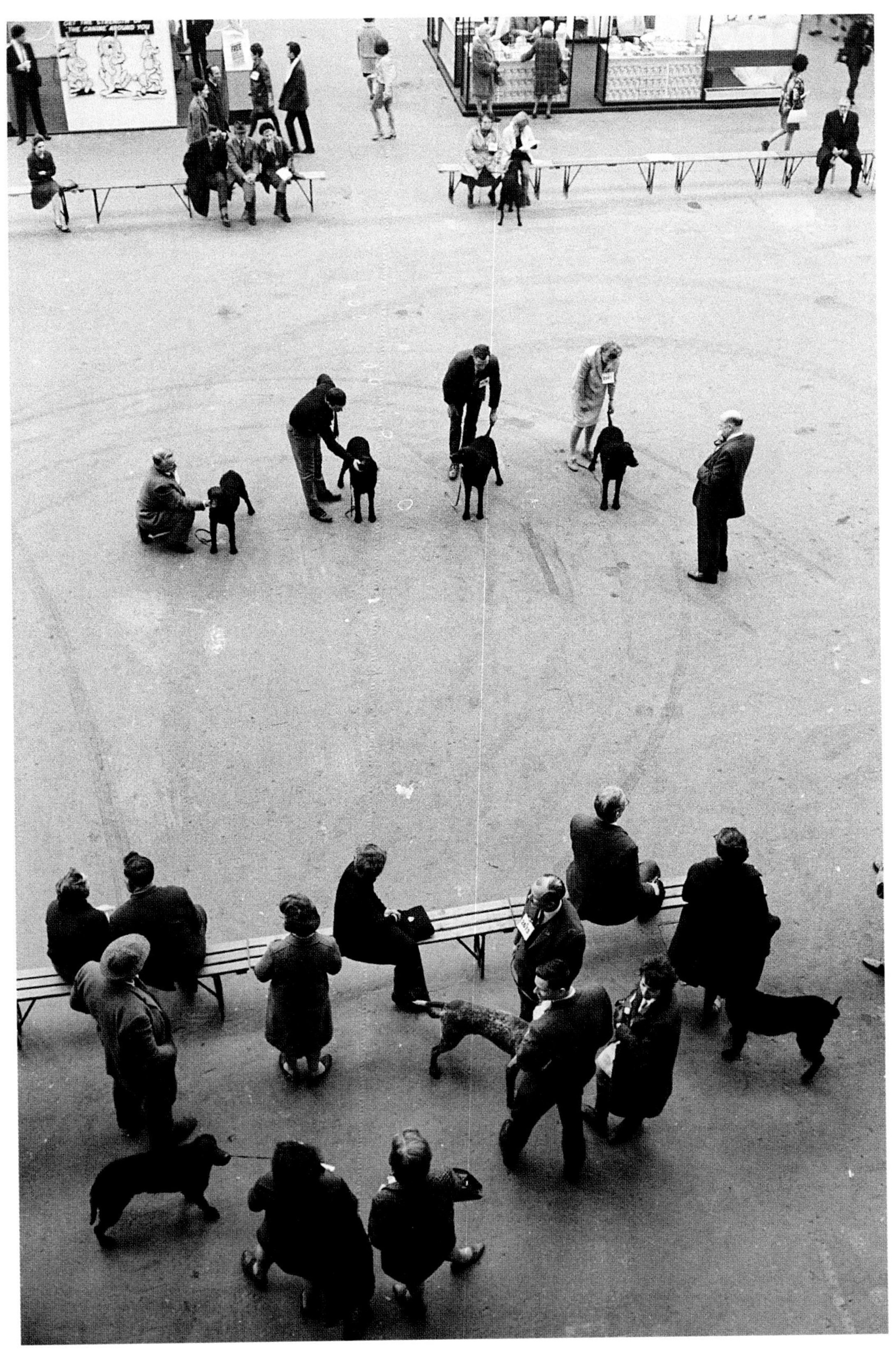

Olympia dog show, London 1965

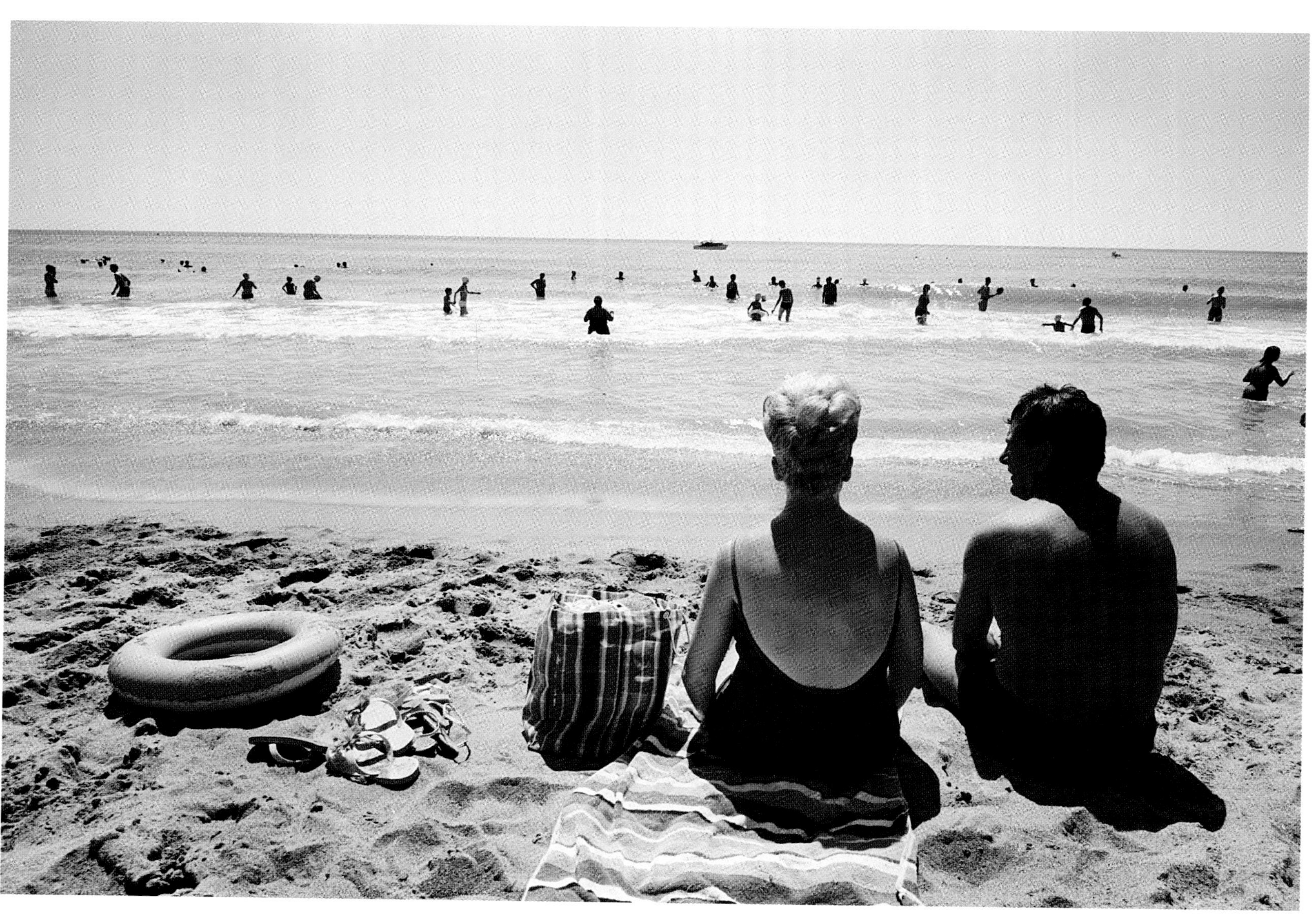

Tourists on Spanish beach, Costa del Sol 1970

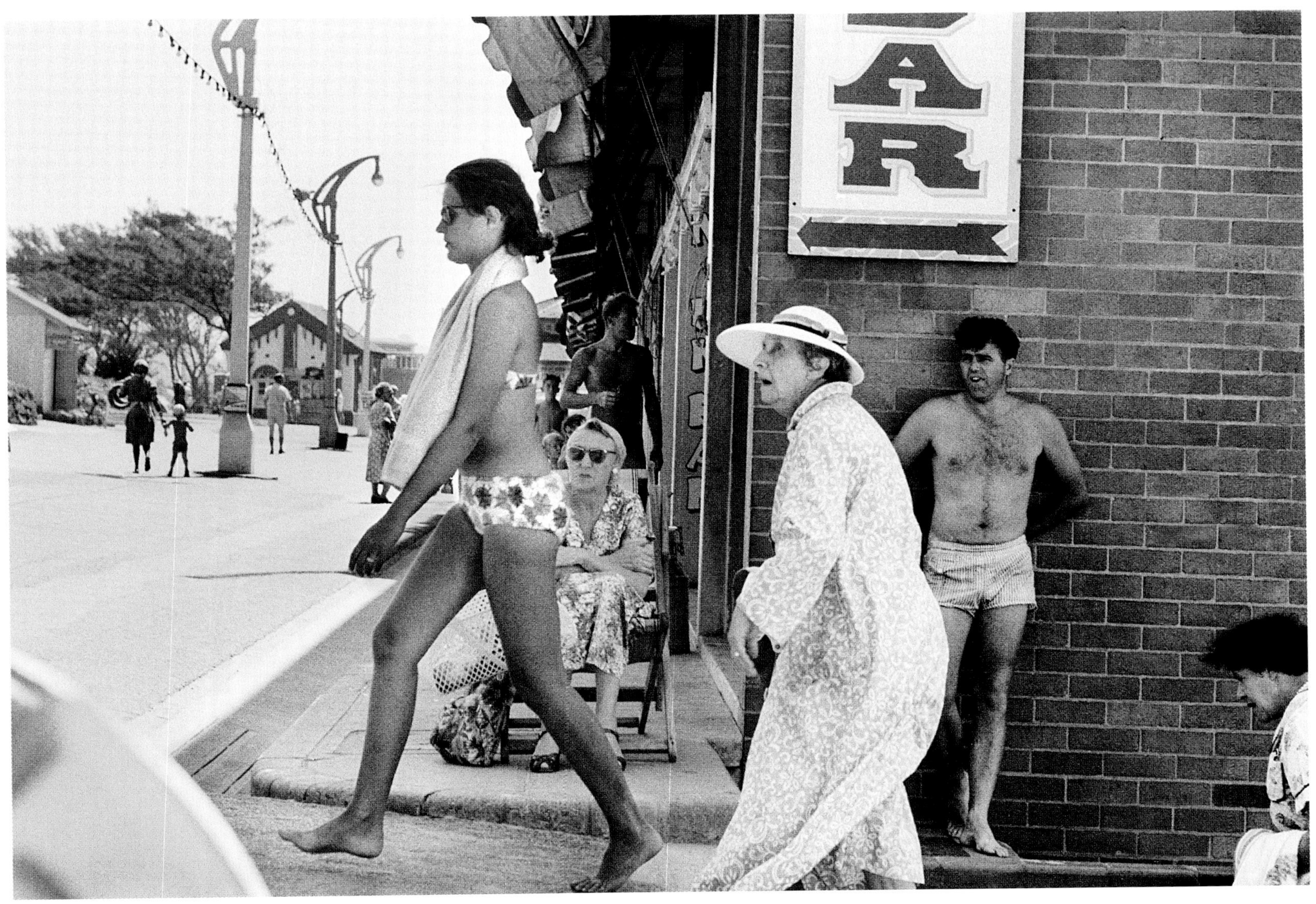

Durban beach 1955

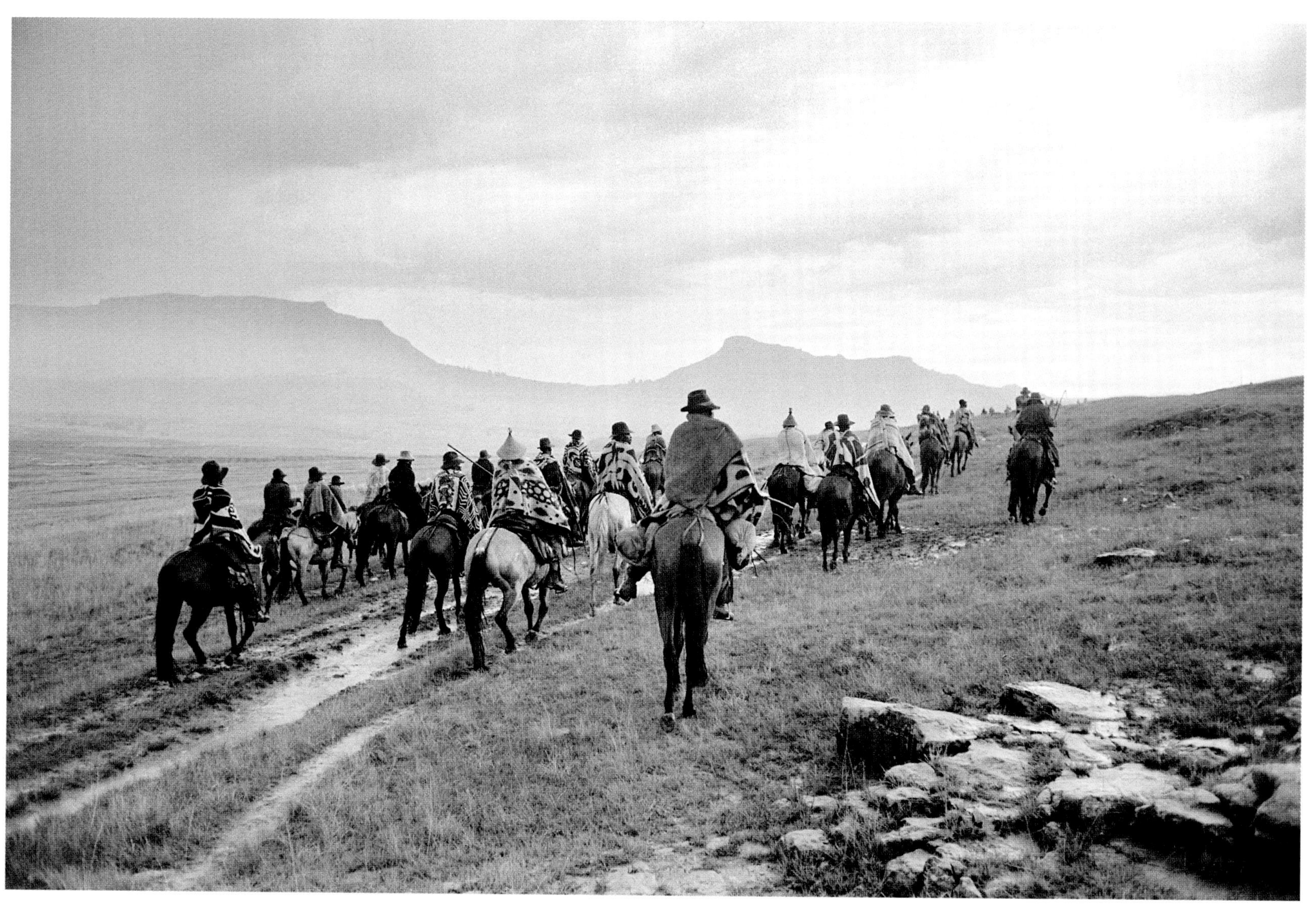

LESOTHO TRIBESMEN 1961

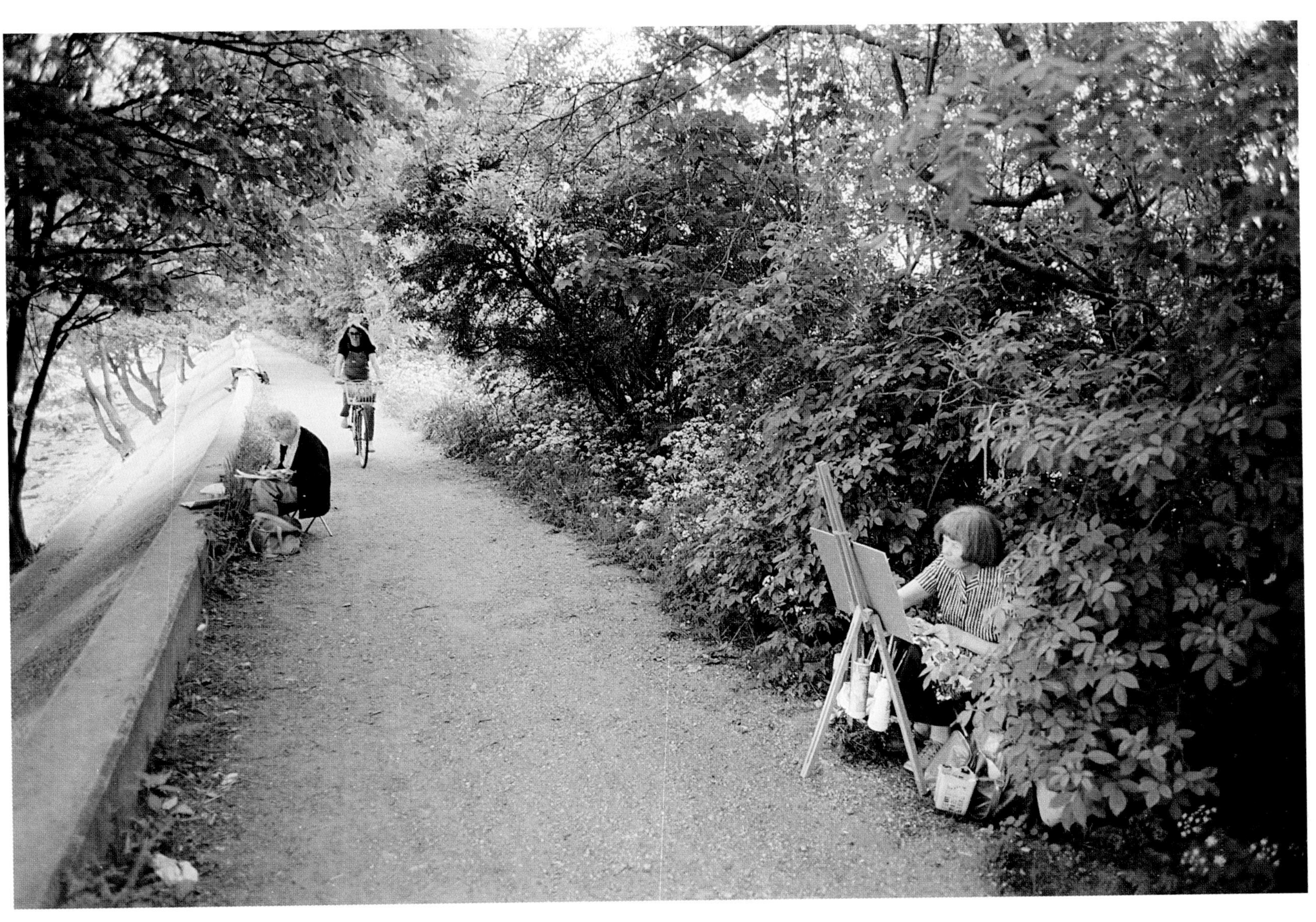

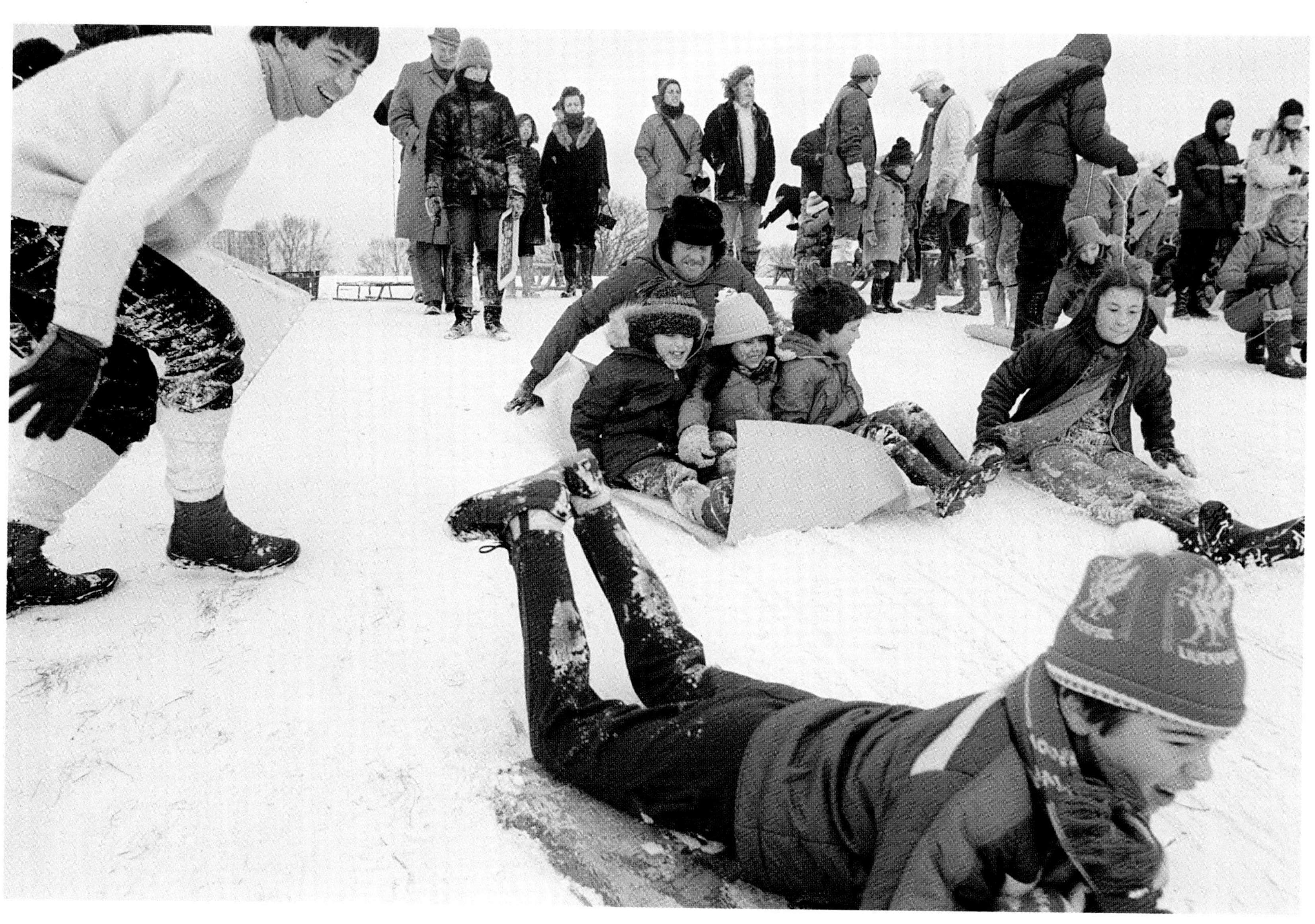

SNOW SLIDE AT PRIMROSE HILL, LONDON 1980

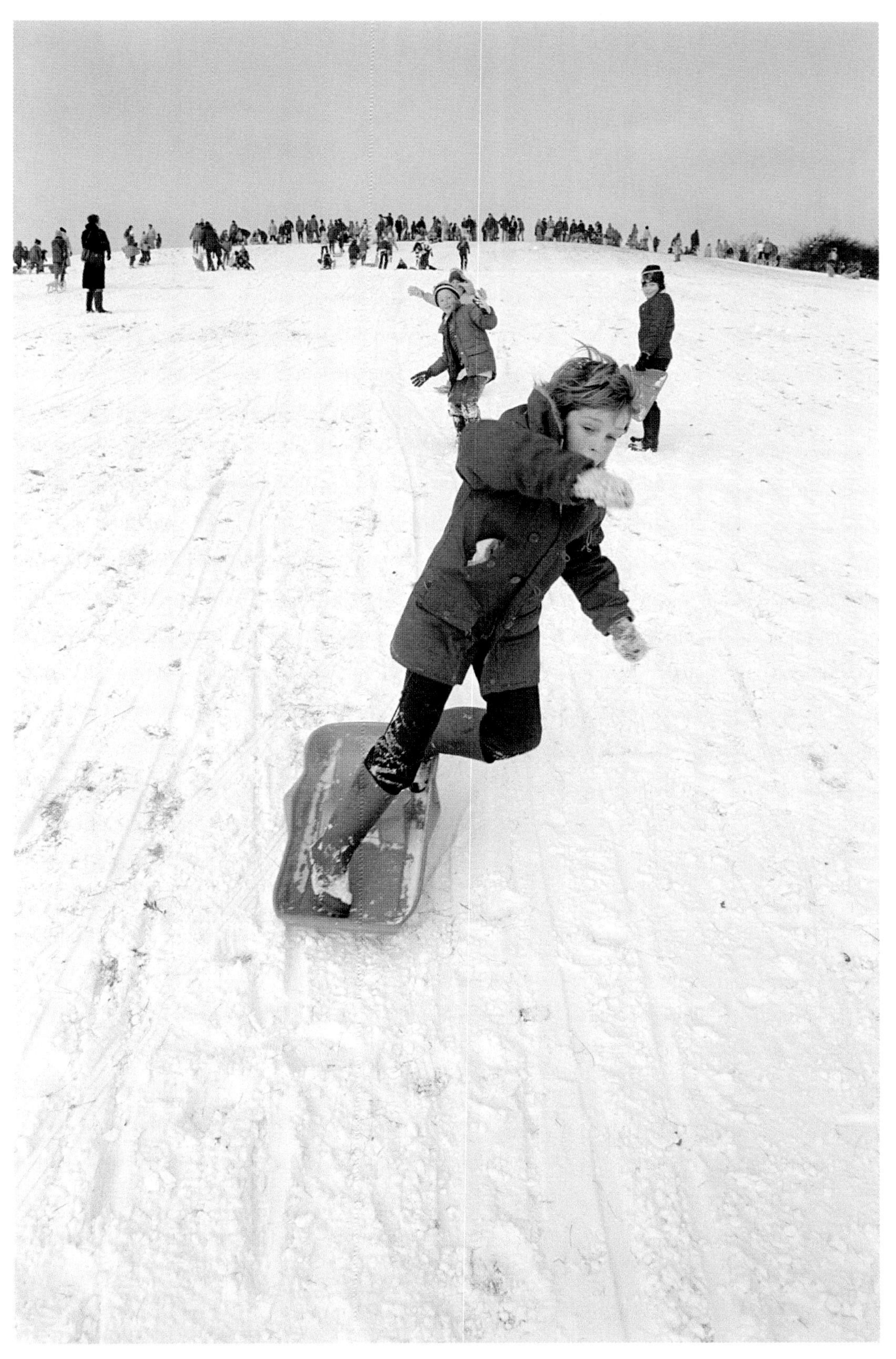

Tray slide at Primrose Hill, London 1980

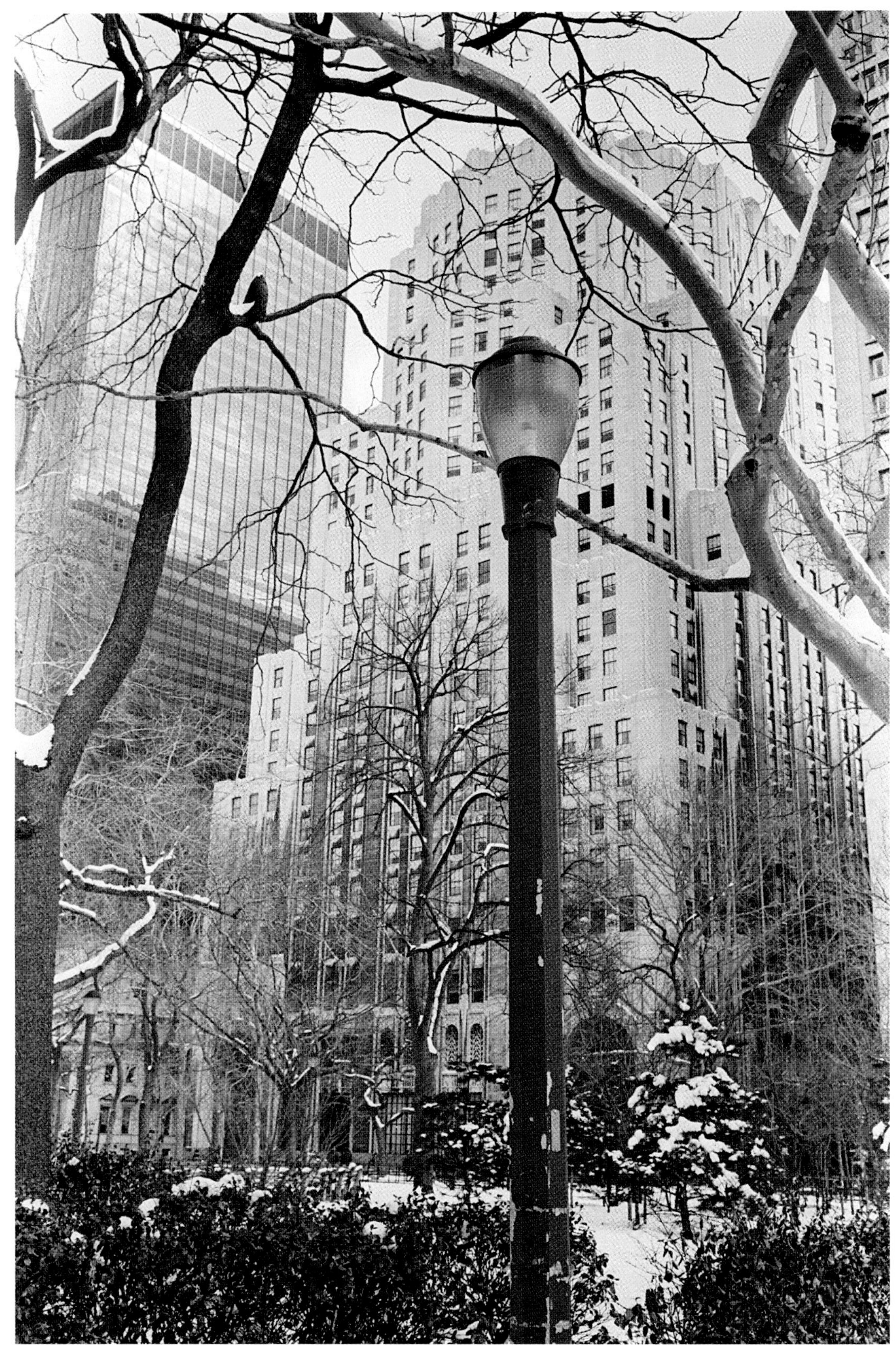

 New York in the snow 1979

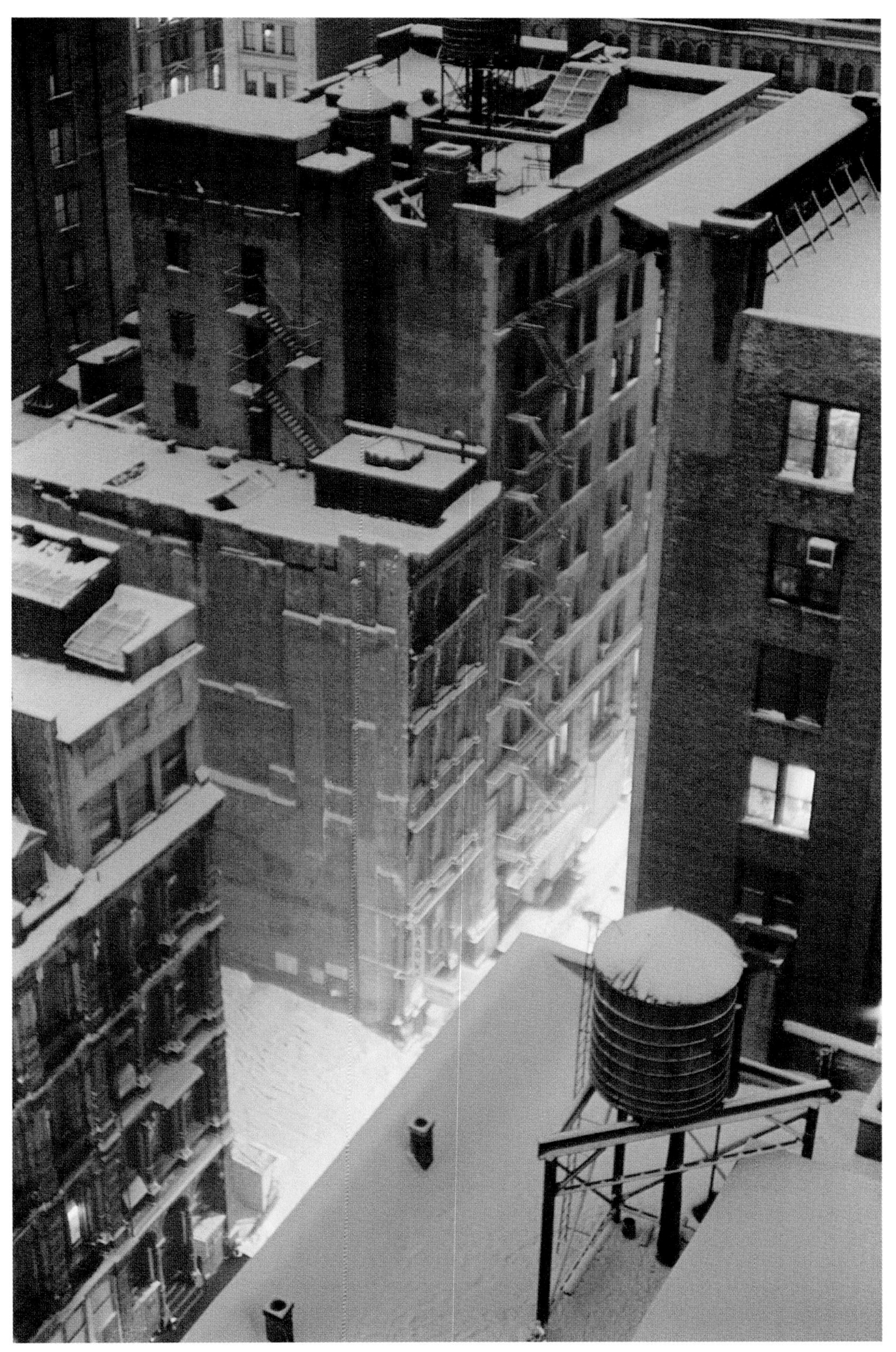

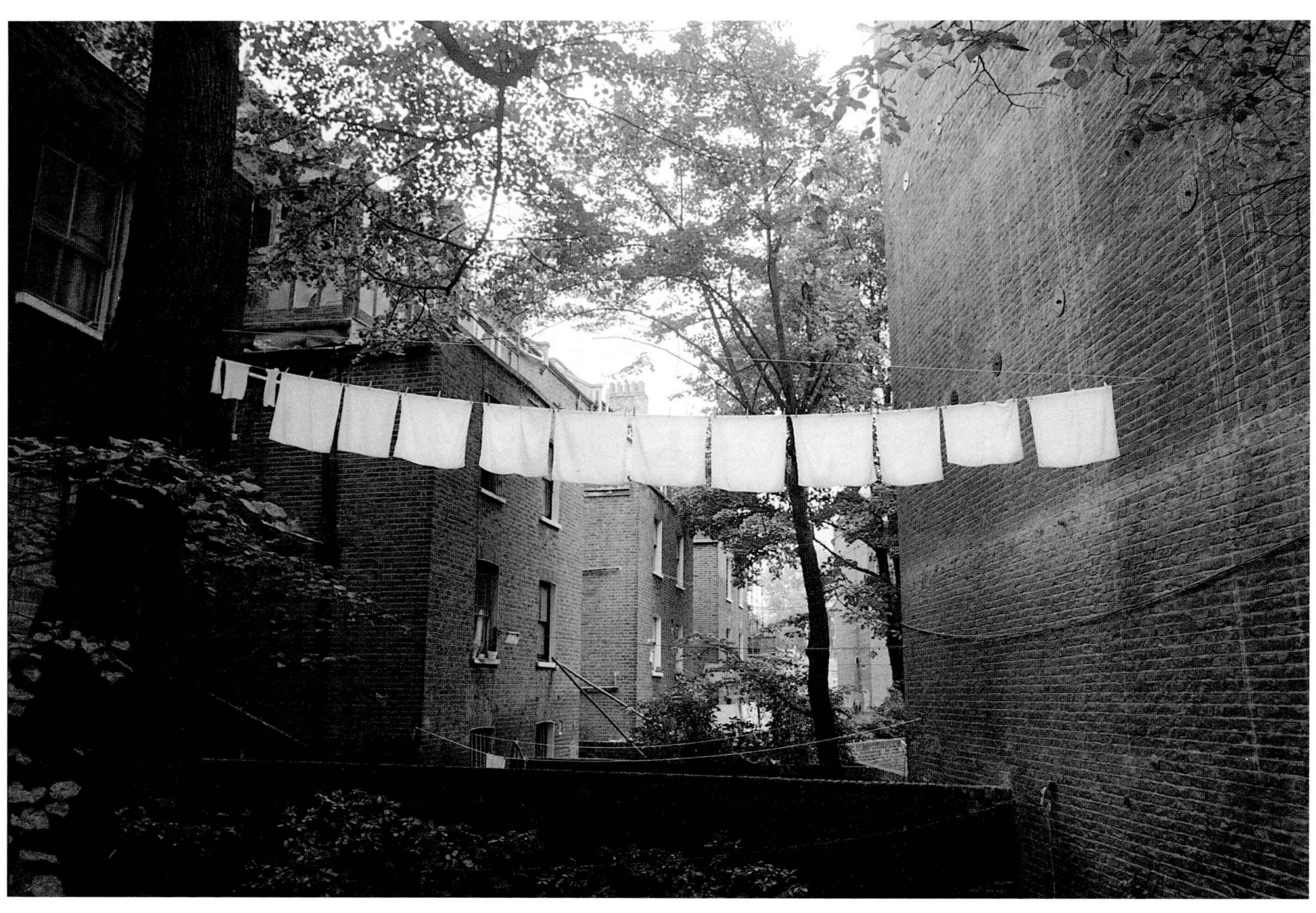

 MAIDE VALE NAPPIES, LONDON 1978

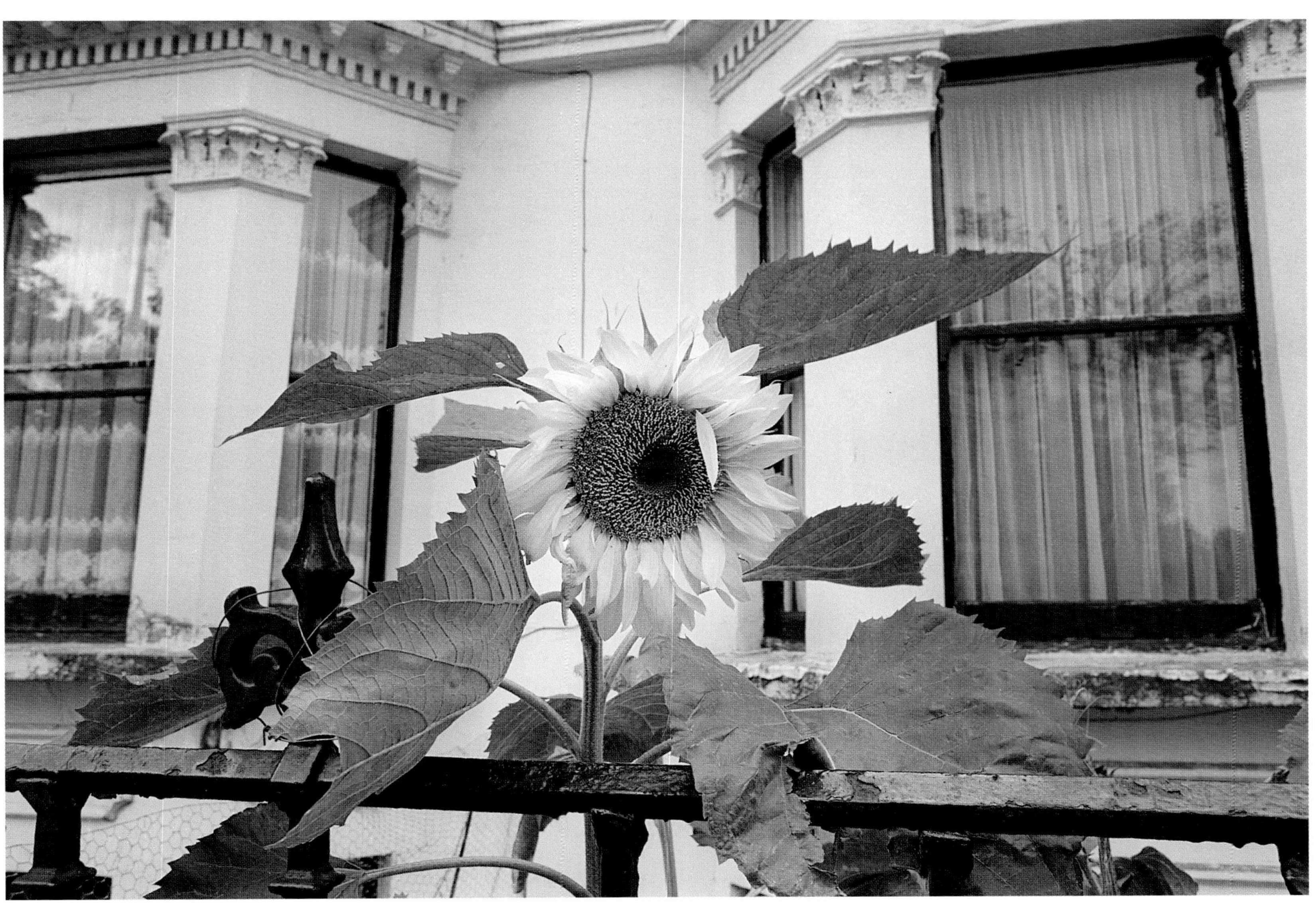

Sunflower in Maide Vale, London 1978

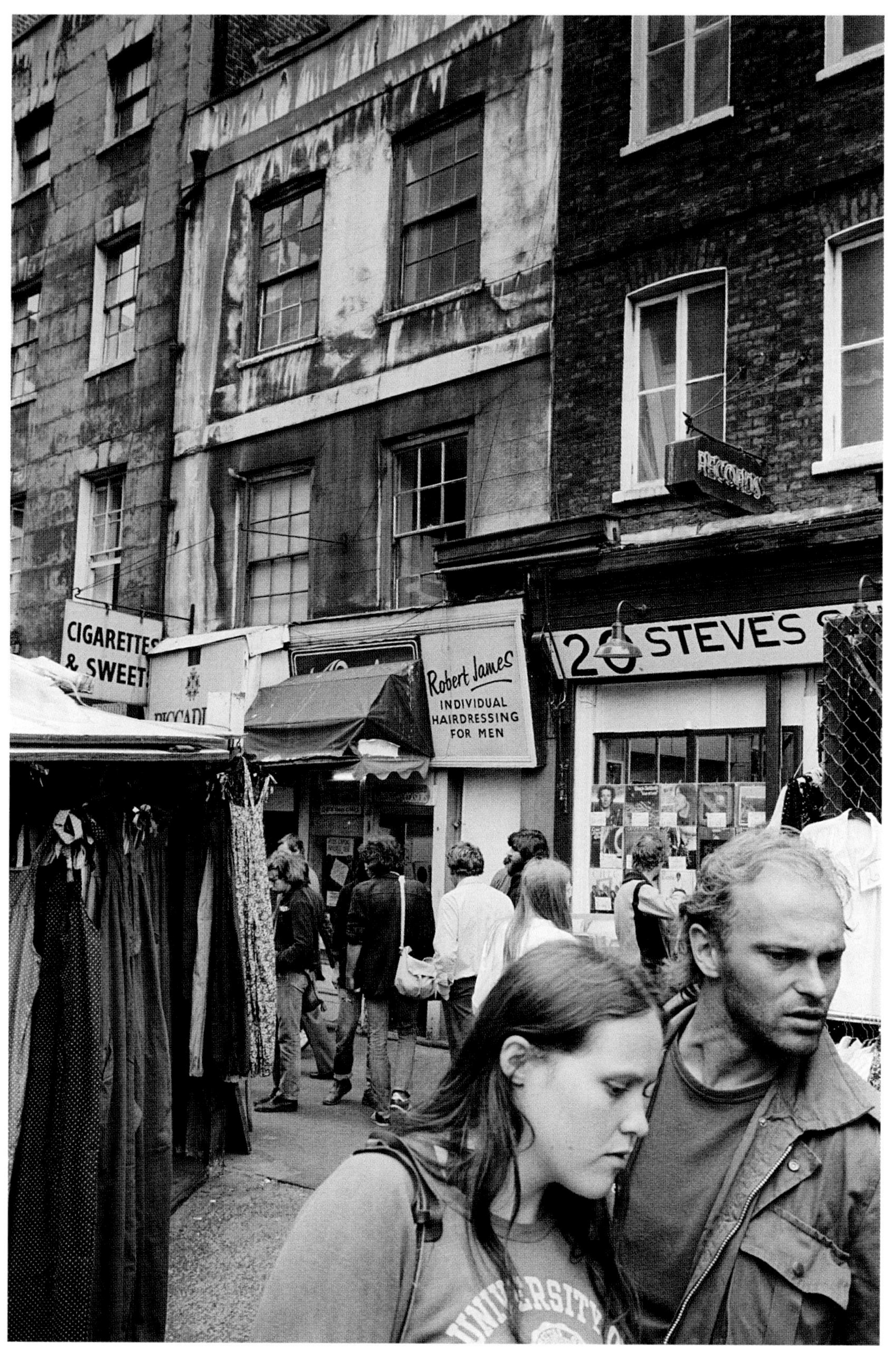

SOHO STREET MARKET, LONDON 1975

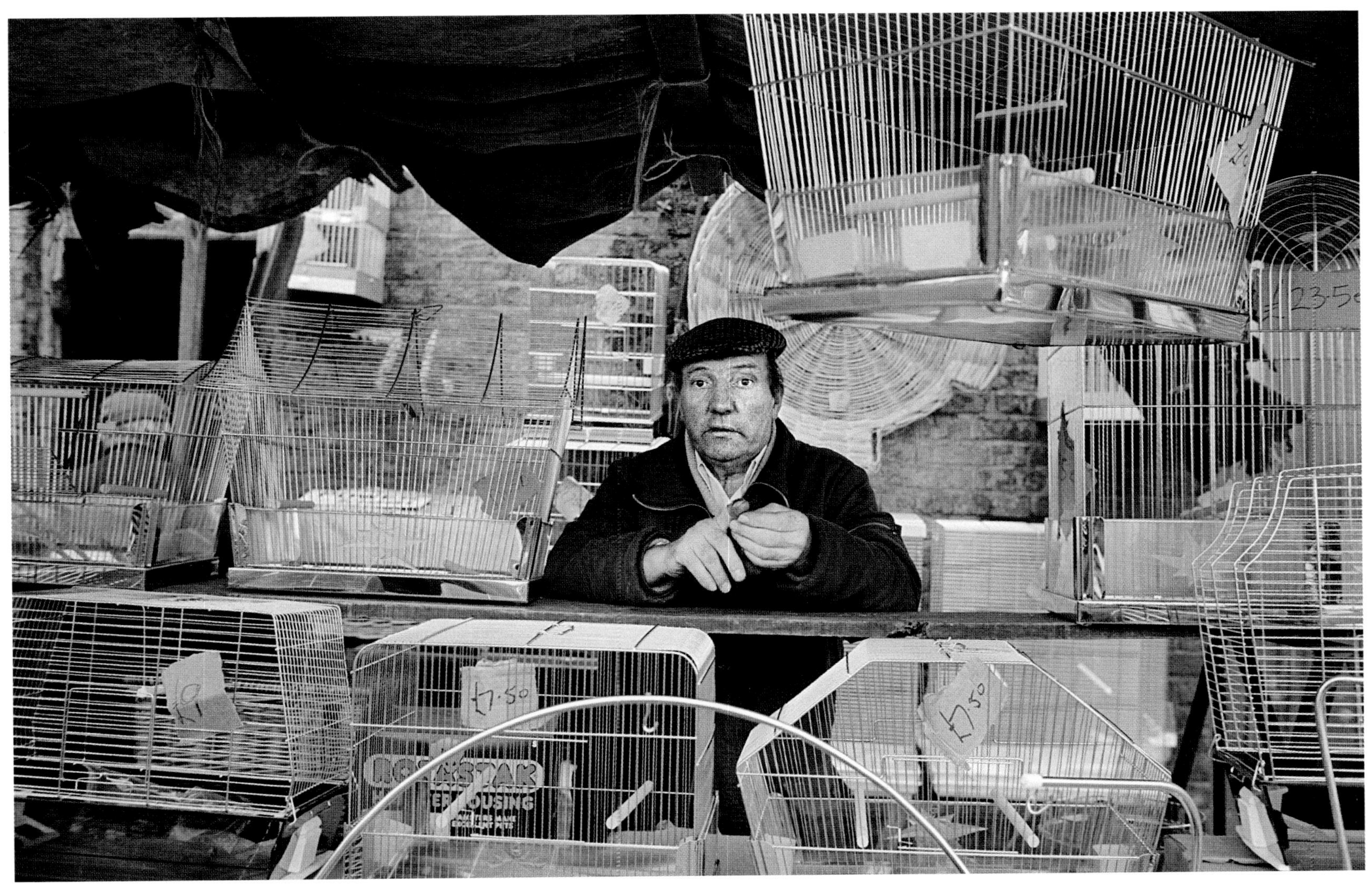

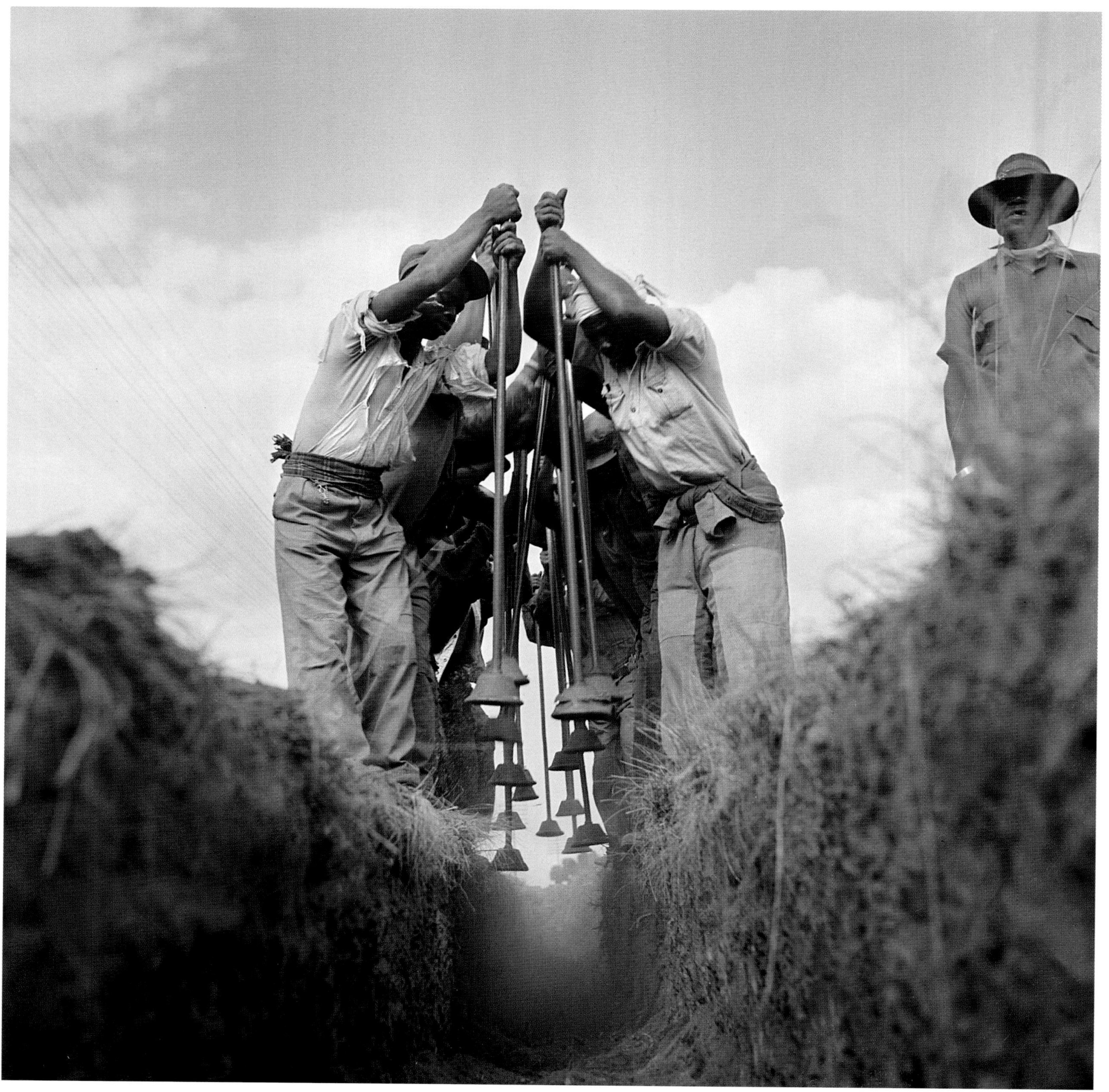

DITCHWORKERS, JOHANNESBURG 1951

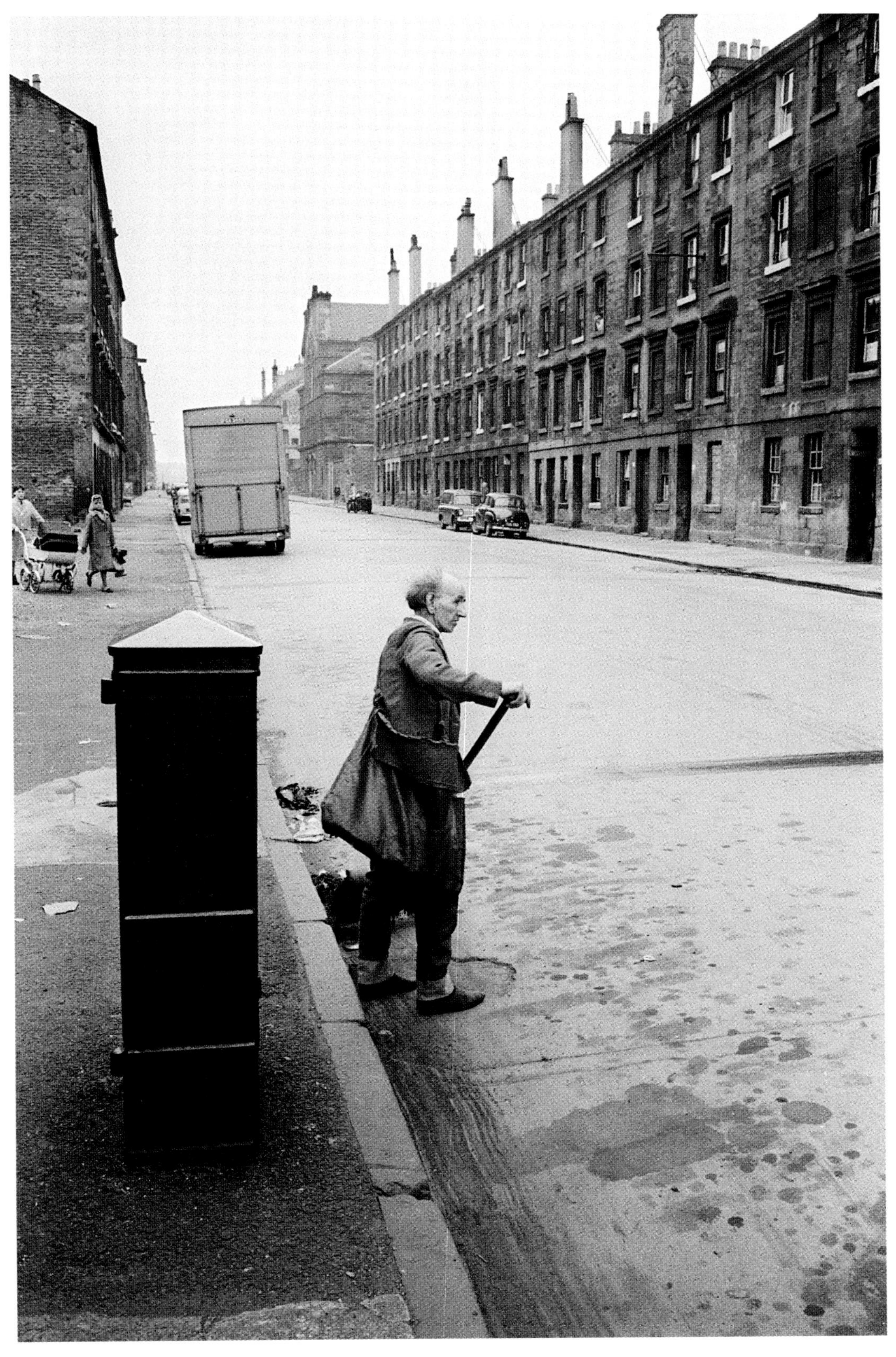

Street cleaner, Glasgow 1968

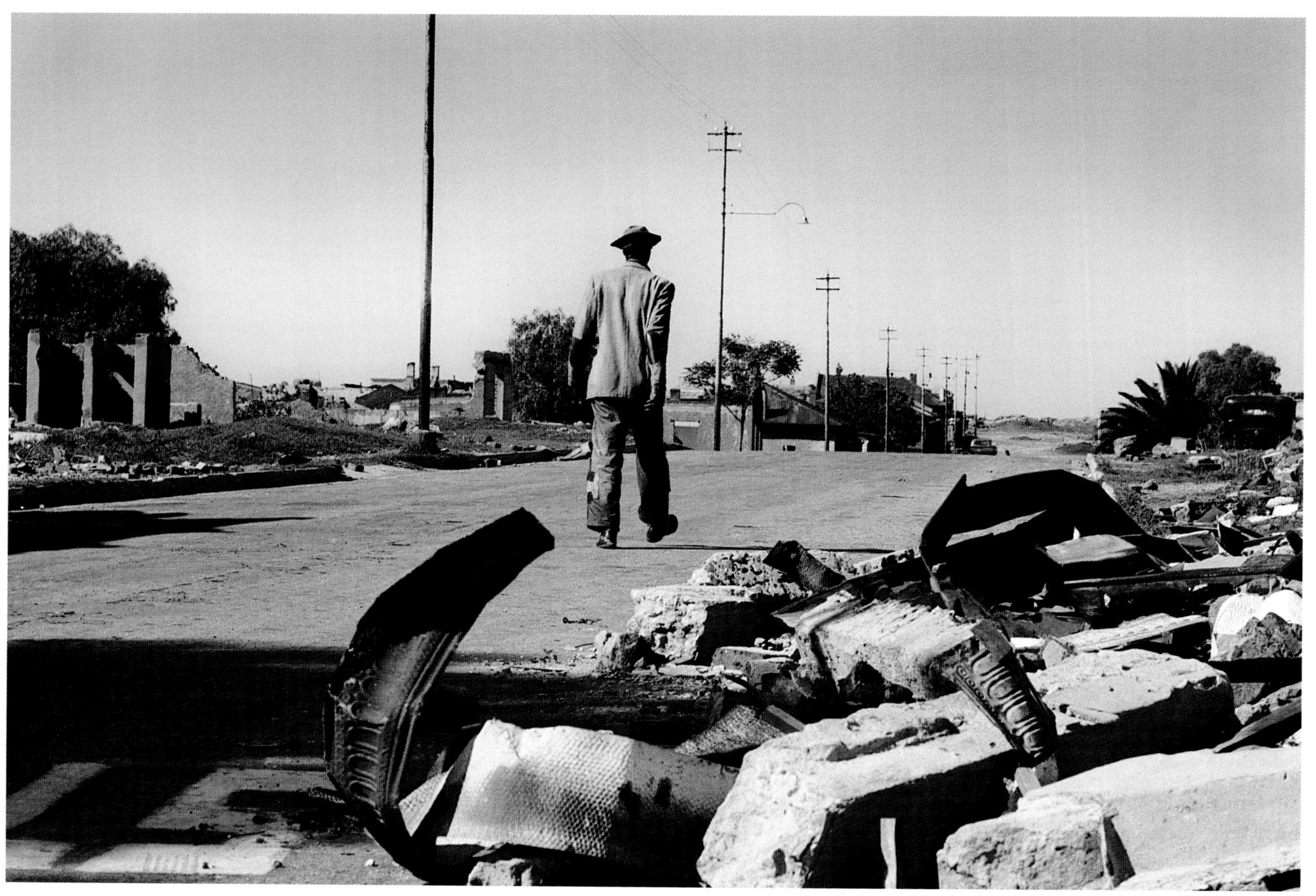

Sophiatown destroyed 1960

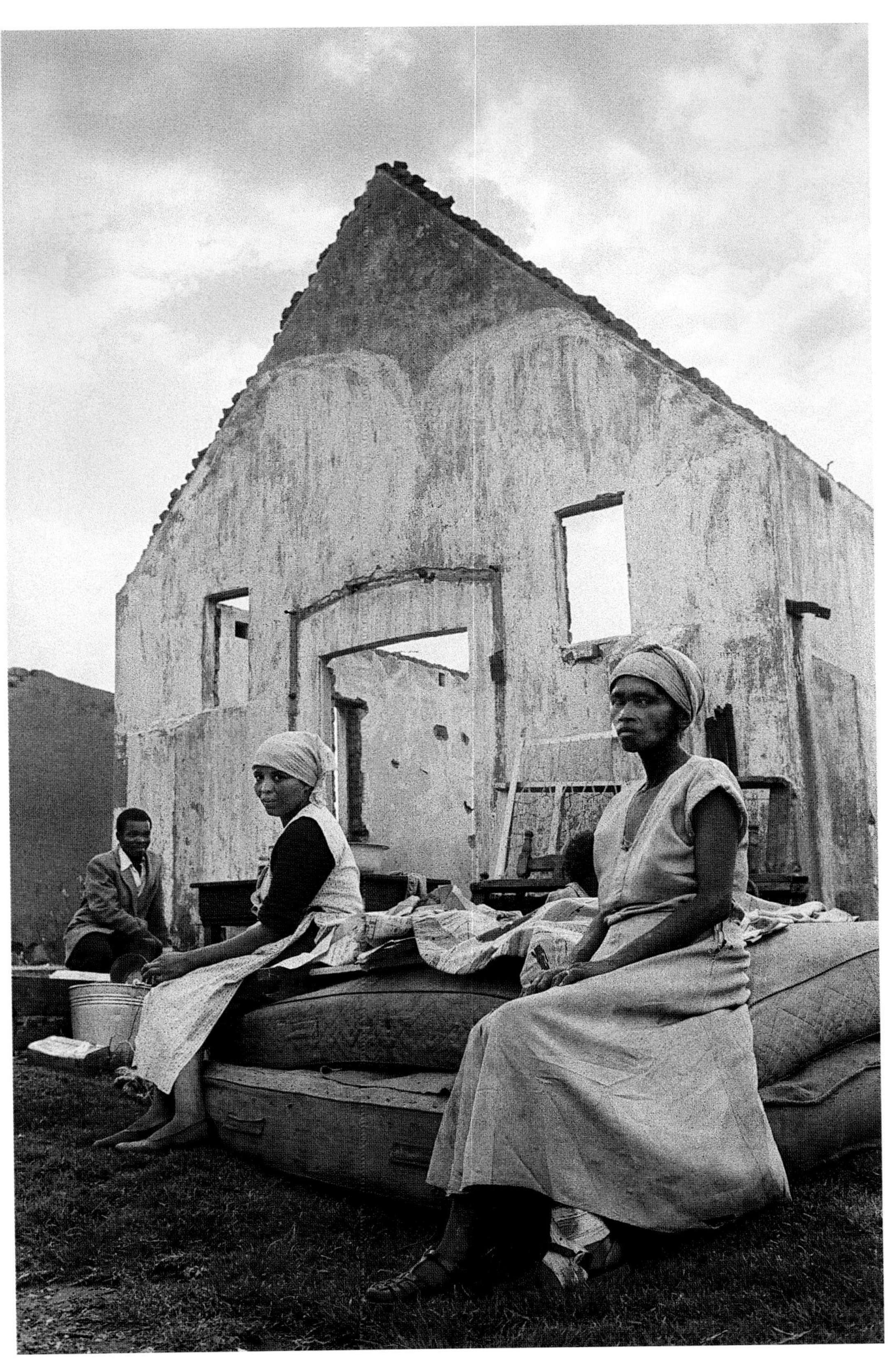

Waiting for the trucks, Sophiatown removals 1959

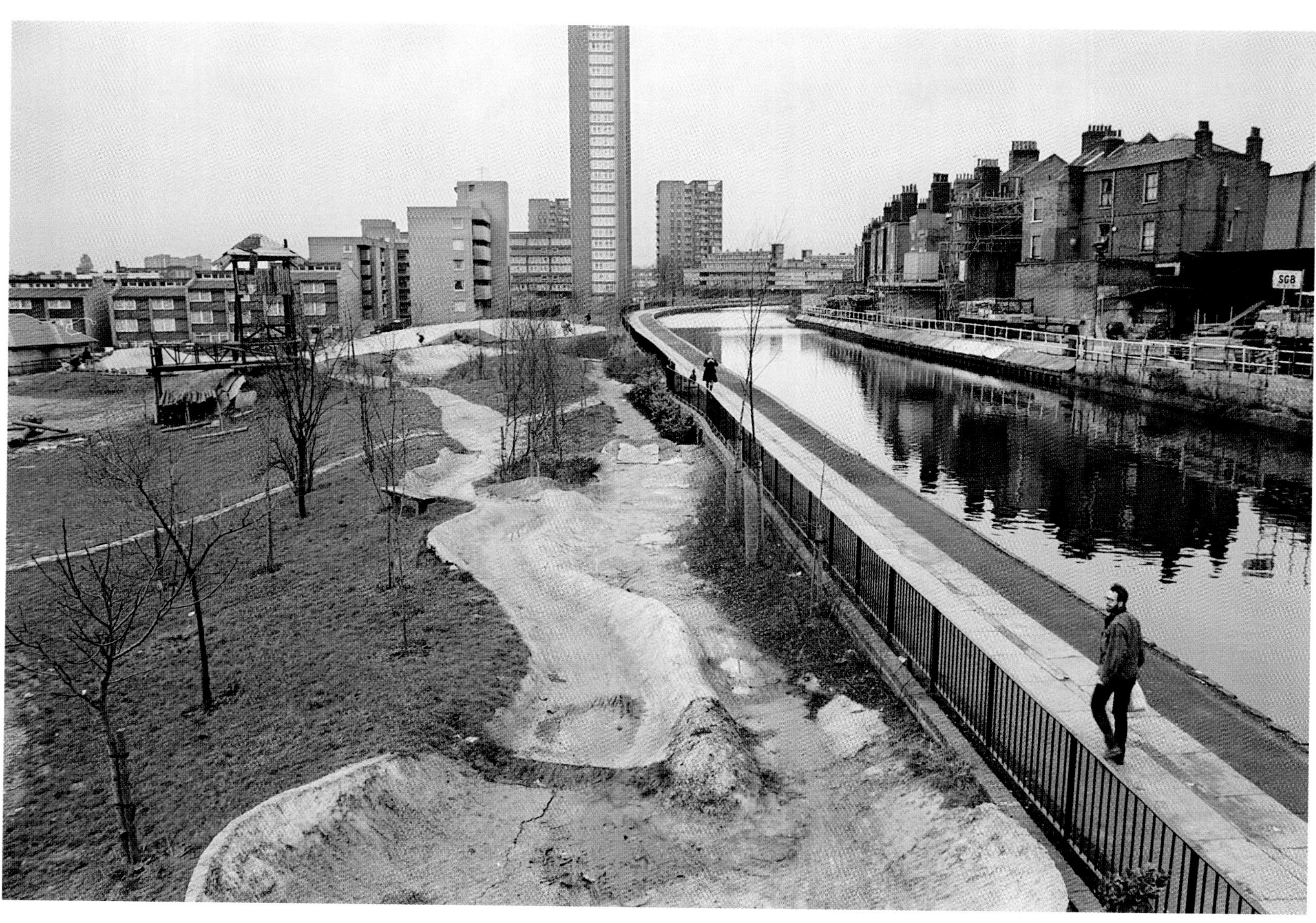

GRAND UNION CANAL, LADBROKE ROAD, LONDON 1977

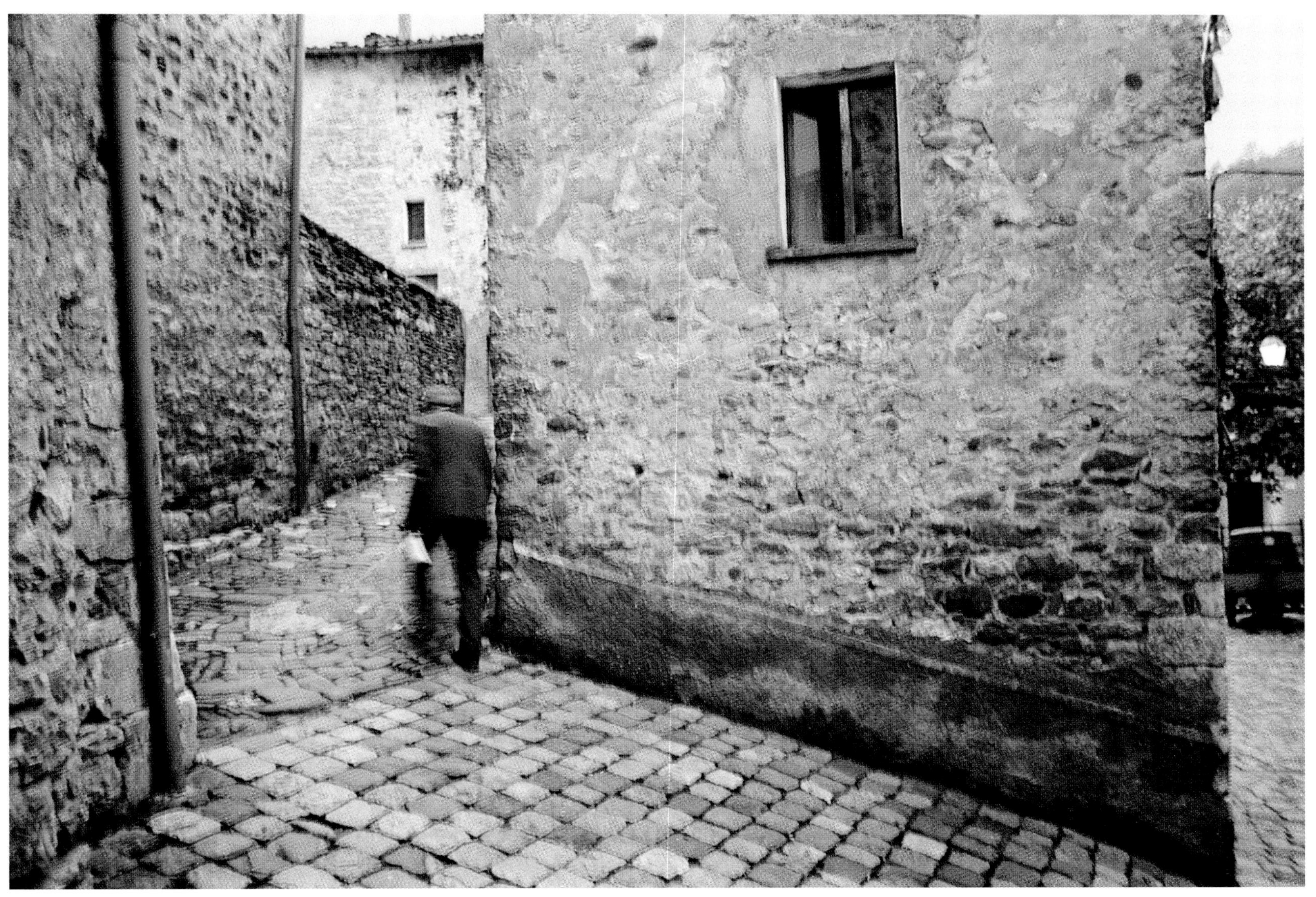

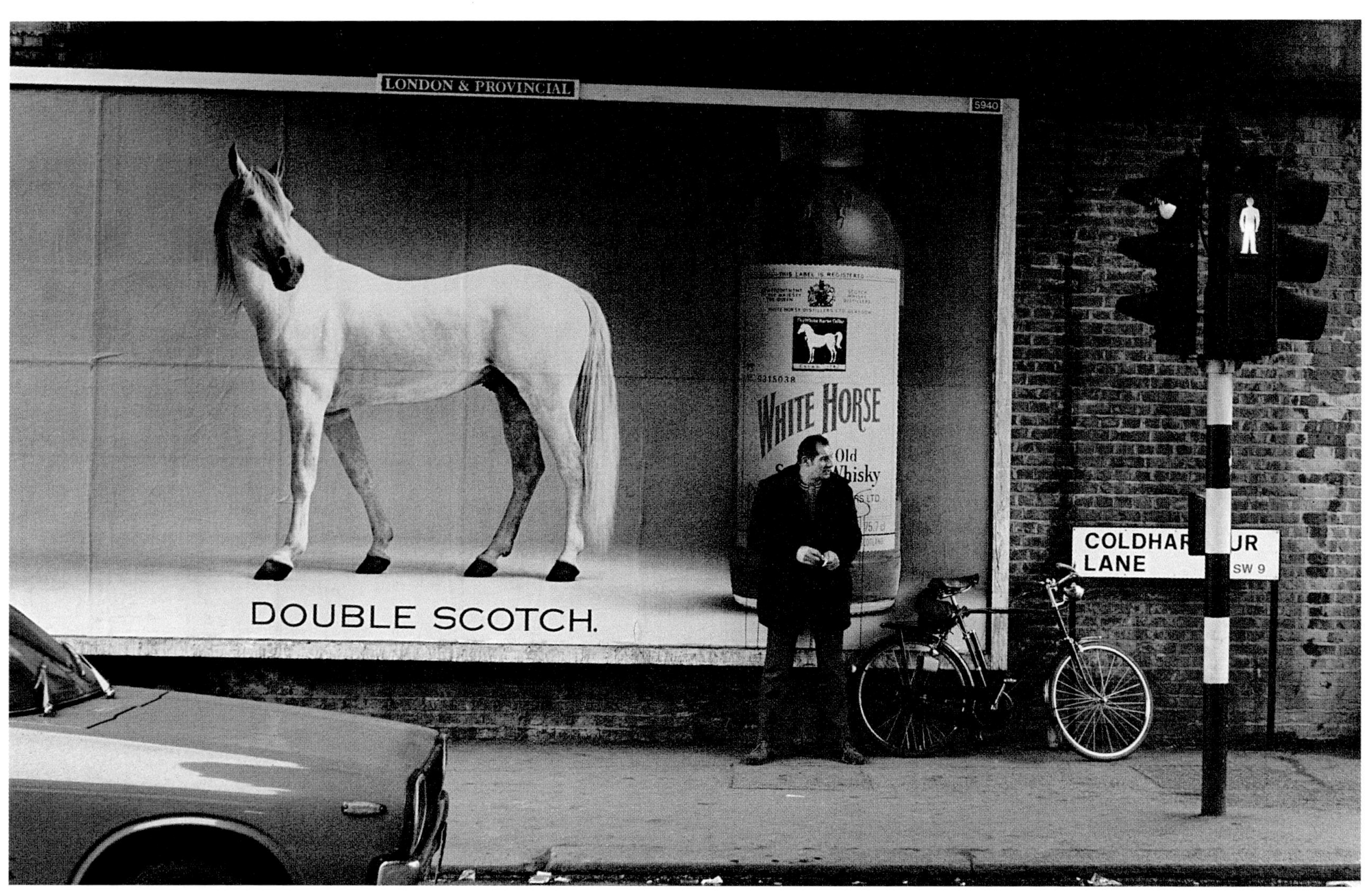

 A HORSE IN COVENT GARDEN, LONDON 1975

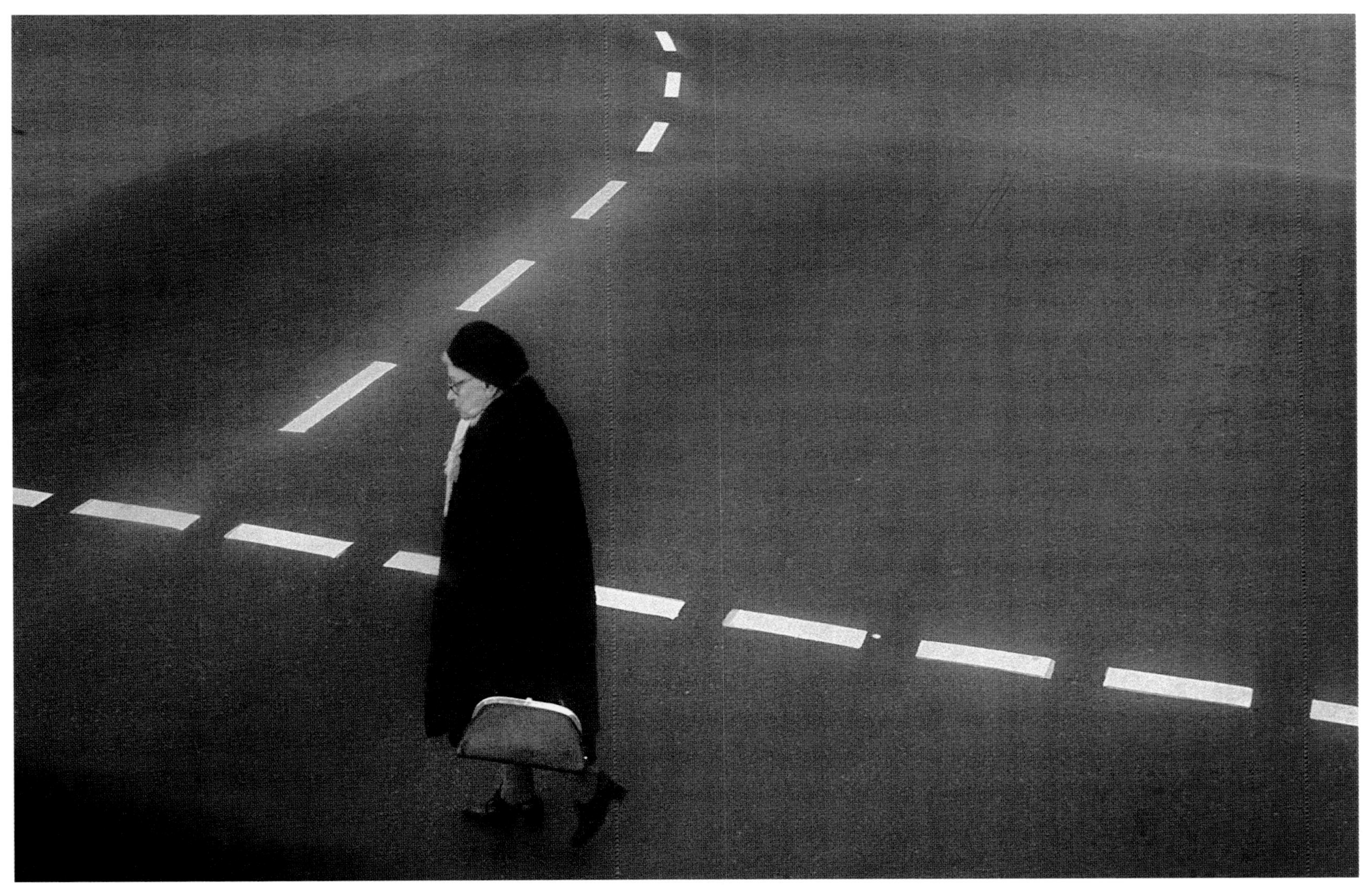

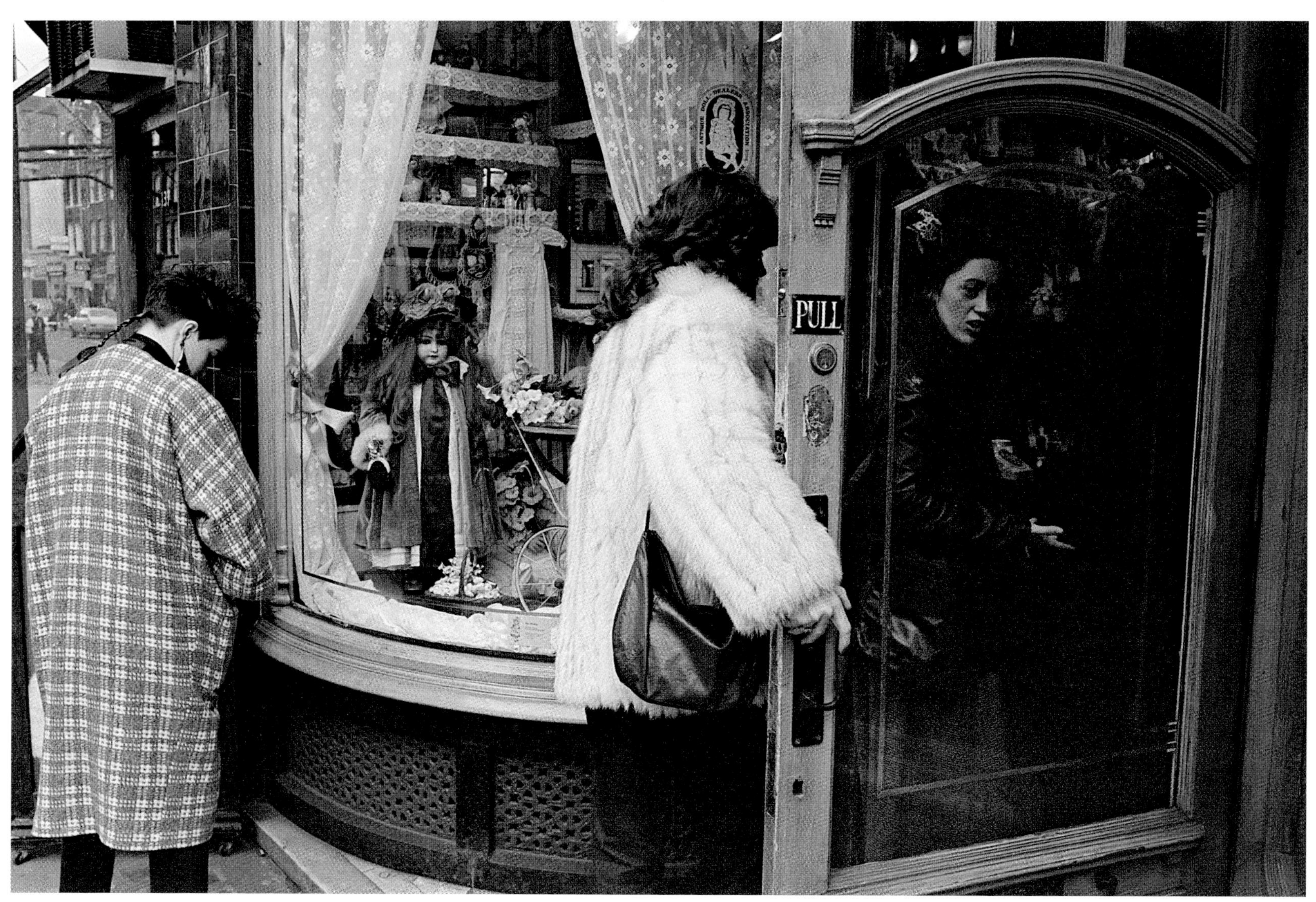

 Shopping in Covent Garden, London 1978

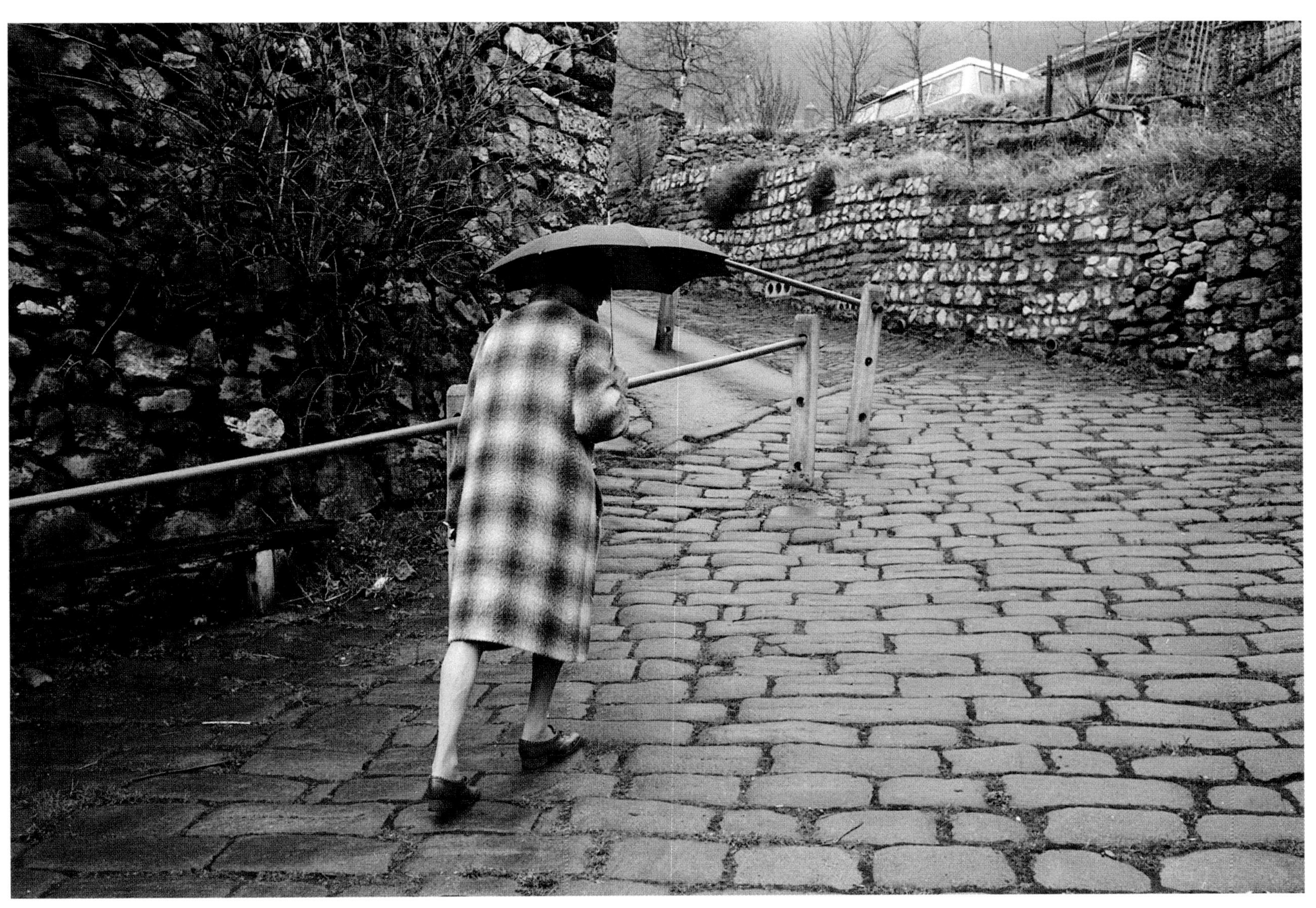

Cobblestone lady, Nottingham, England 1978

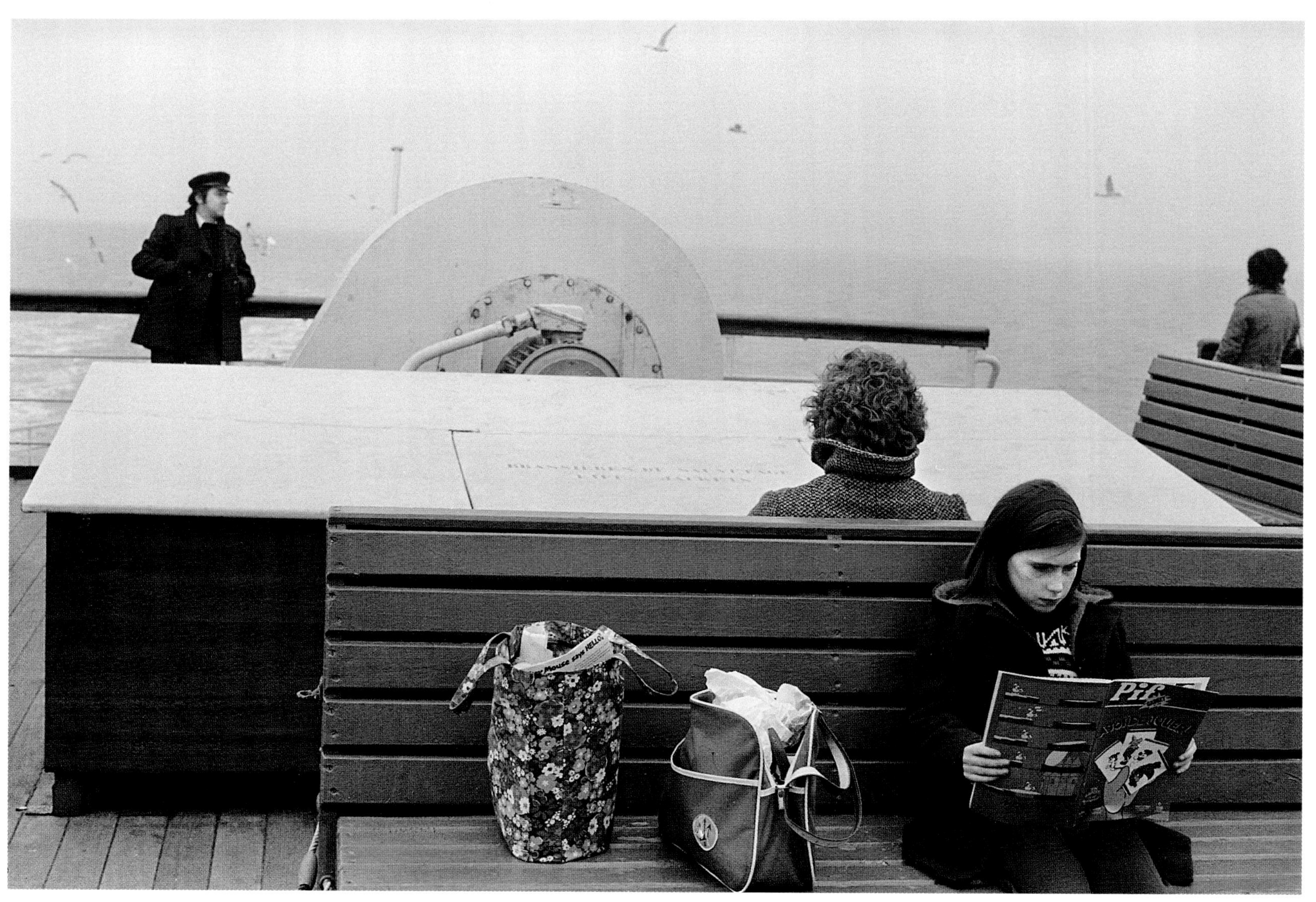

    Channel crossing 1975

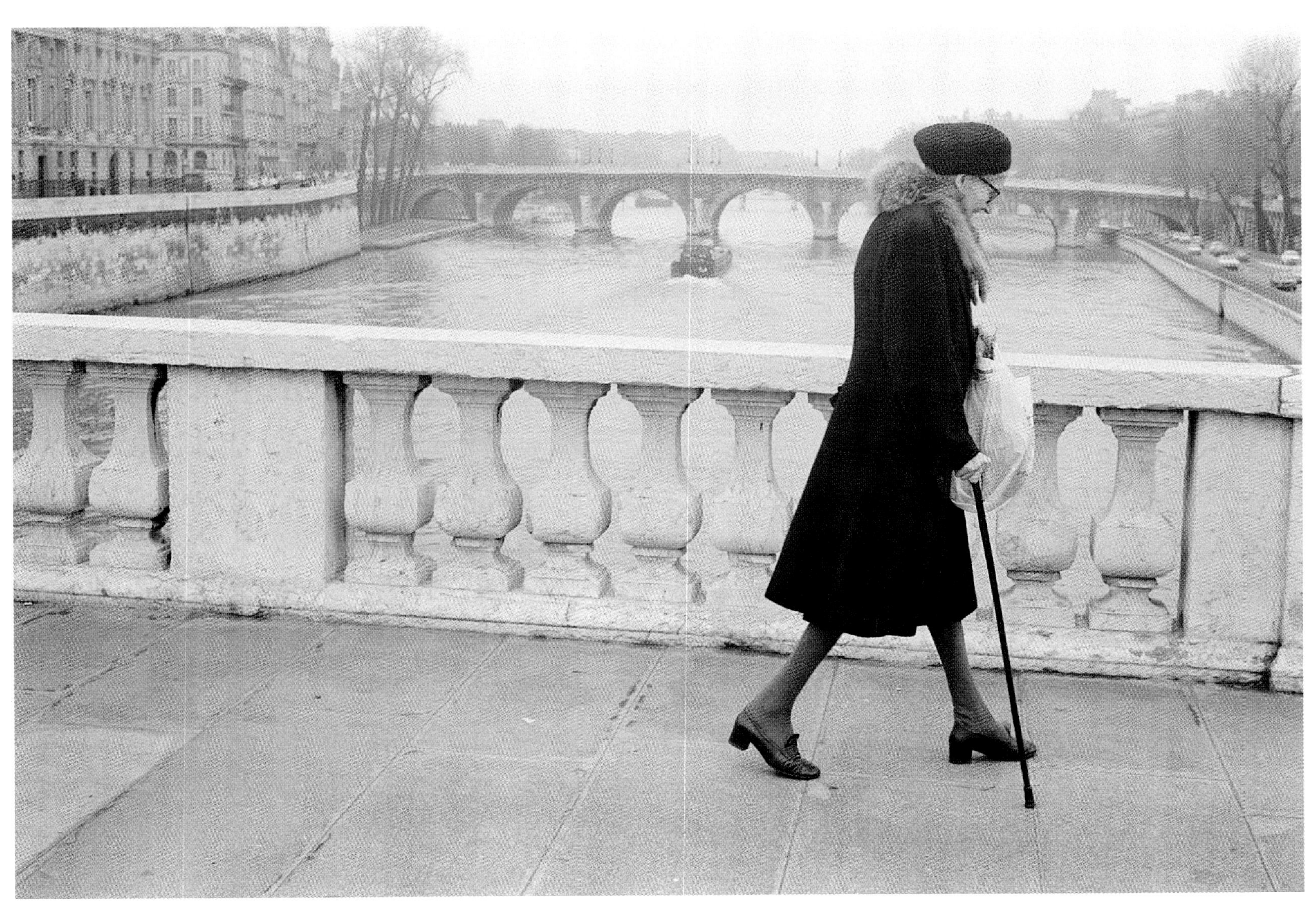

PARISIENNE ON BRIDGE 1975

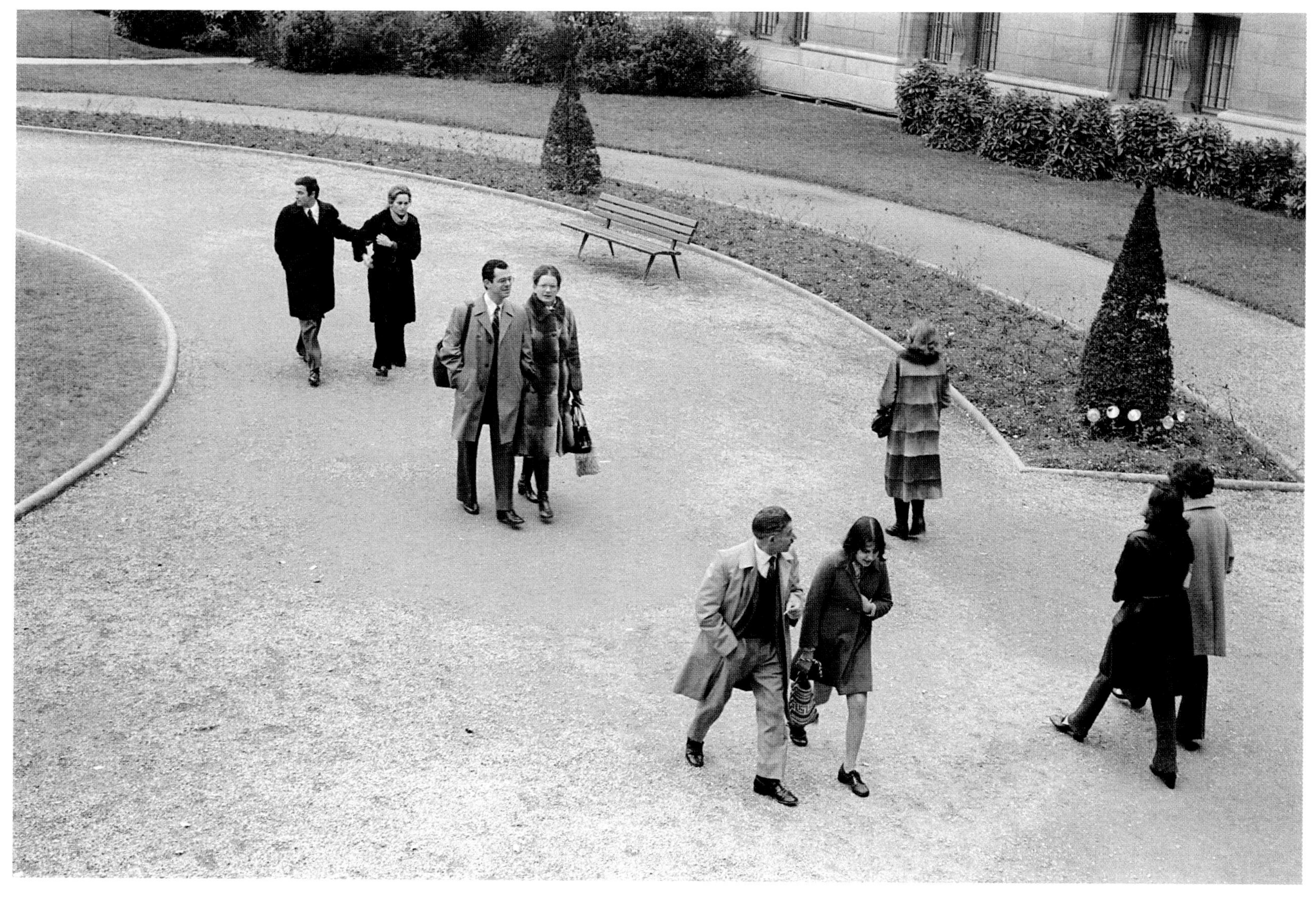

PARIS PARK 1980

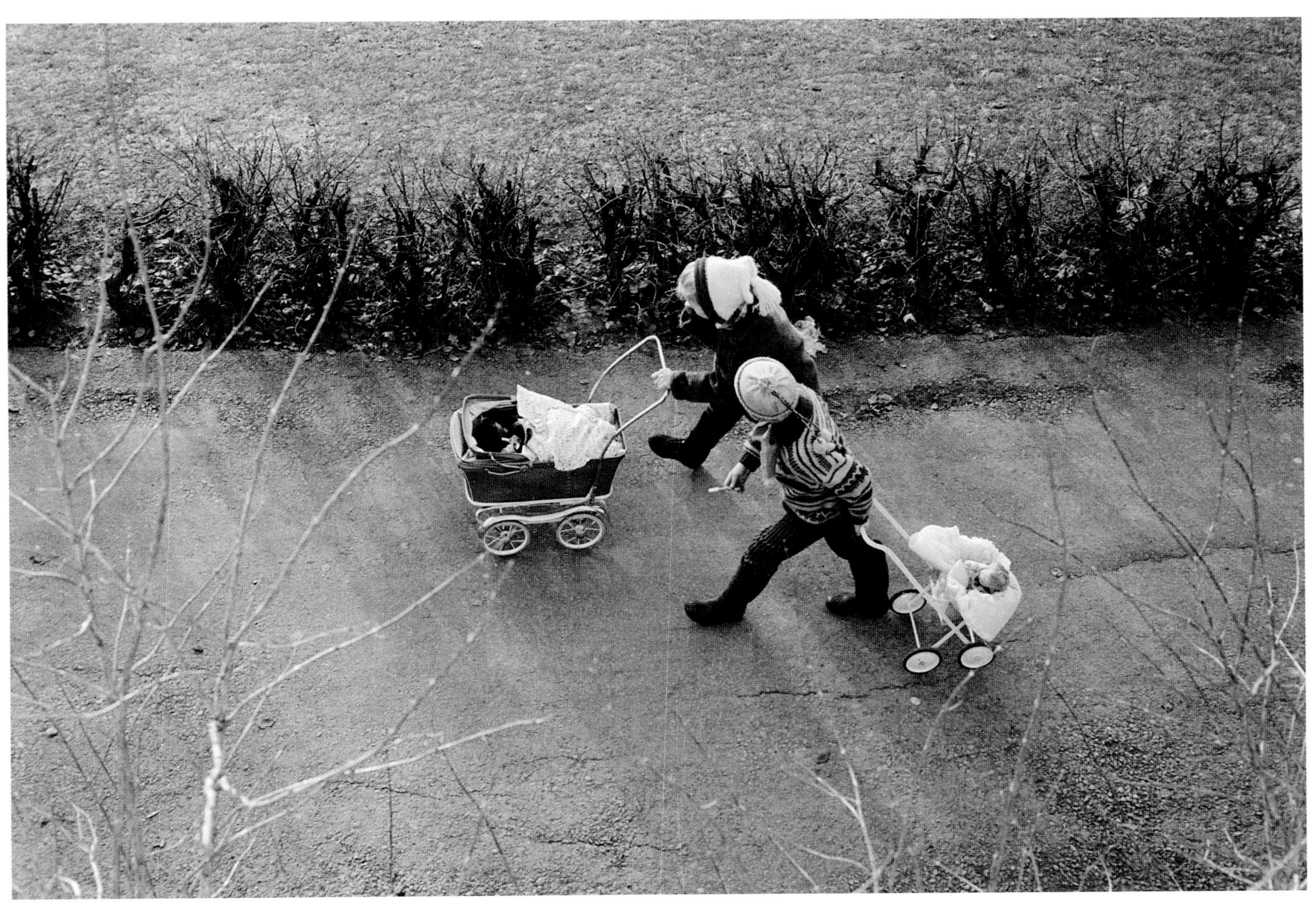

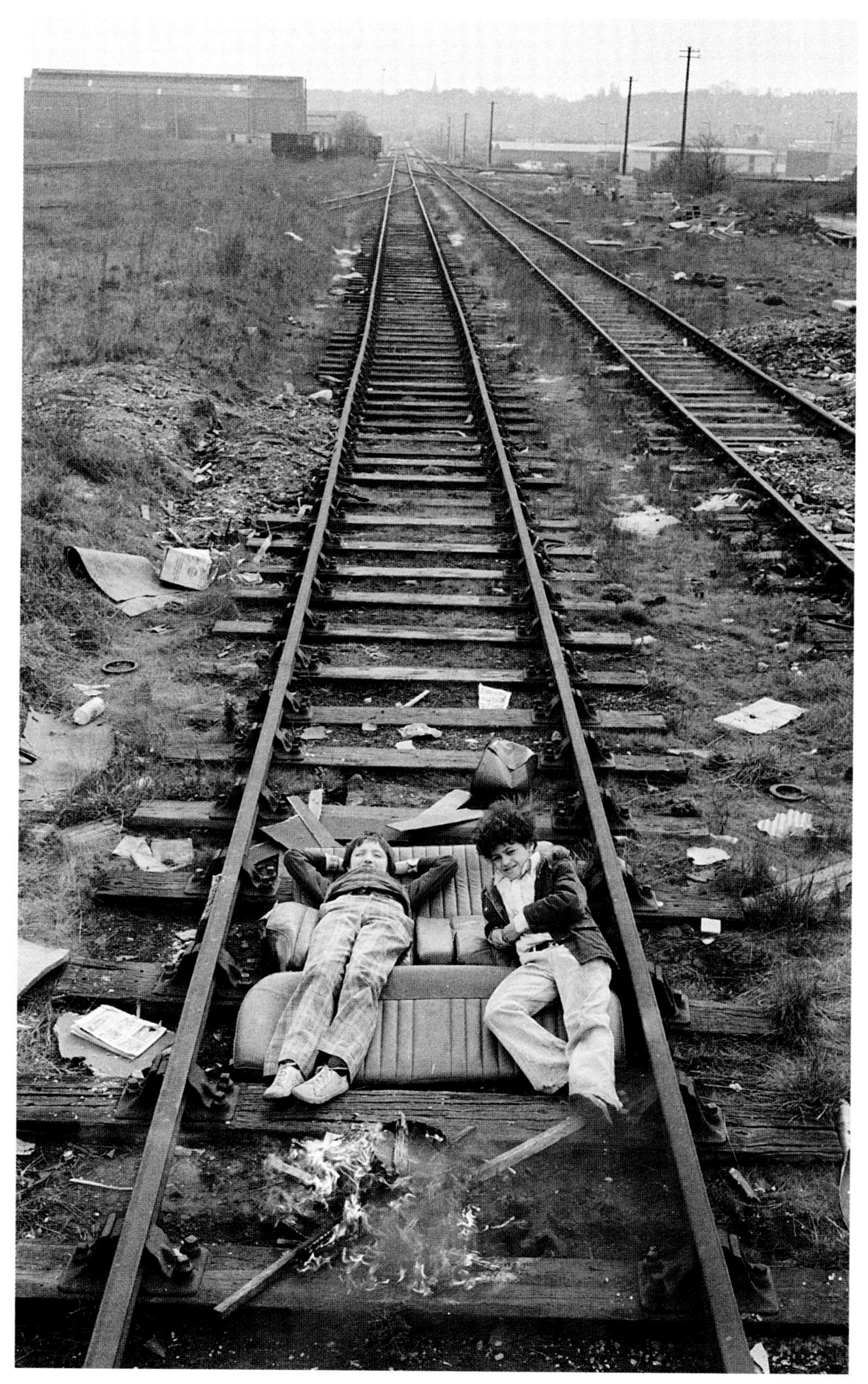

THE END OF THE LINE, LONDON DOCKS 1974

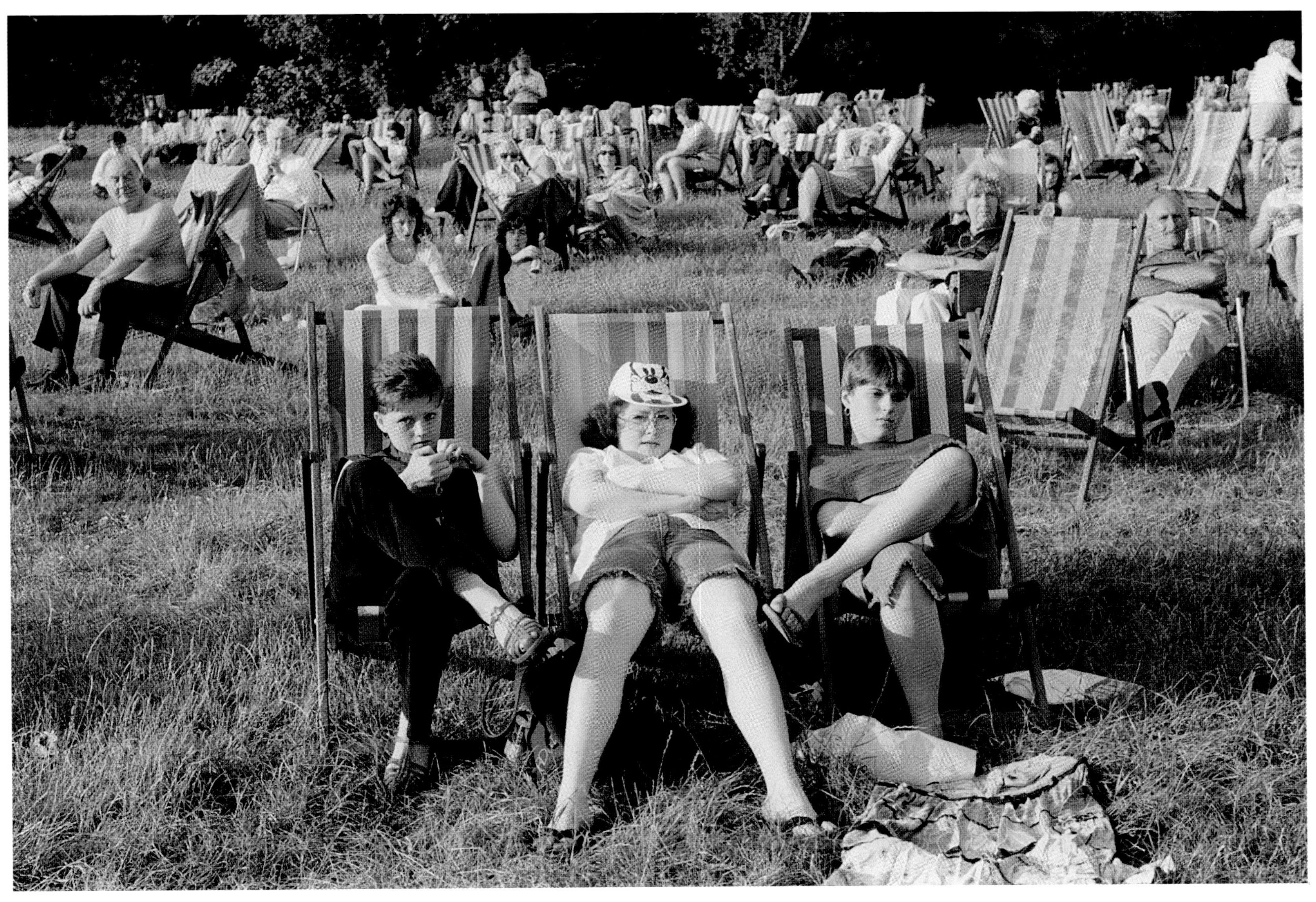

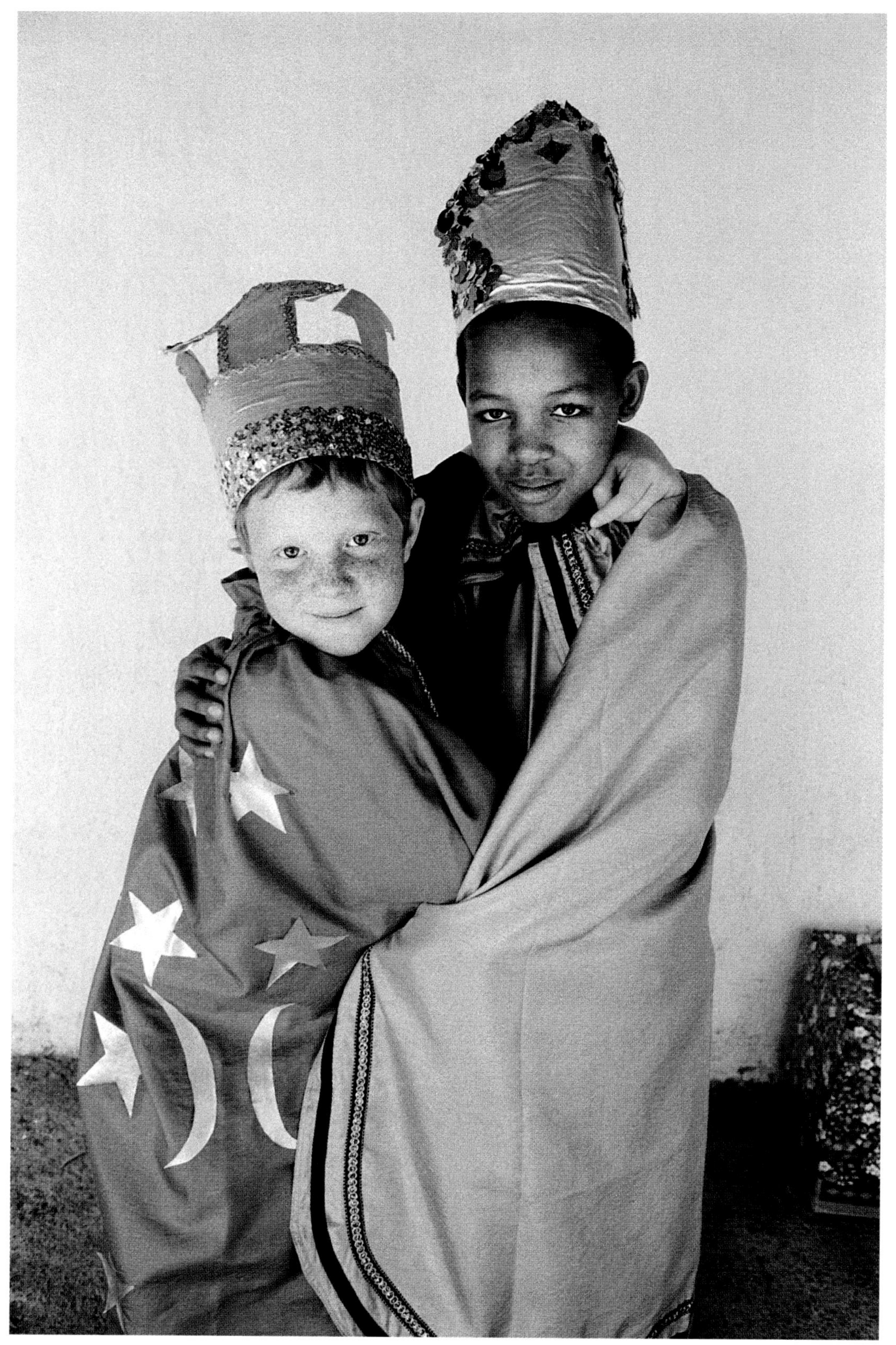

CHARLIE & PAUL, NATIVITY PLAY, JOHANNESBURG 1996

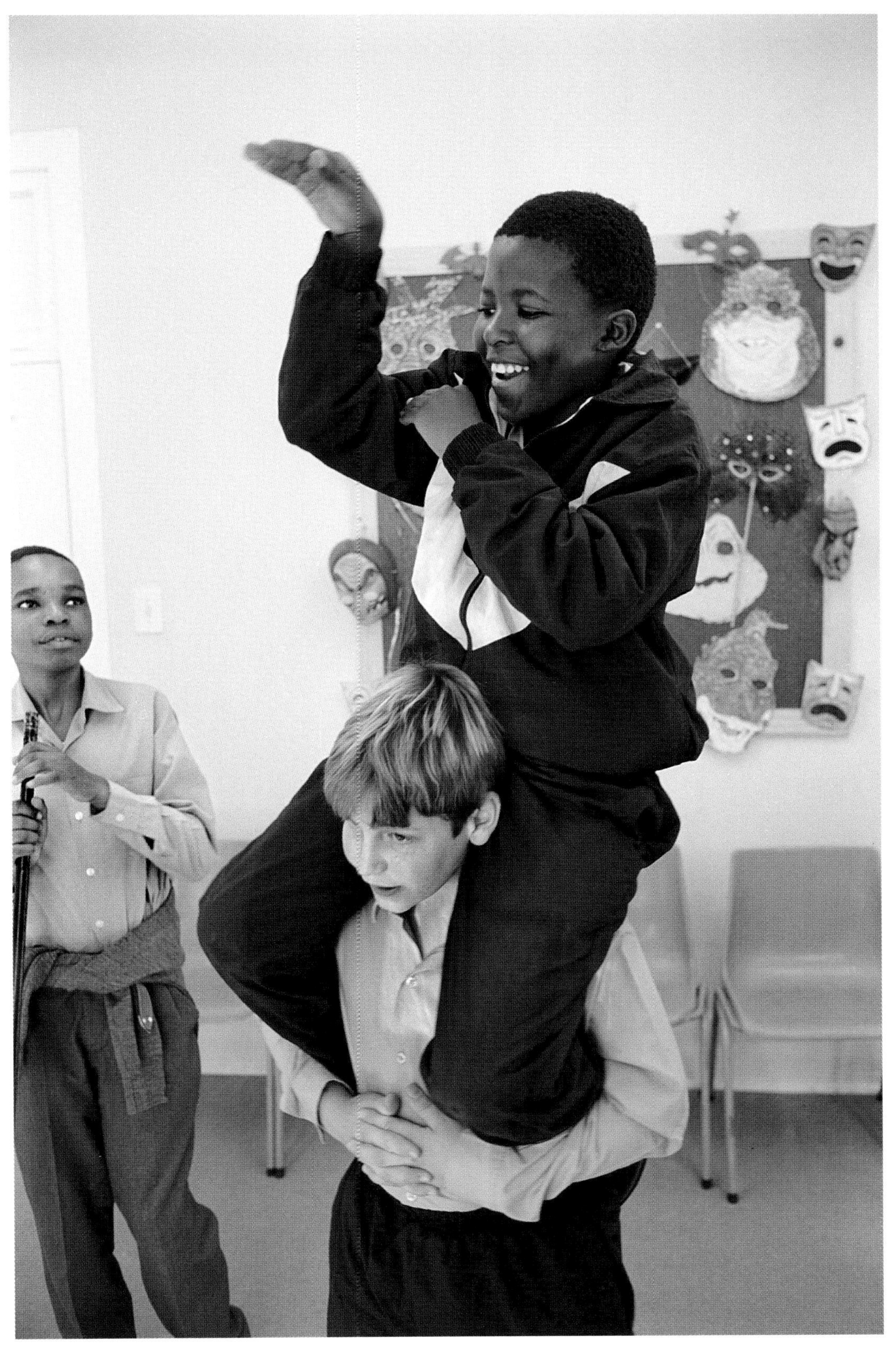

Rehearsing for school play, Johannesburg 1998

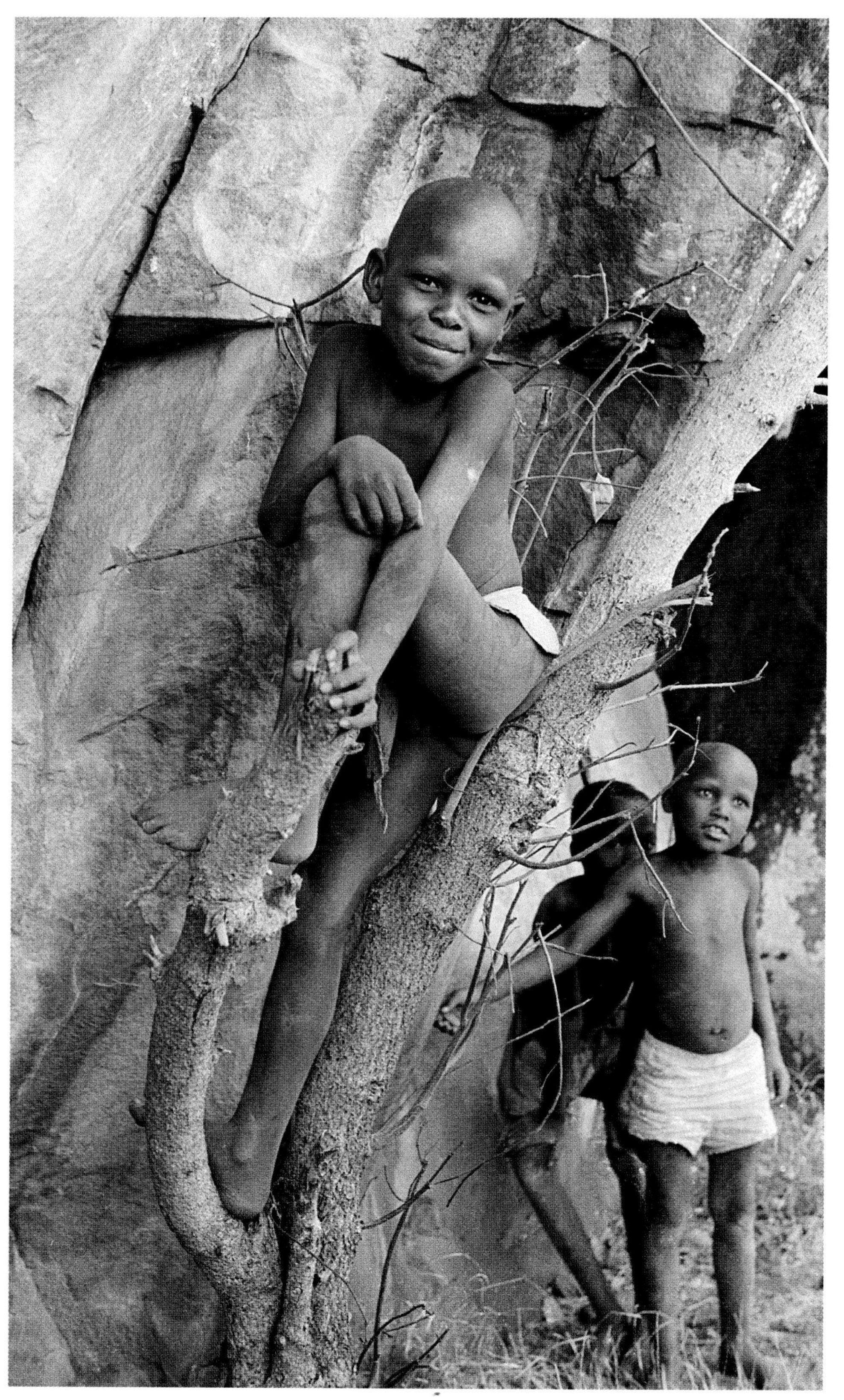

Botswana boys 1973

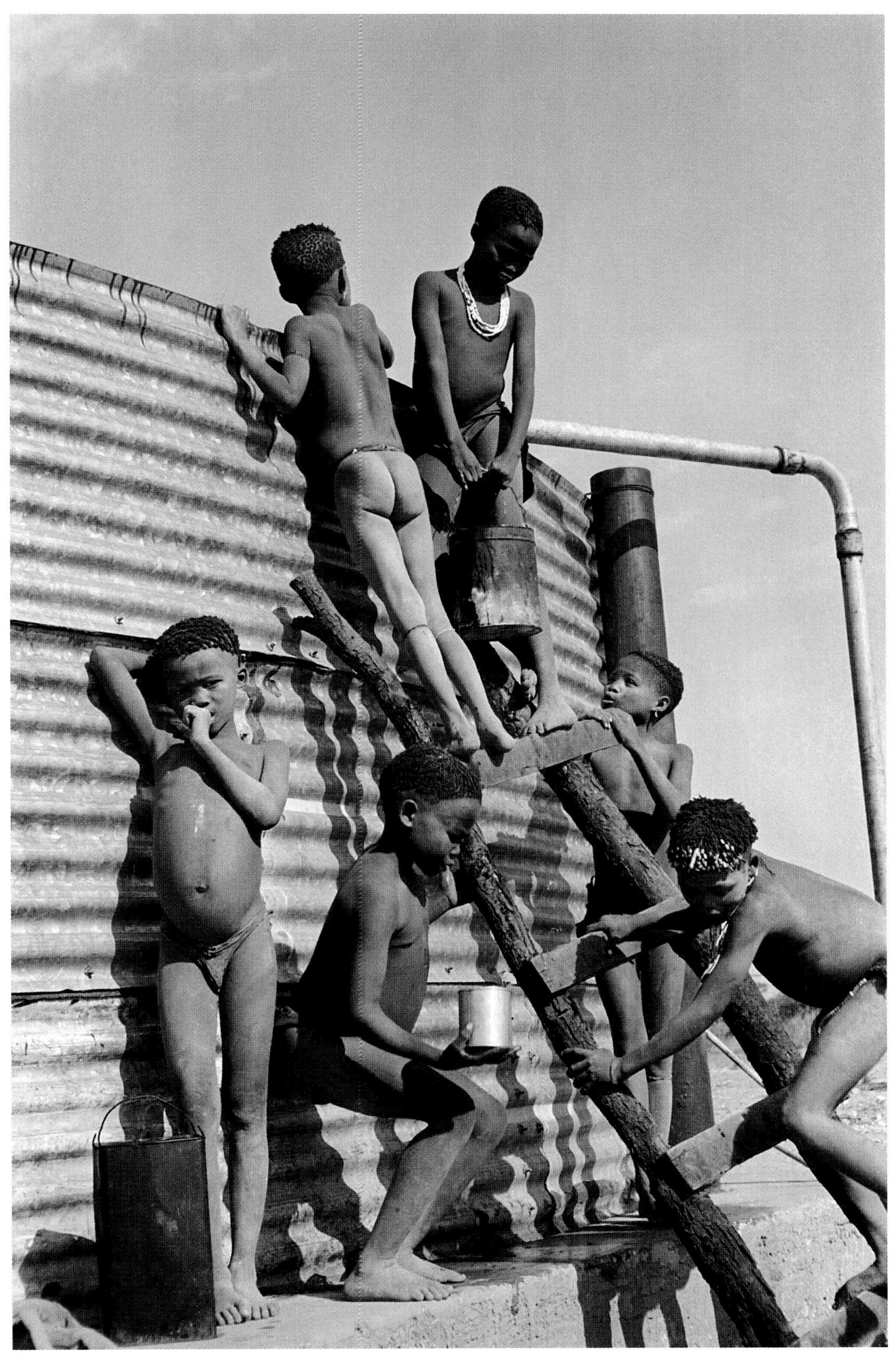

San boys gathering water at Lone Tree, Kalahari 1959

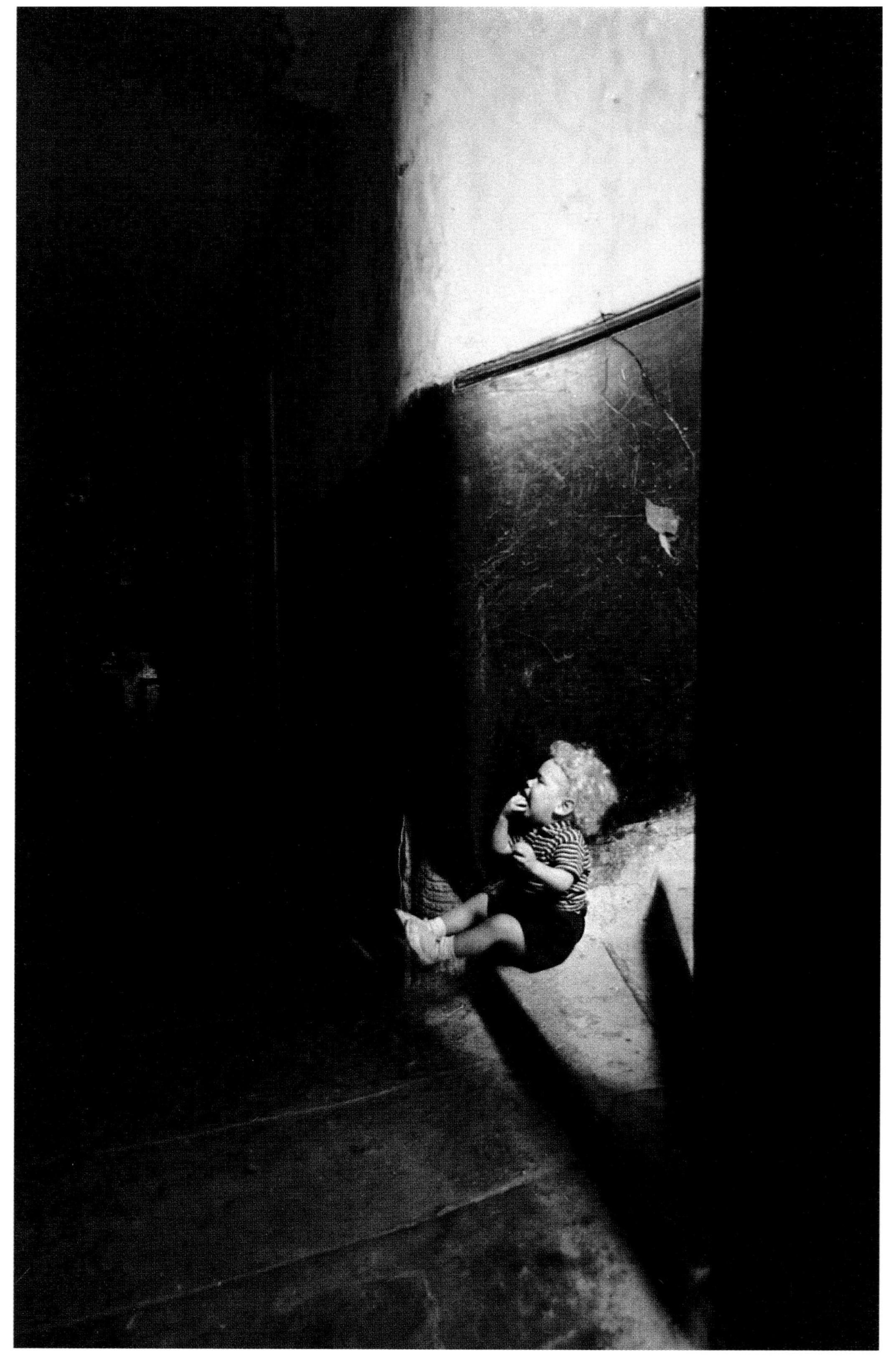

GLASGOW STAIRCASE 1968

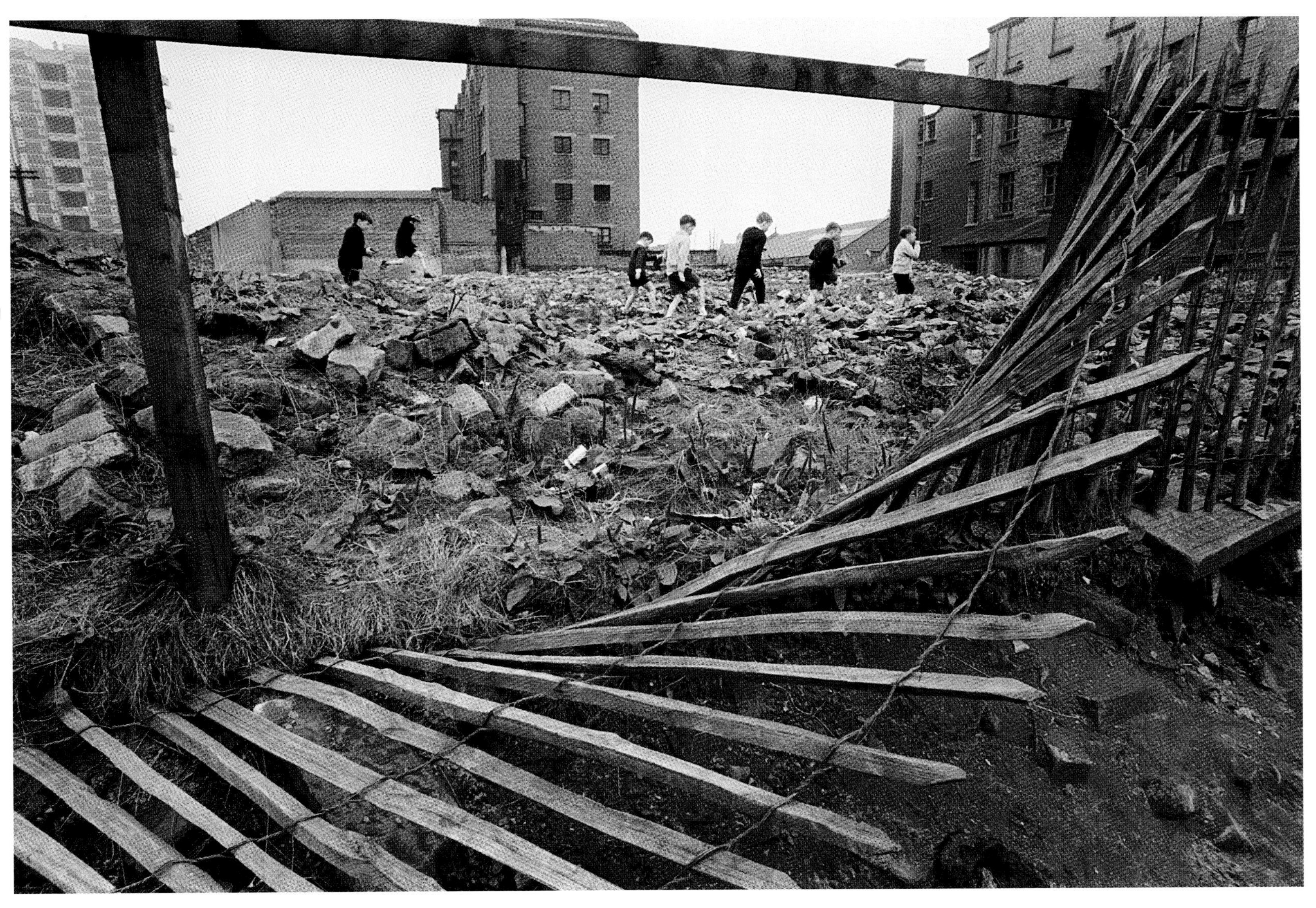

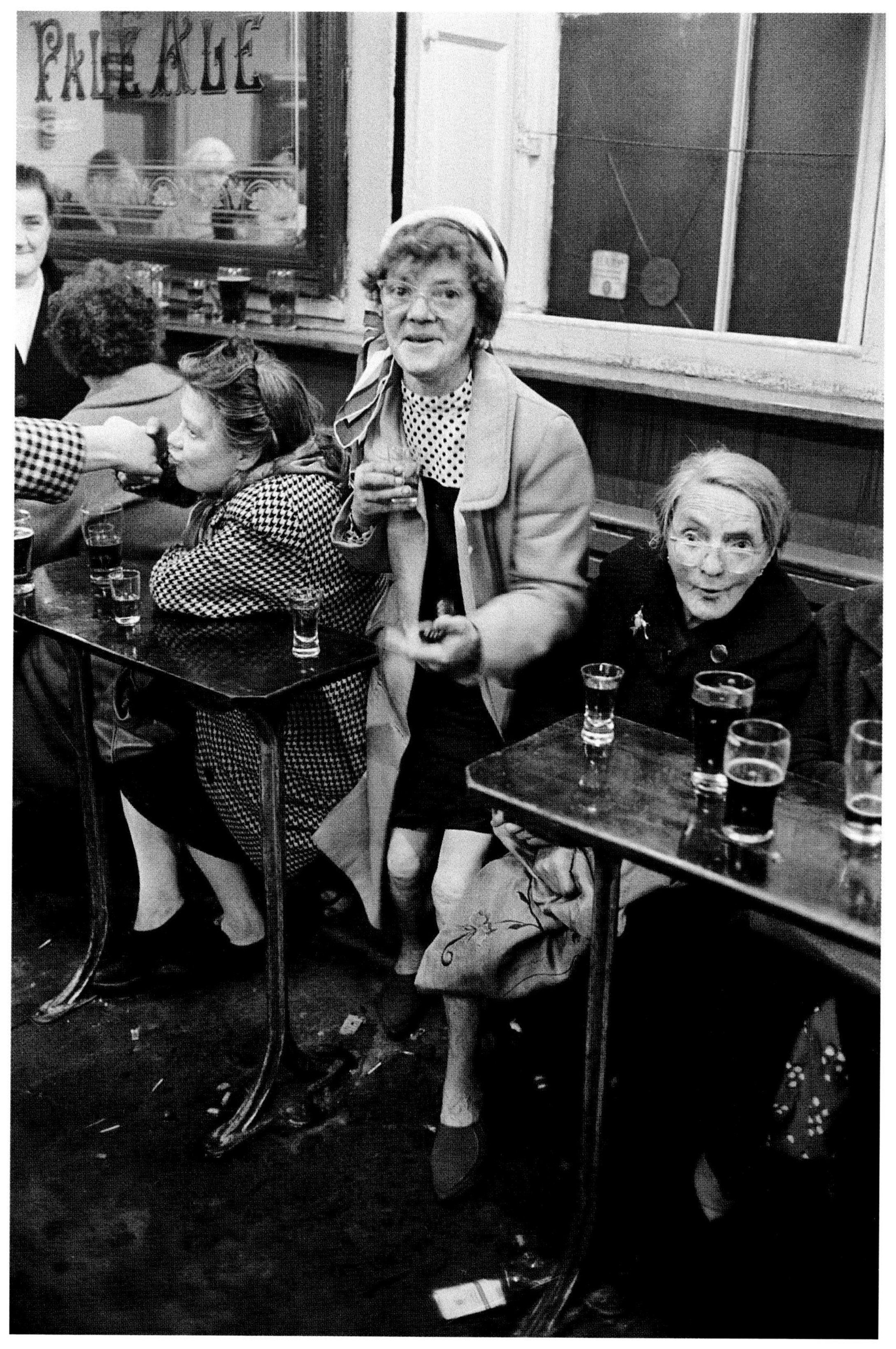

 Sherry drinkers, Gorbals, Glasgow 1968

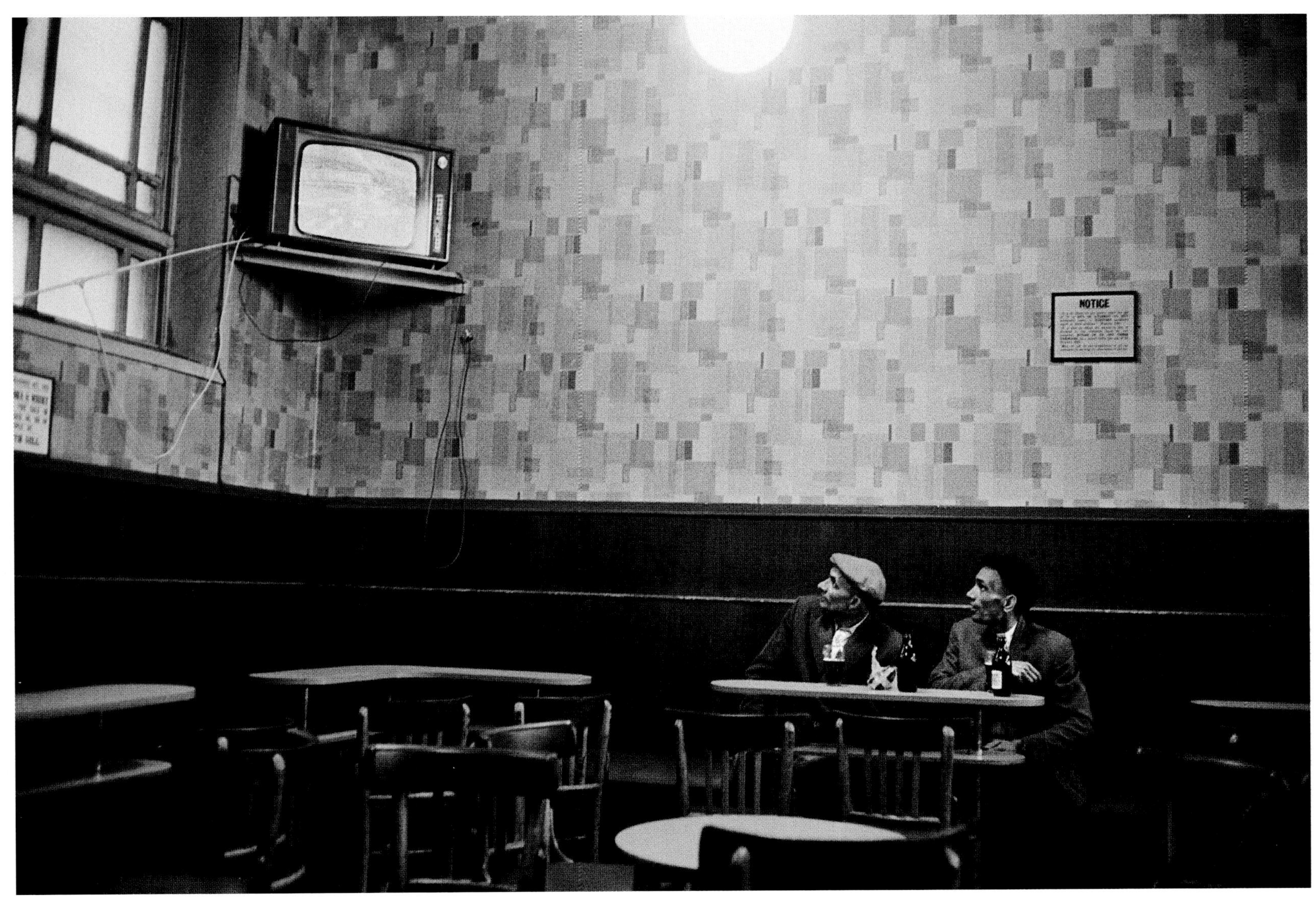

Pub TV, Gorbals, Glasgow 1968

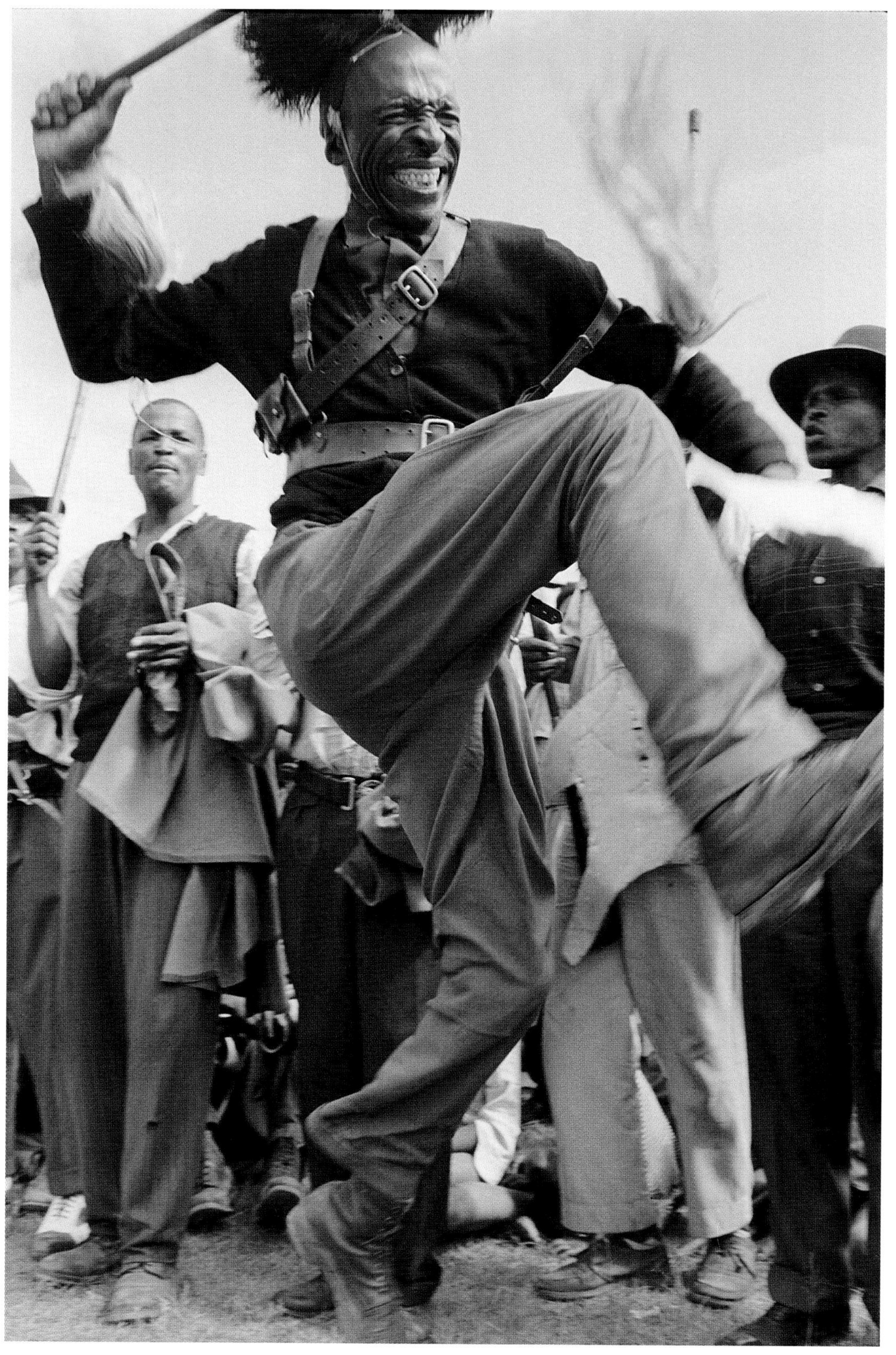

Lesotho independence celebrations 1960

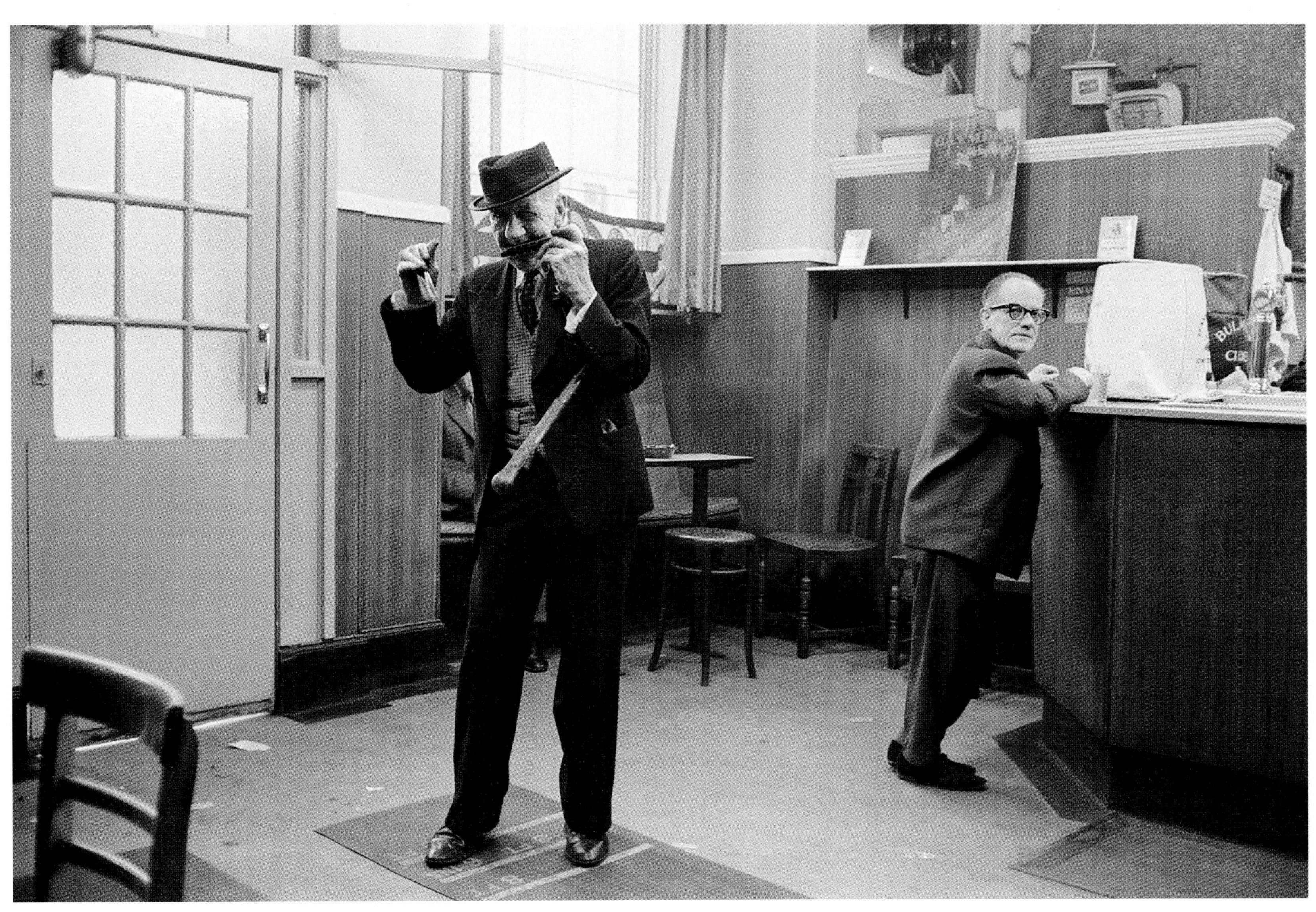

Song and dance man, Gorbals, Glasgow pub 1968

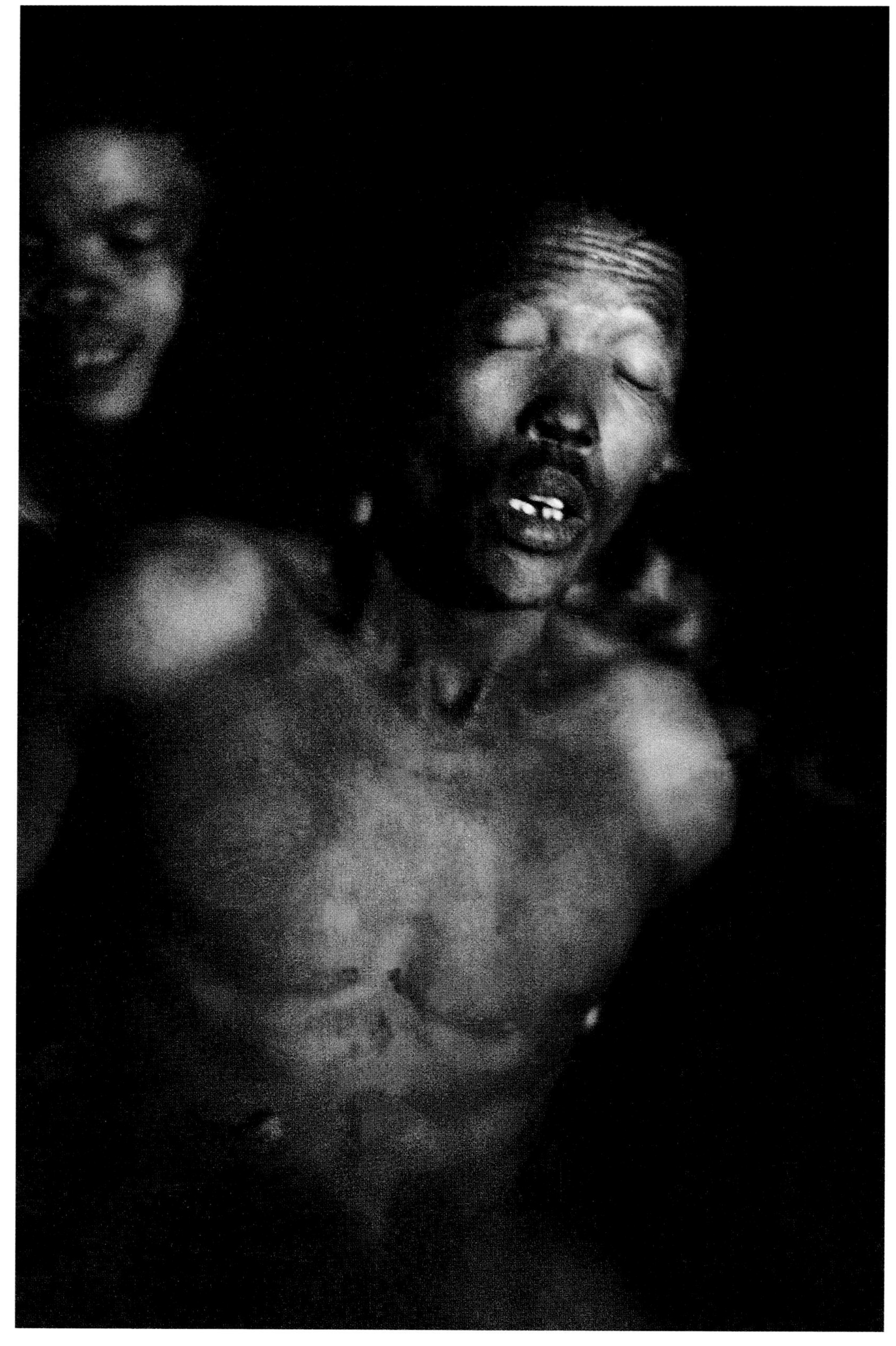

  The San trance dance, Kalahari 1959

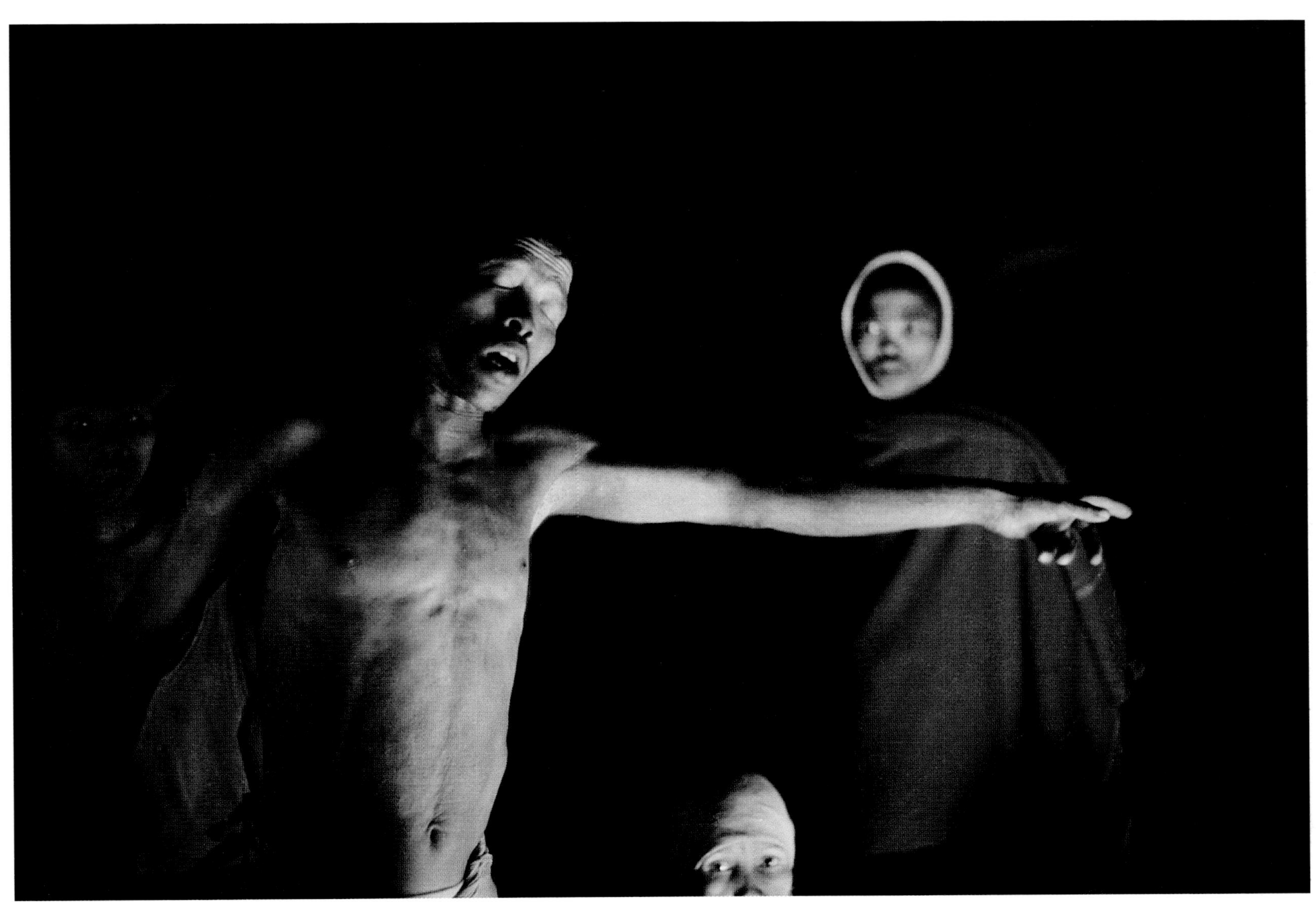

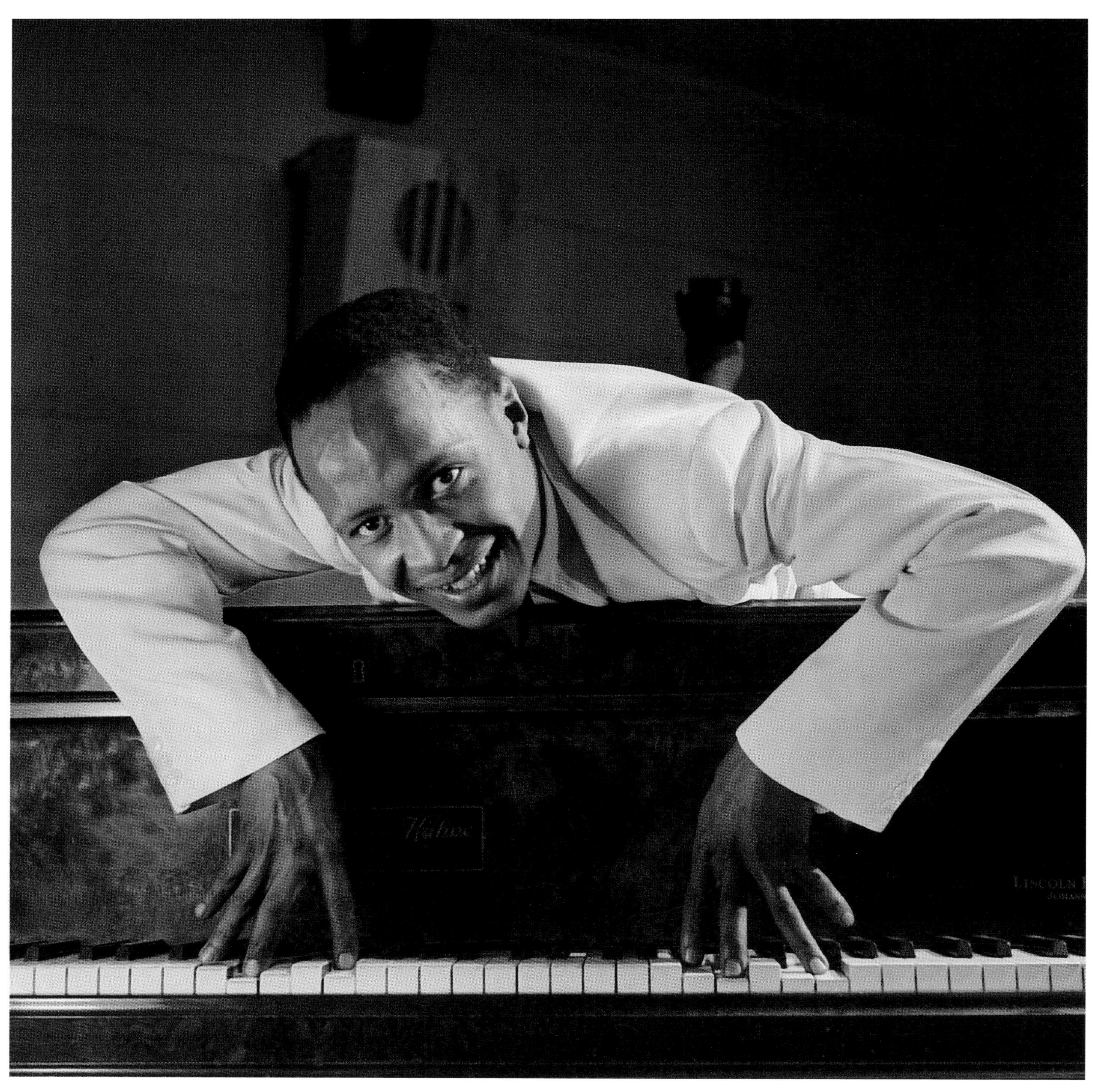

"PIANO FINGERS" — BOYCIE GWELE BIG BAND PLAYER,
JOHANNESBURG 1952

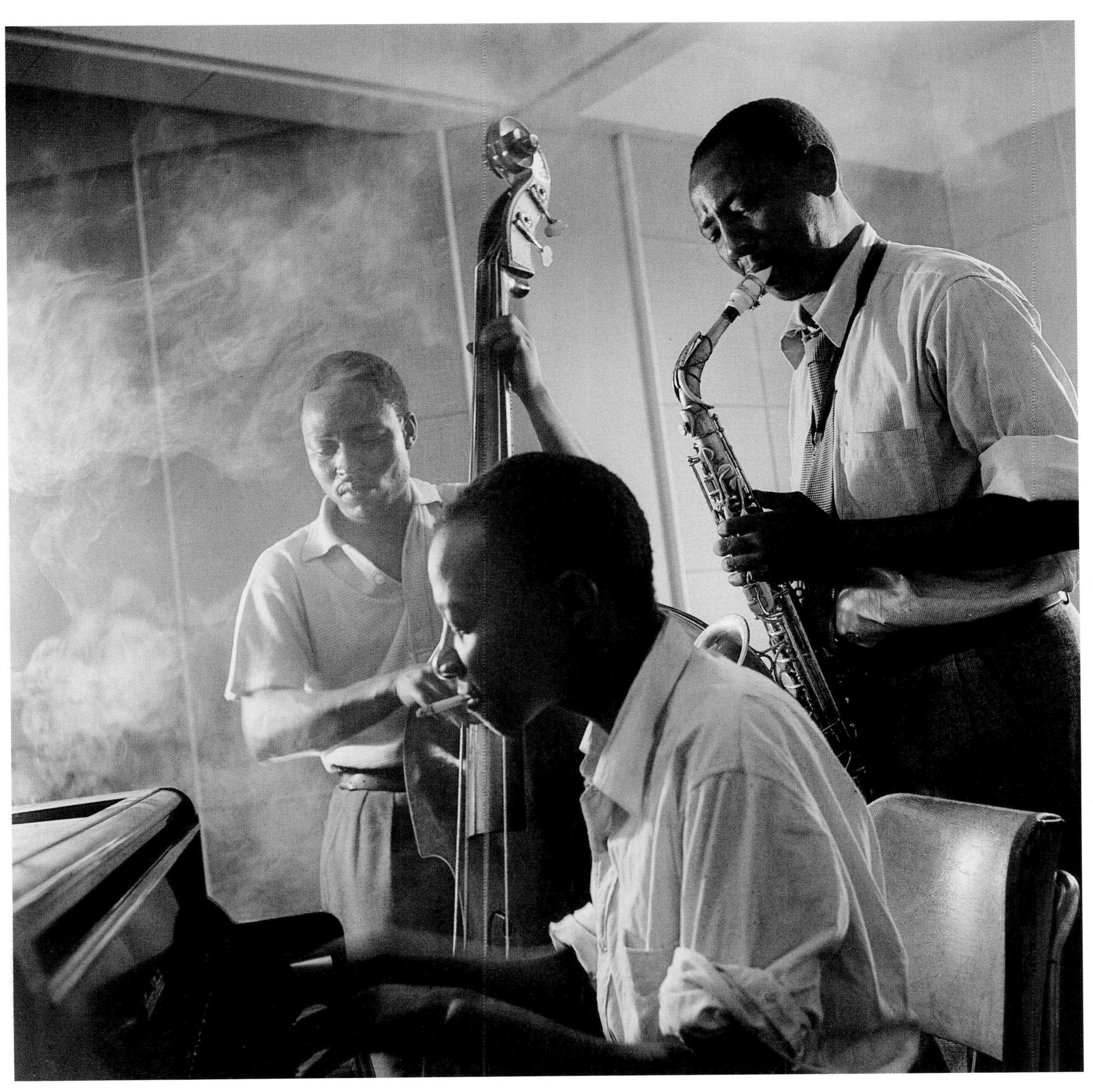

THE JAZZOLOMOS — JACOB "MZALA" LEPERS (BASS),
BEN "GWIGWI" MRWEBI (ALTO SAX), SOL "BEEGEEPEE" KLAASTE (PIANO), JOHANNESBURG 1953

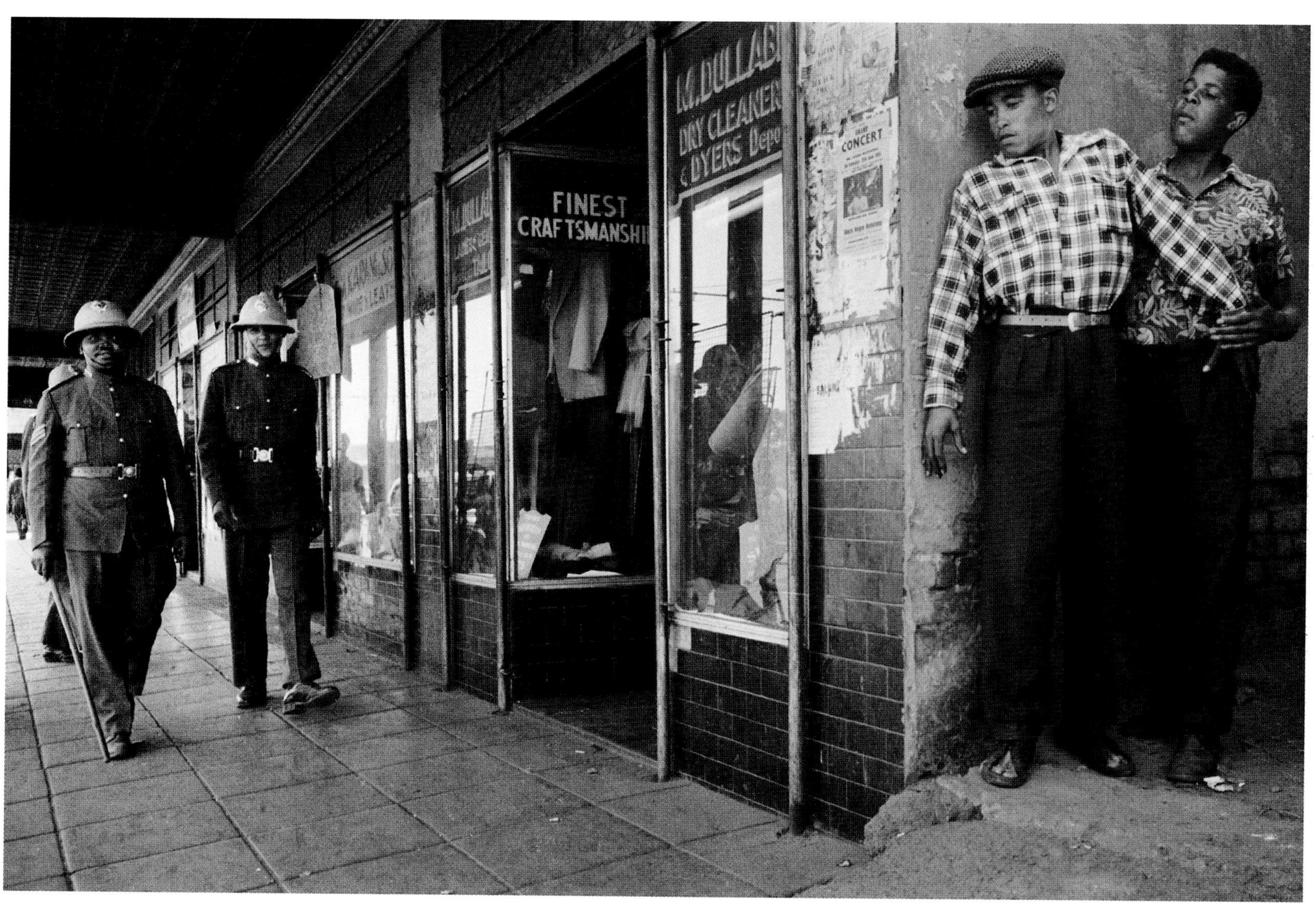

 AVOIDING THE PASS, JOHANNESBURG 1955

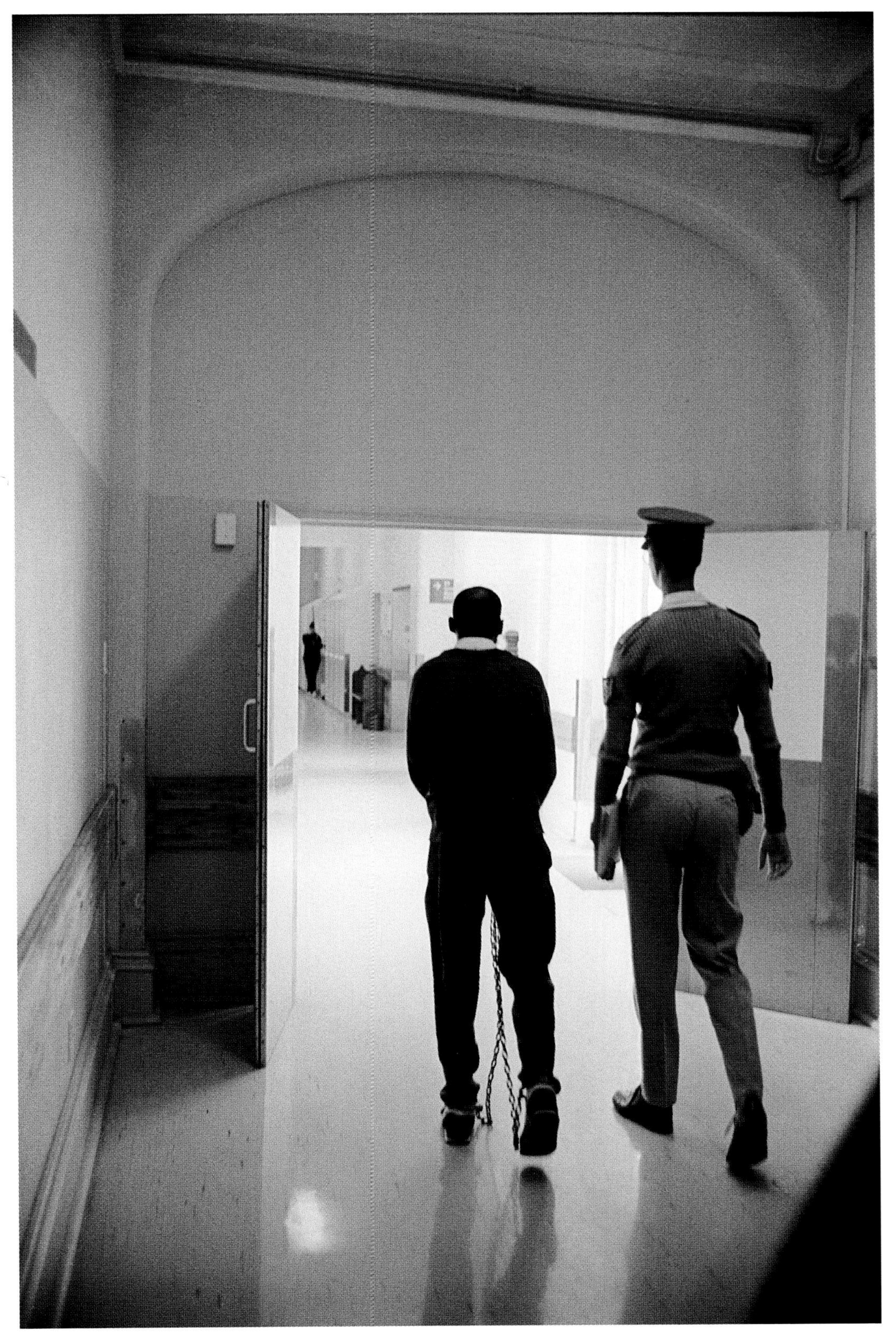

Robben Island prisoner on hospital visit, Cape Town 1993

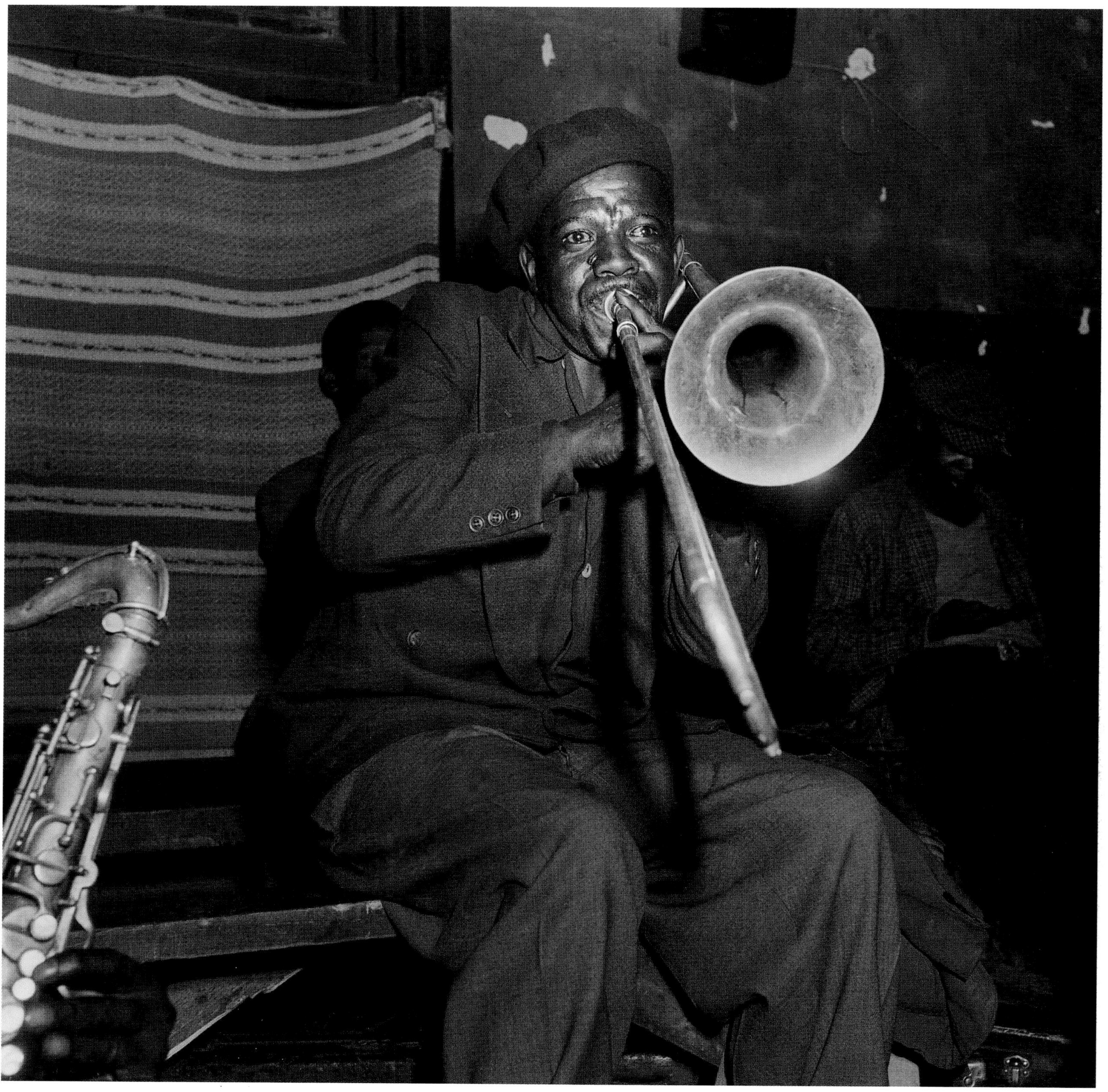

   VI NKOSI, JOHANNESBURG 1951

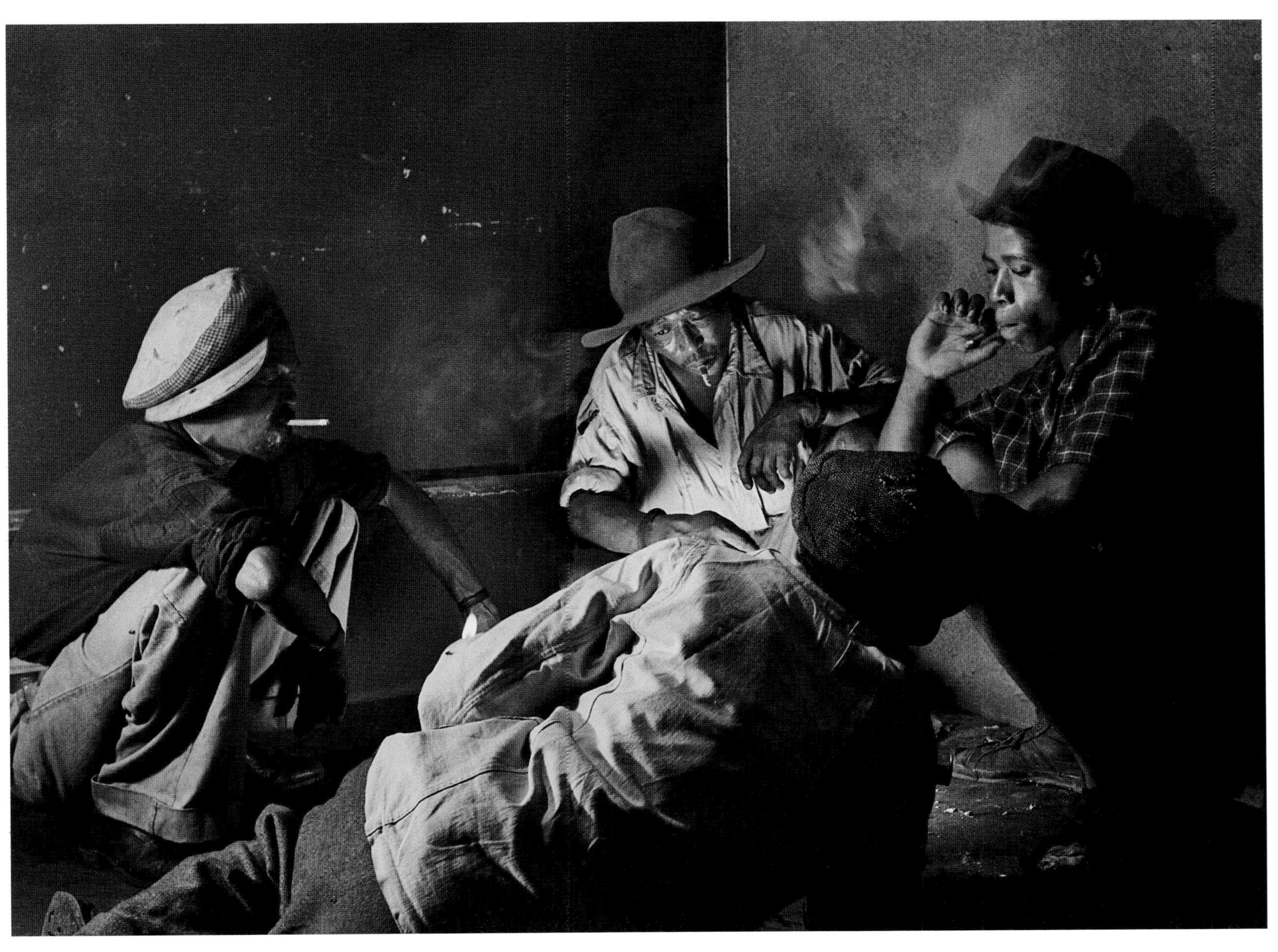

Gamblers in a smoky corner in Sophiatown 1955

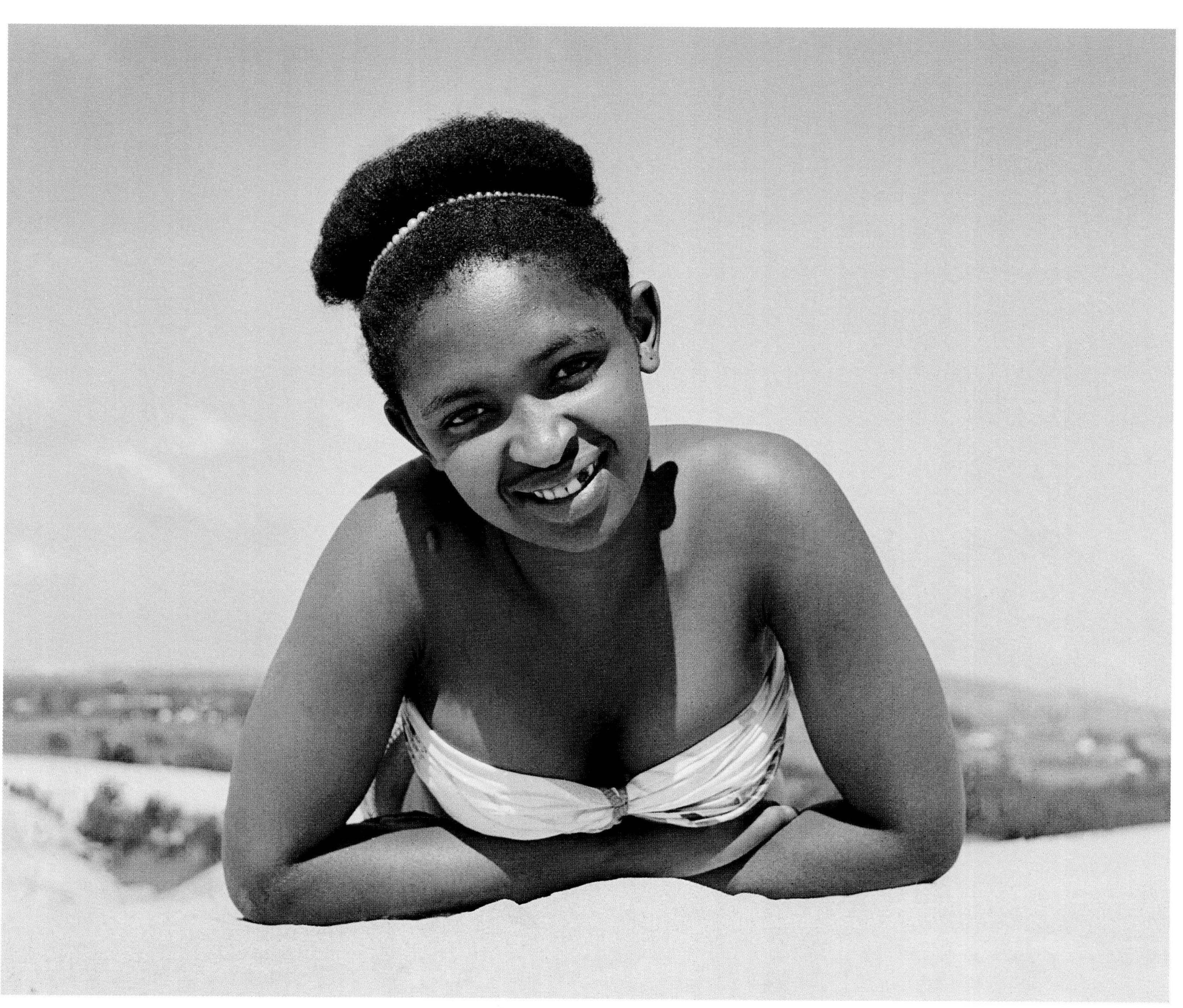

   Dolly Rathebe, South African jazz and blues queen, on a shoot for magazine cover, Johannesburg 1952

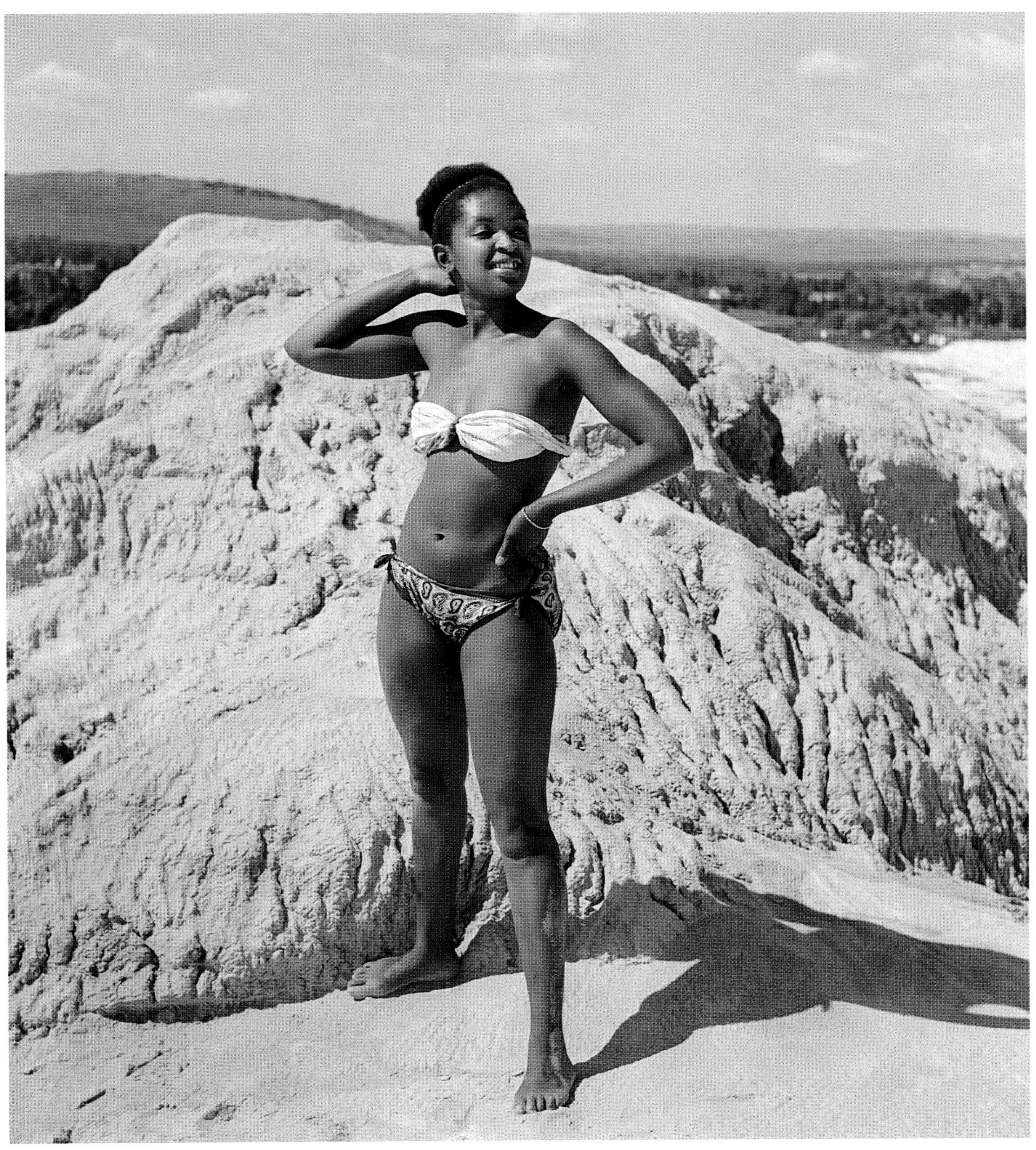

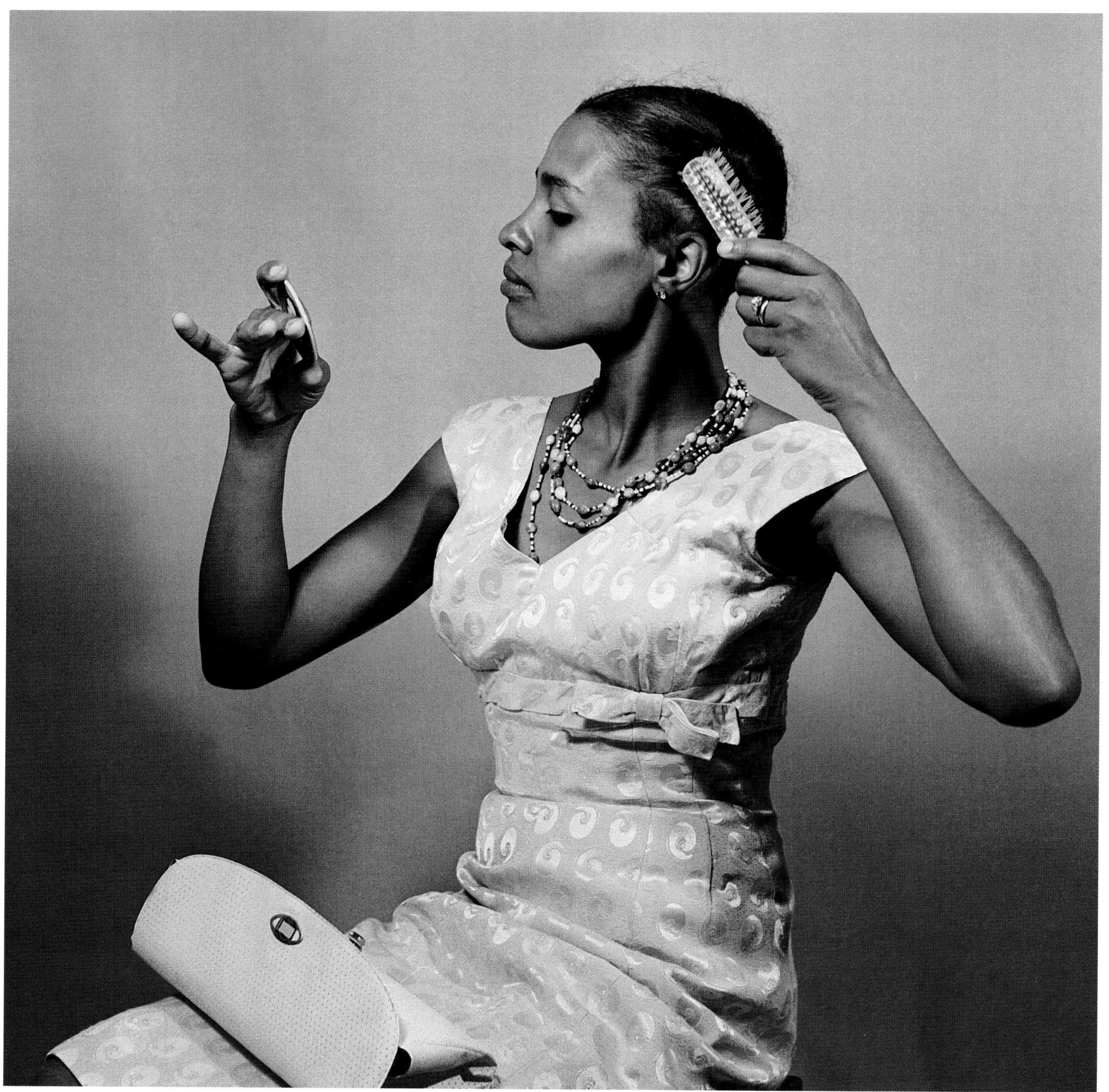

Priscilla Mtimkulu, Johannesburg 1954

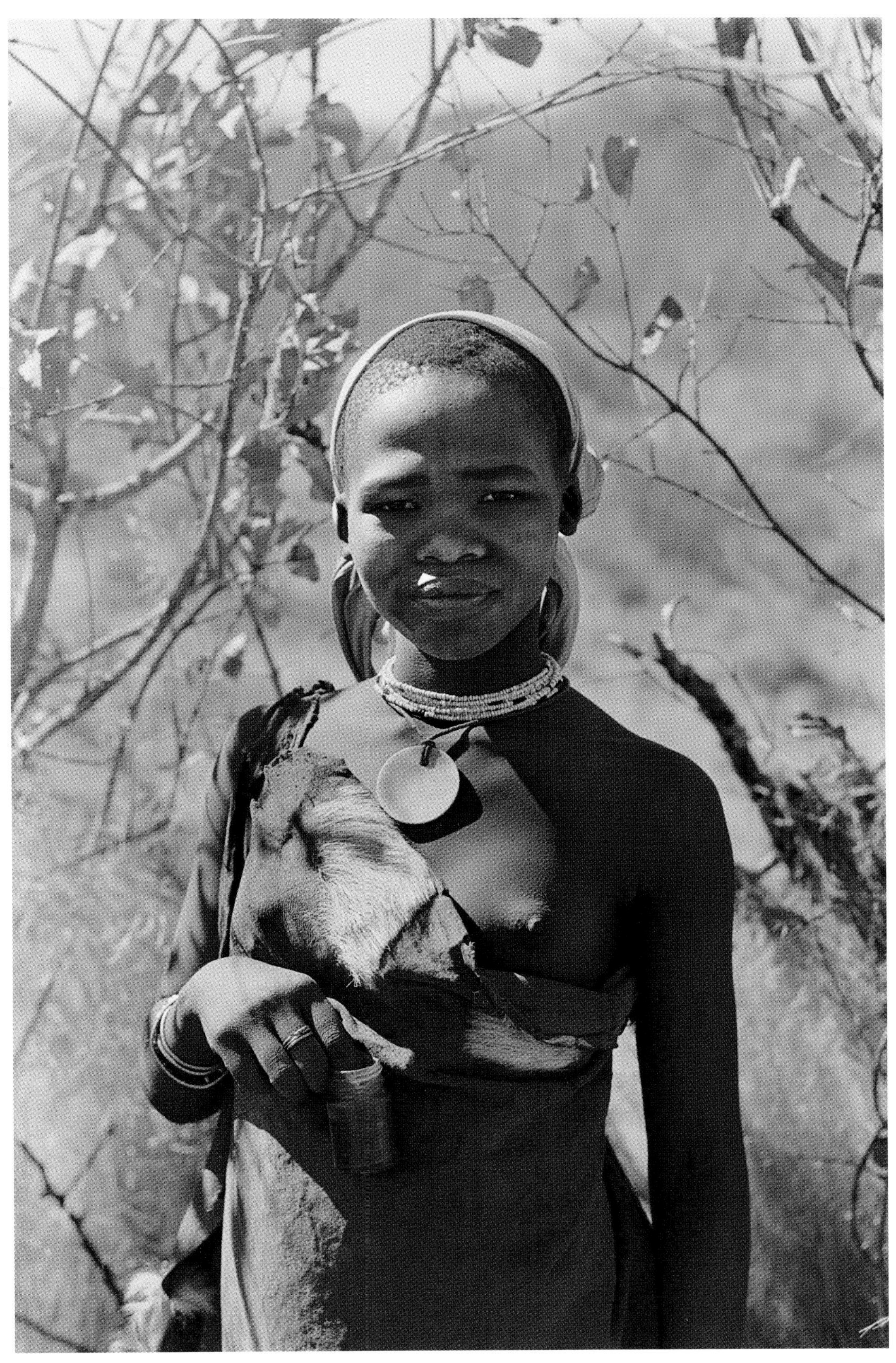

San girl, Kalahari 1959

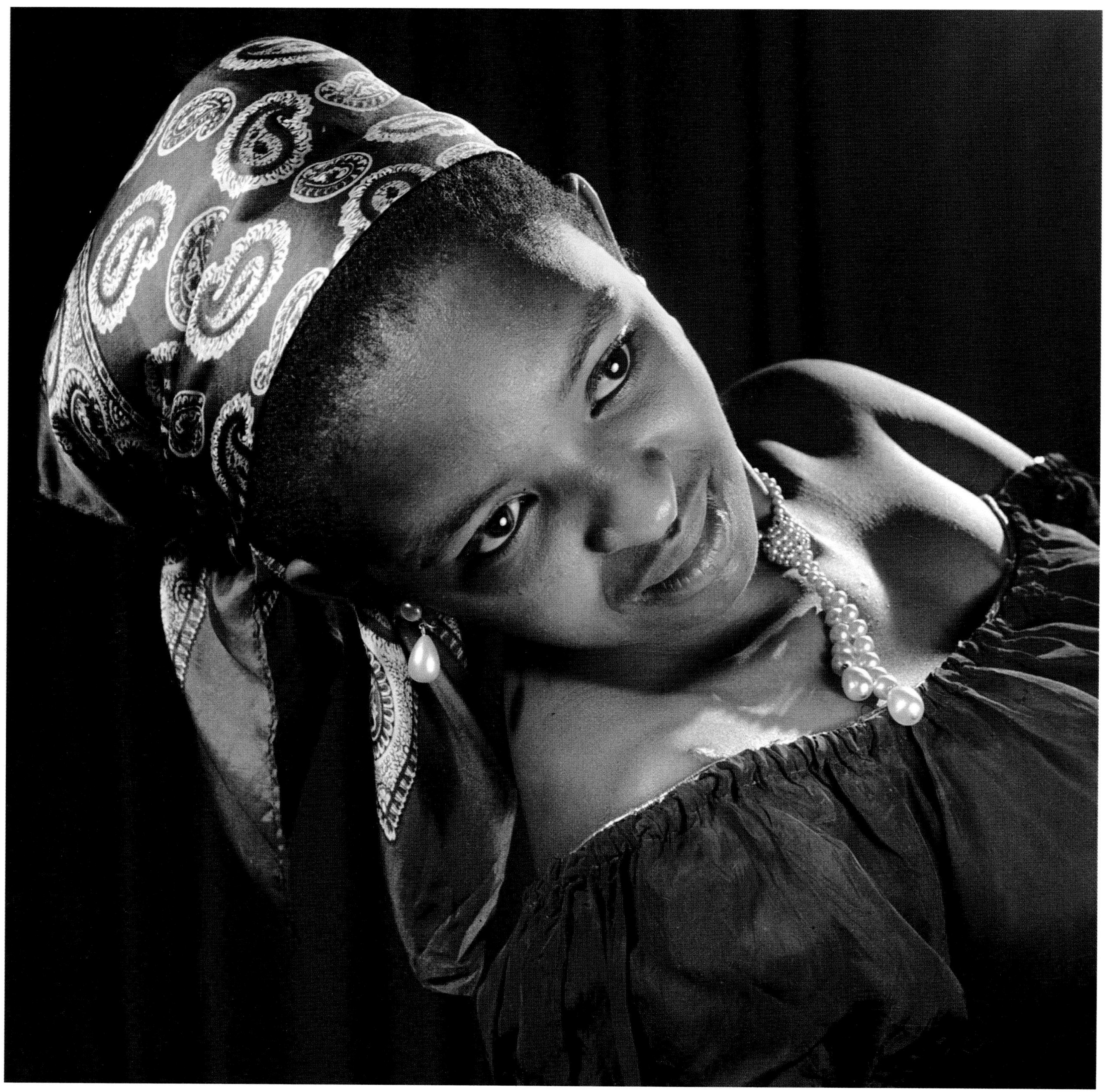

   BLUES QUEEN DOLLY RATHEBE, JOHANNESBURG 1955

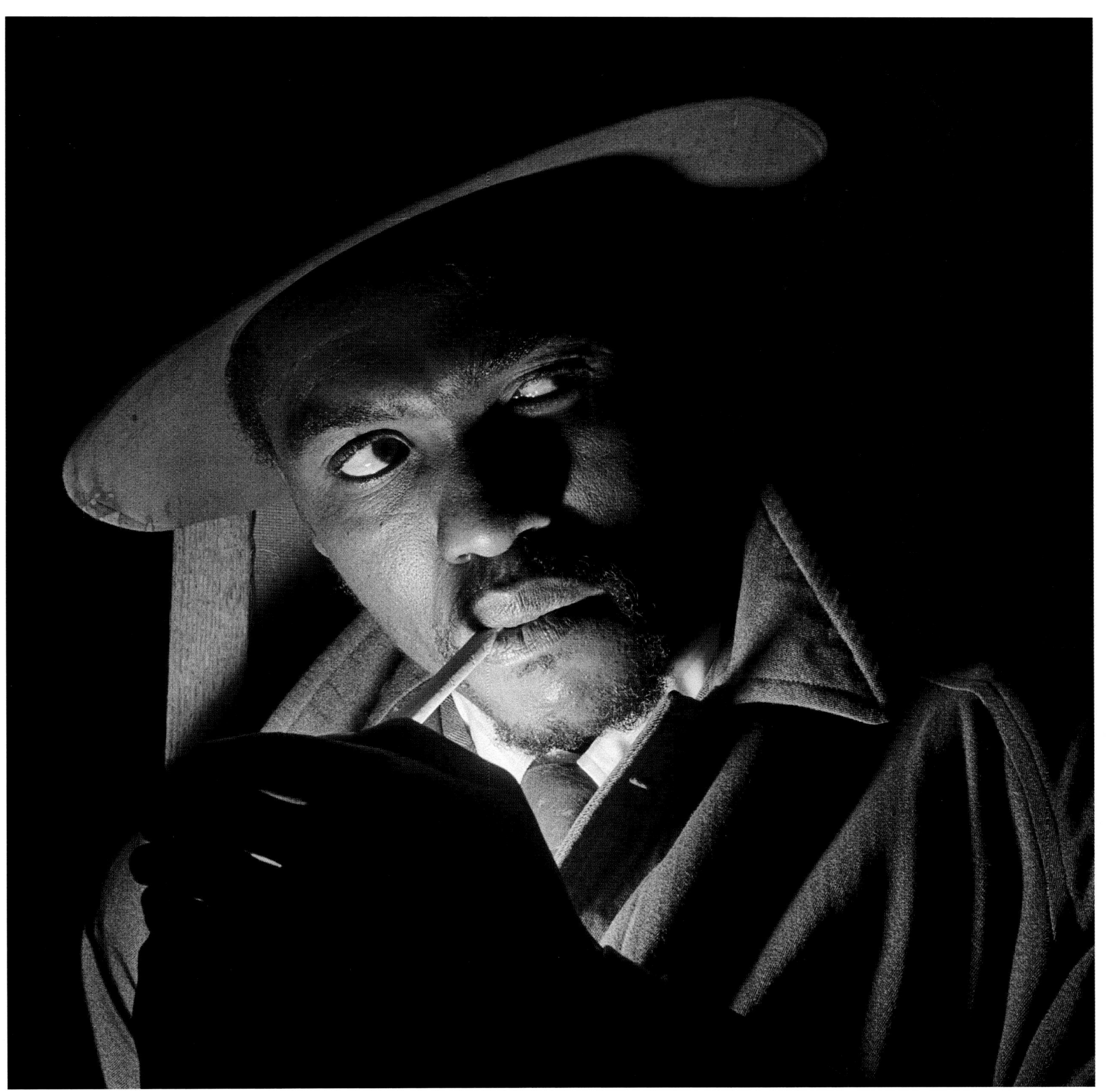

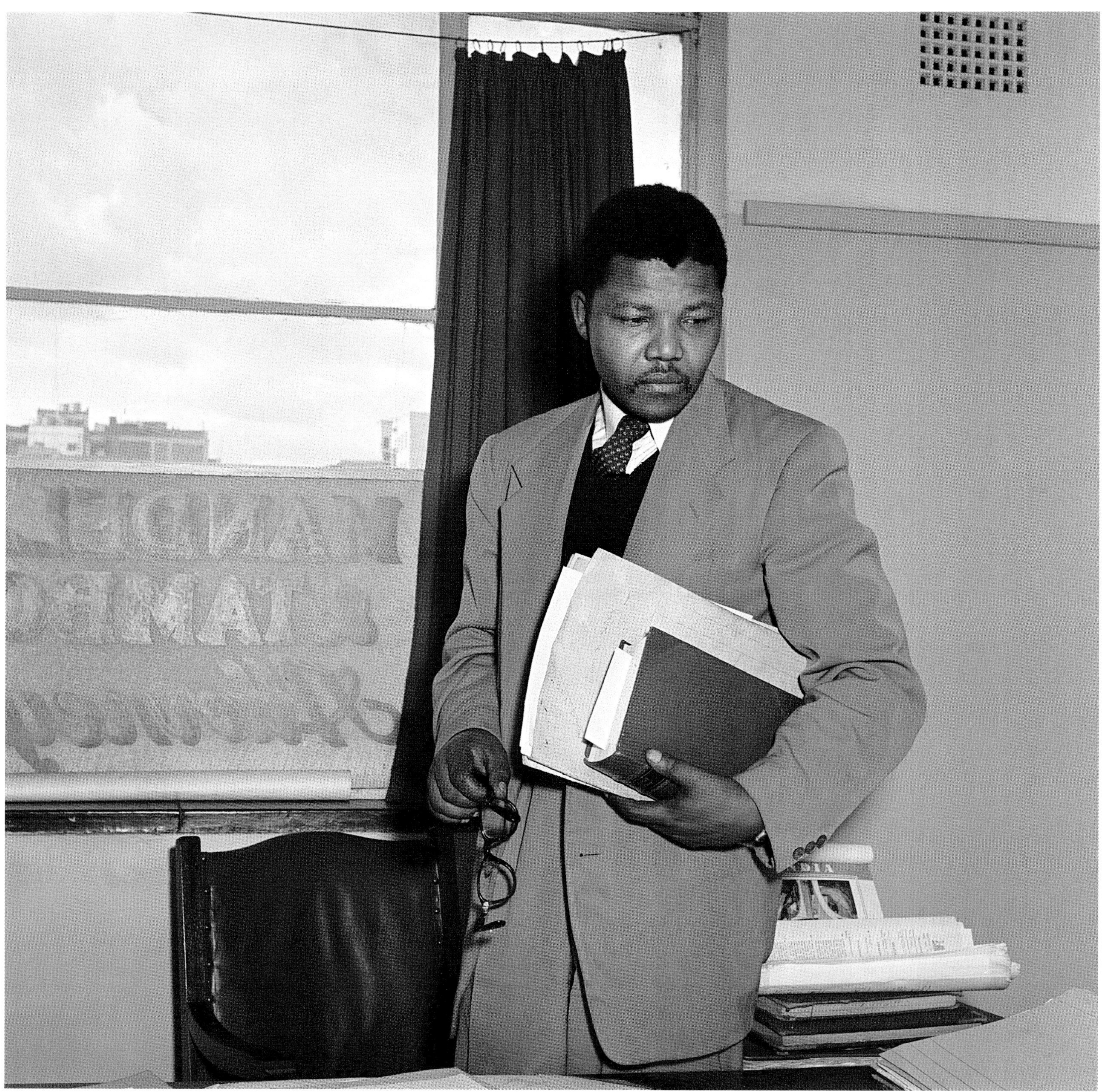

 Nelson Mandela in his law office, Johannesburg 1952

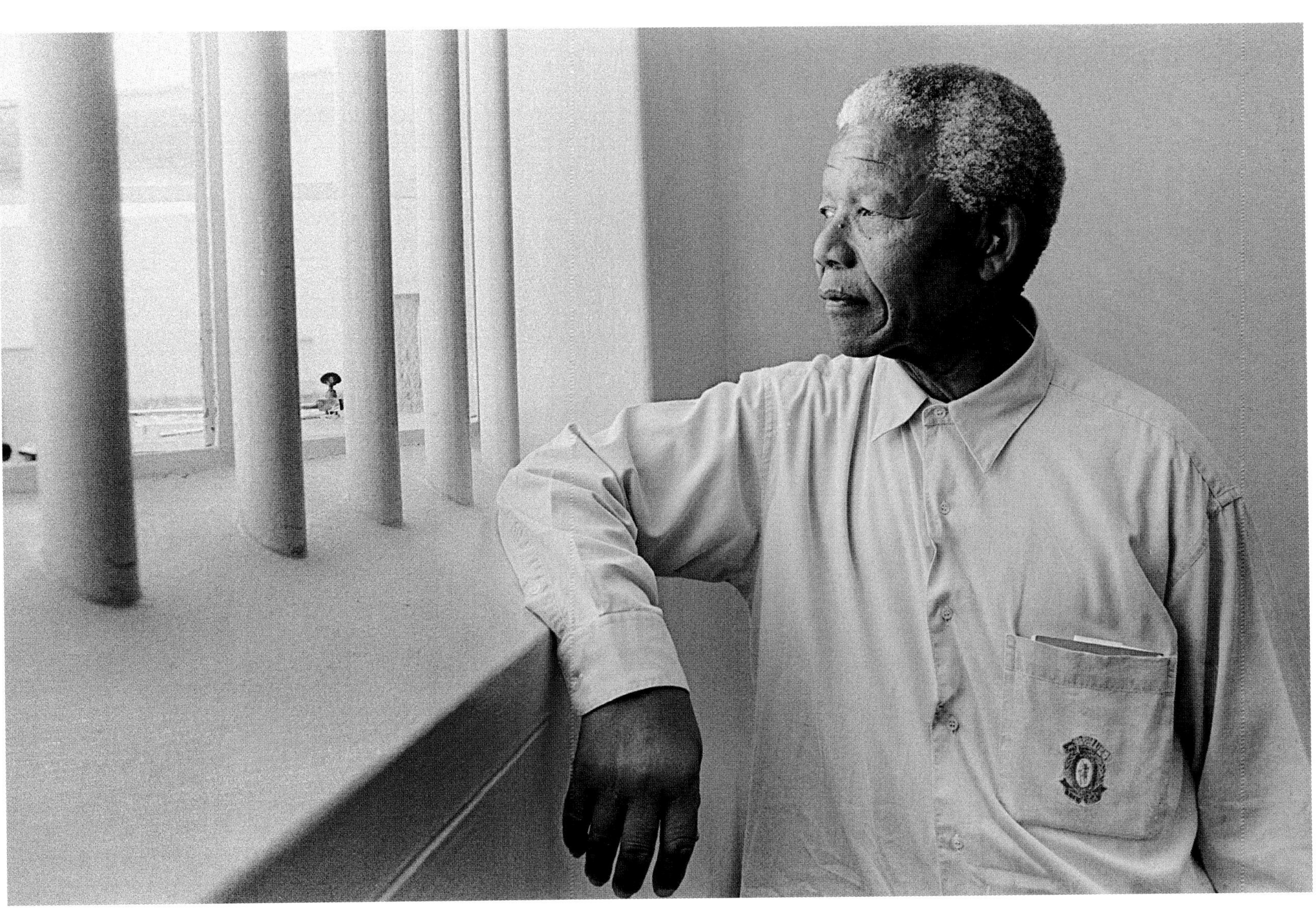

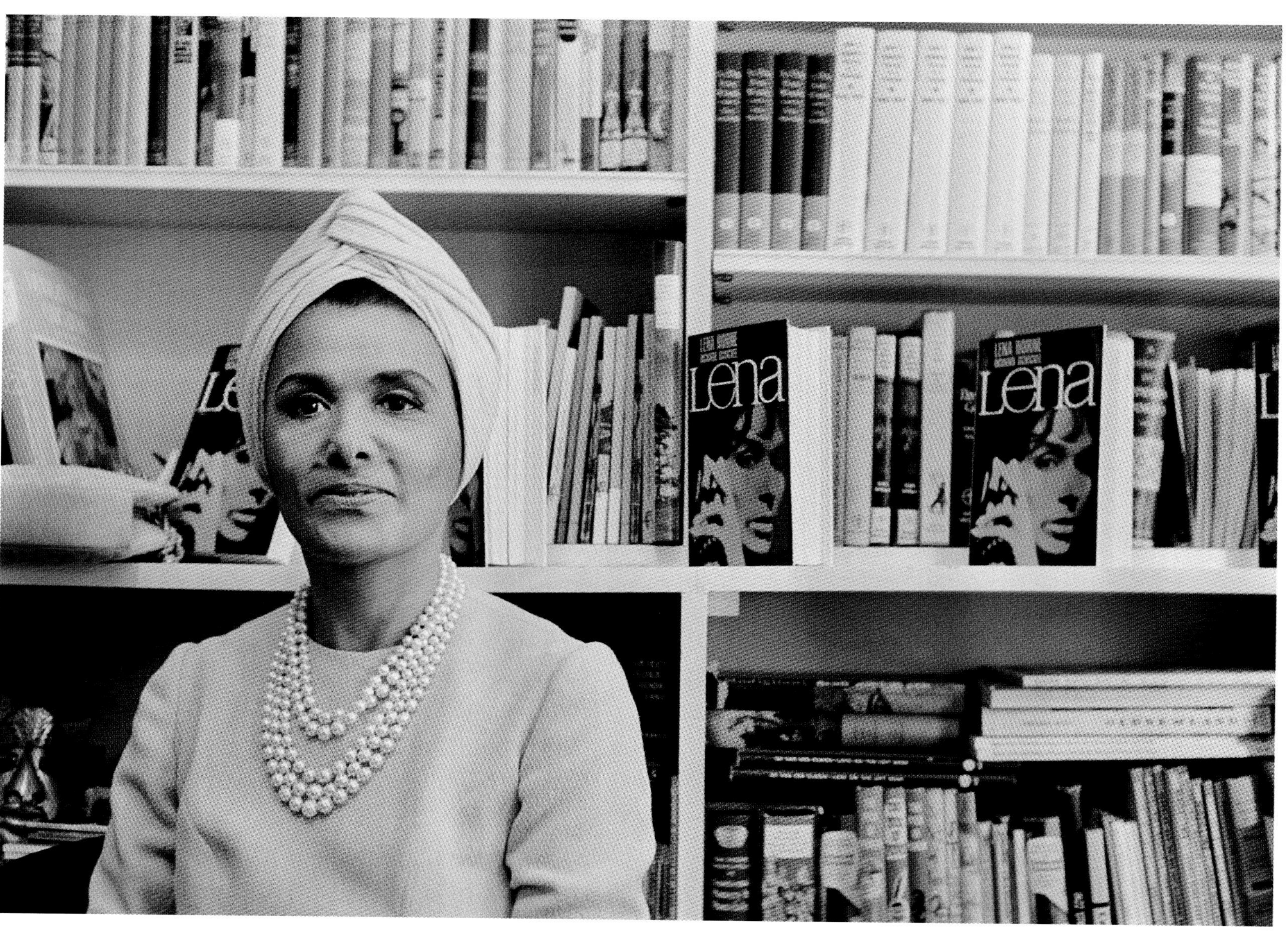

LENA HORNE, LONDON 1967

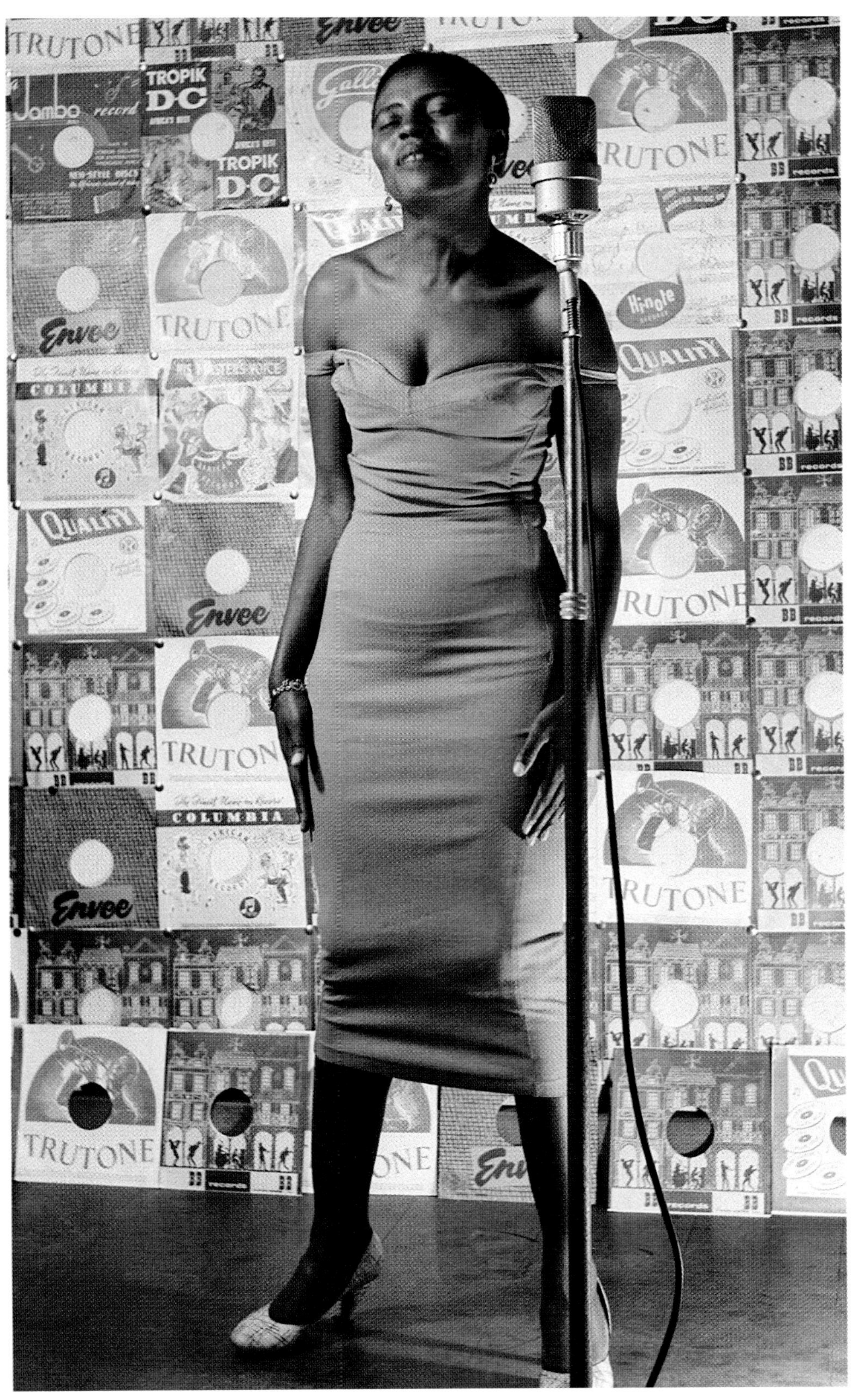

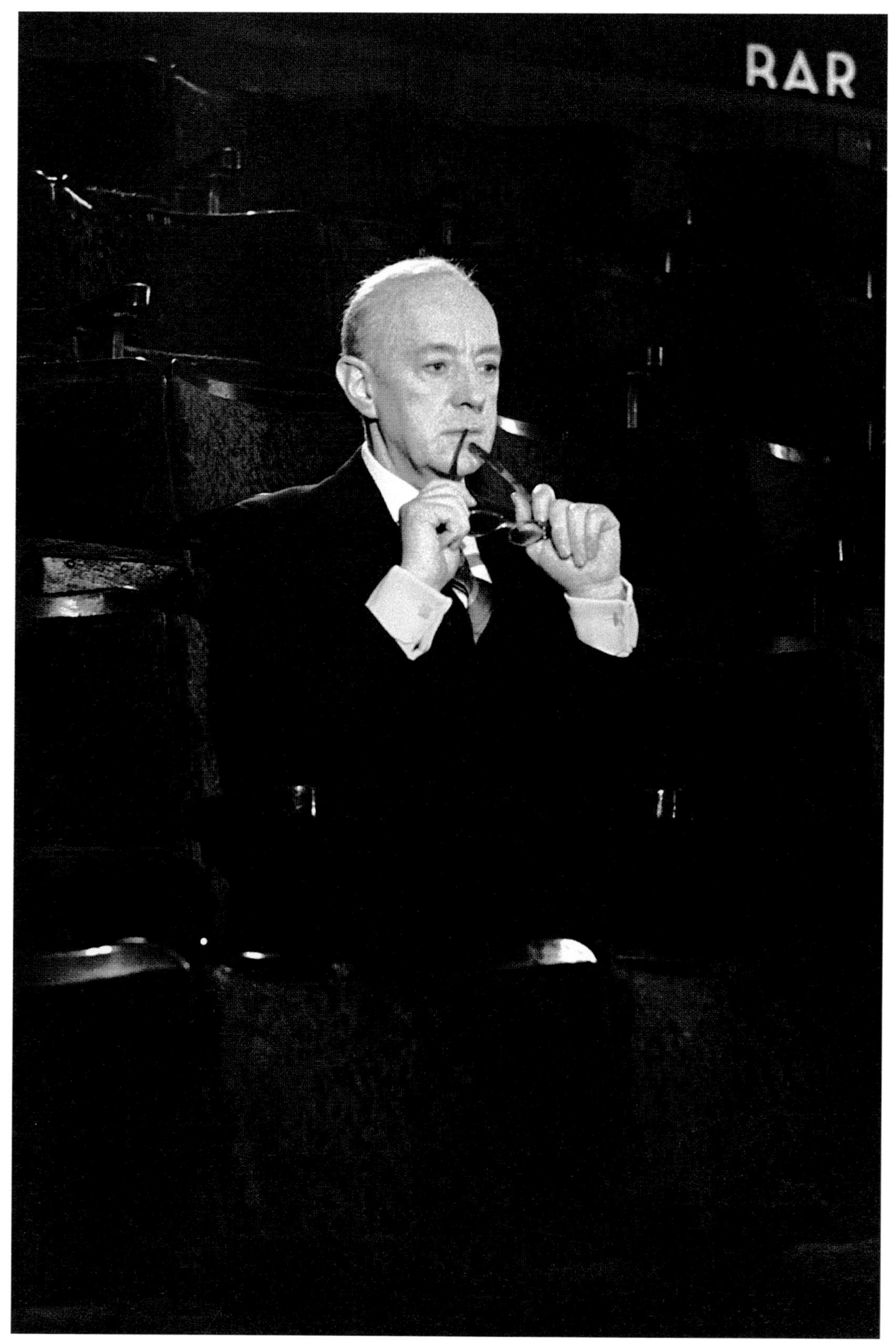

 SIR ALEC GUINNESS, LONDON 1968

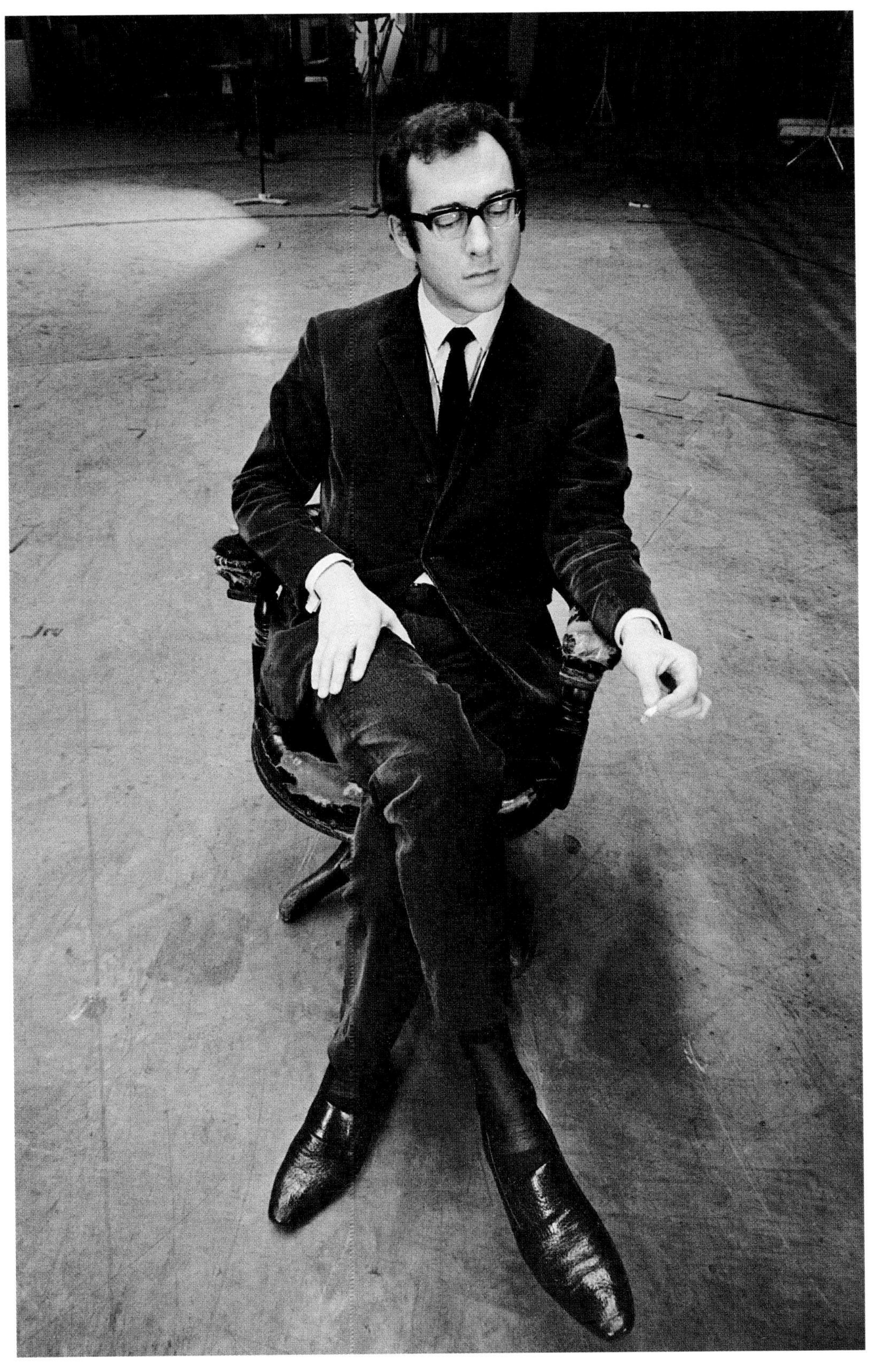

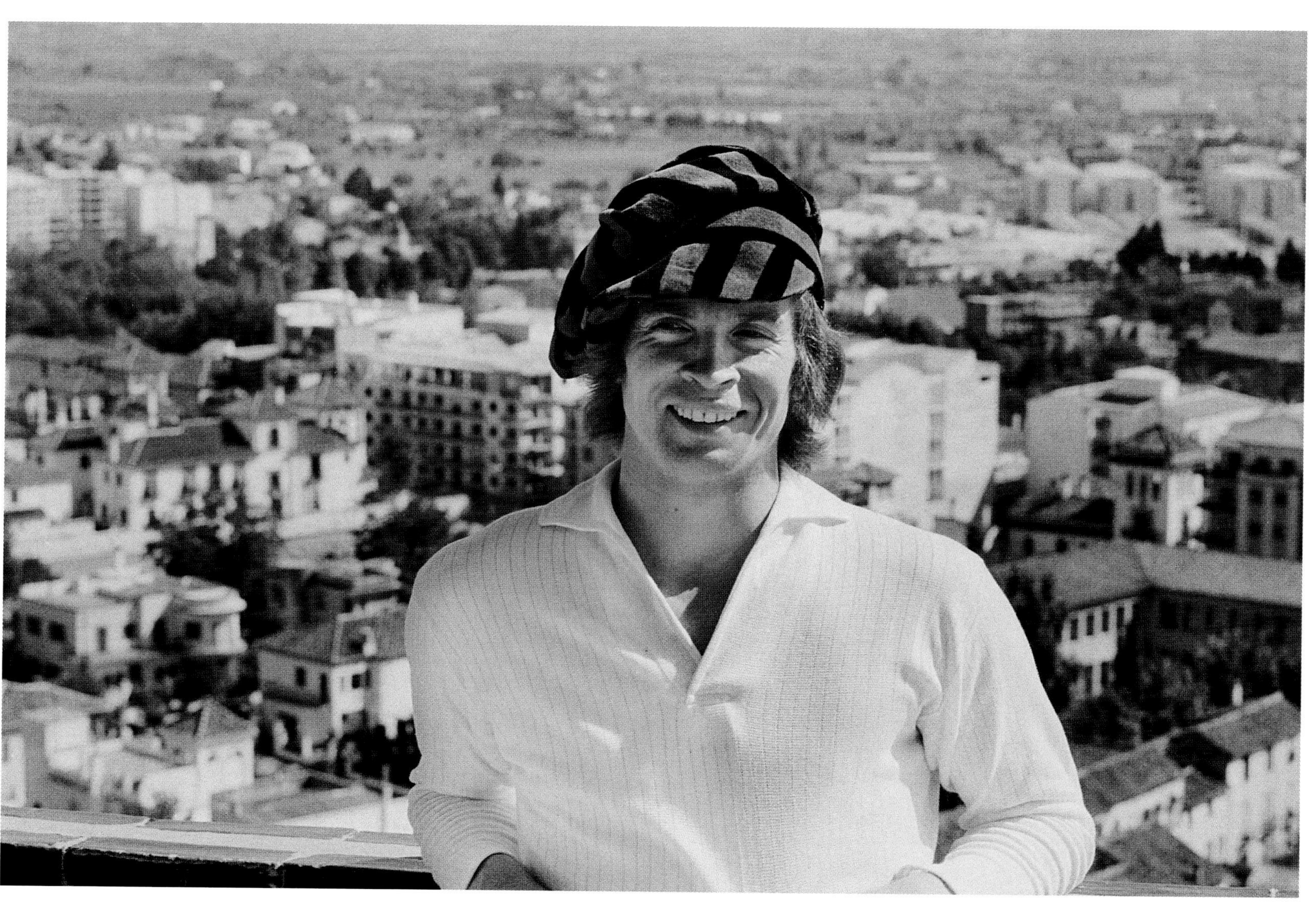

RUDOLF NUREYEV, GRENADA, SPAIN 1970

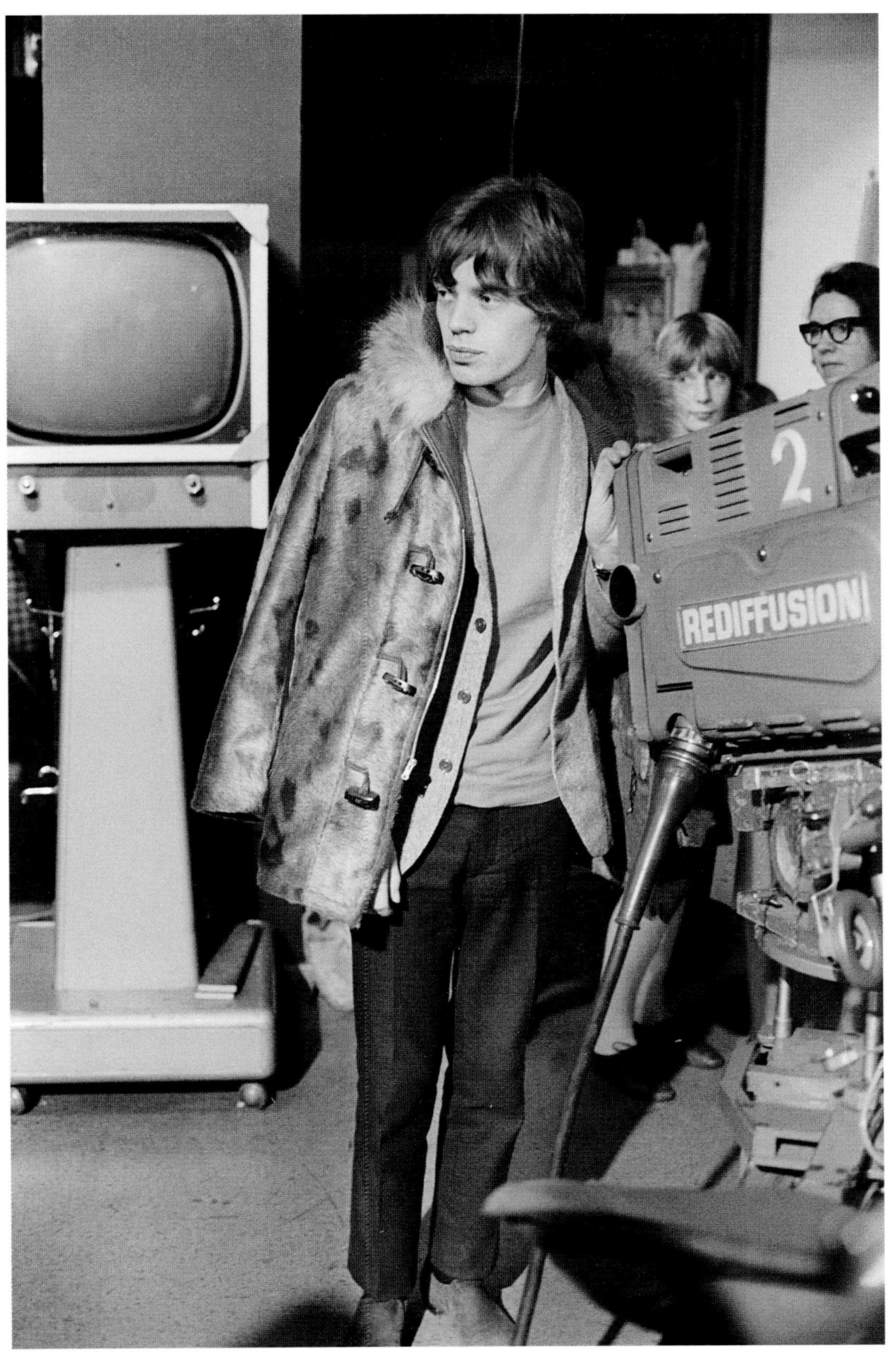

MICK JAGGER AT THE READY STEADY GO STUDIOS 1966

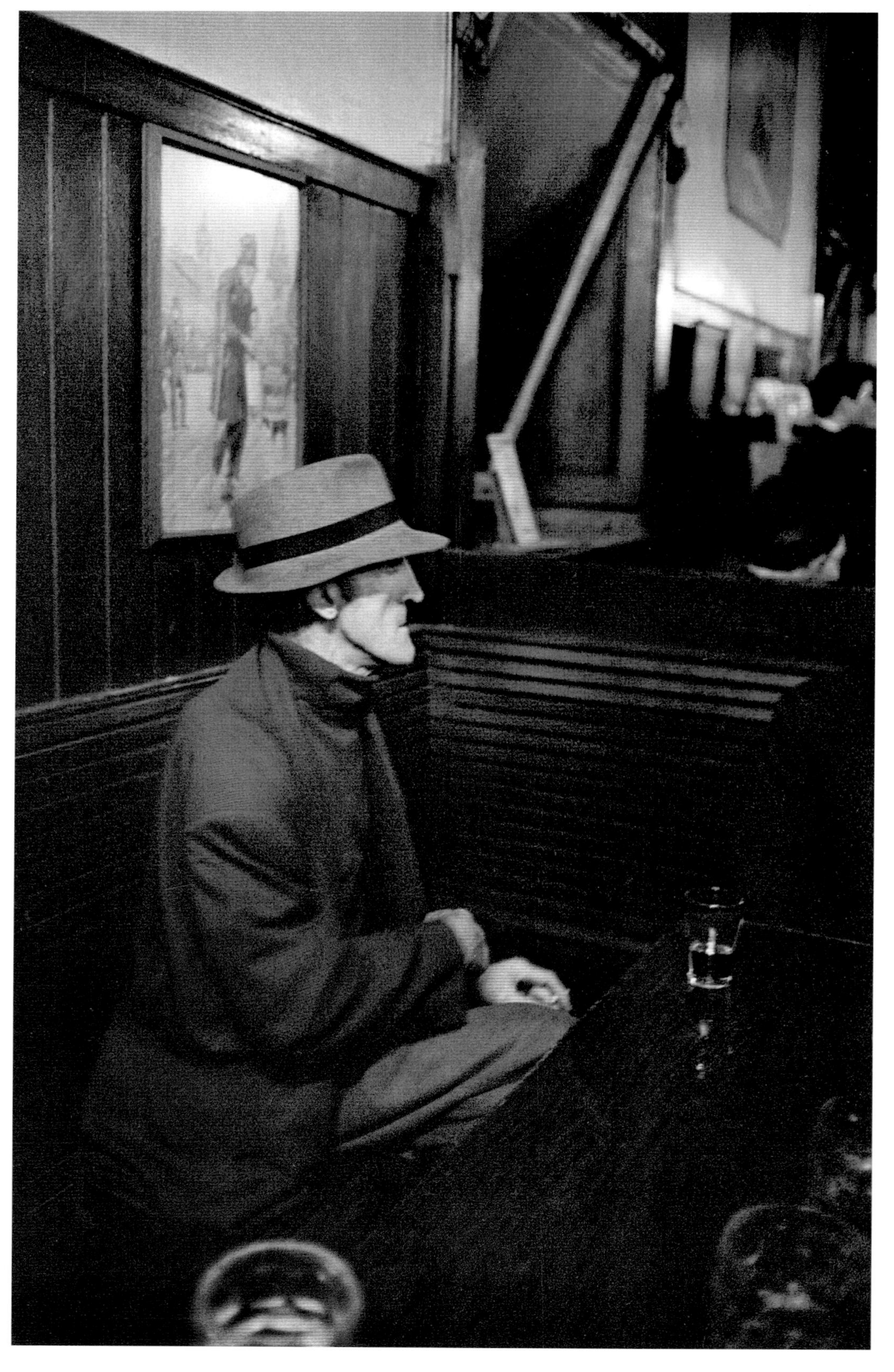

A Glasgow pub 1968

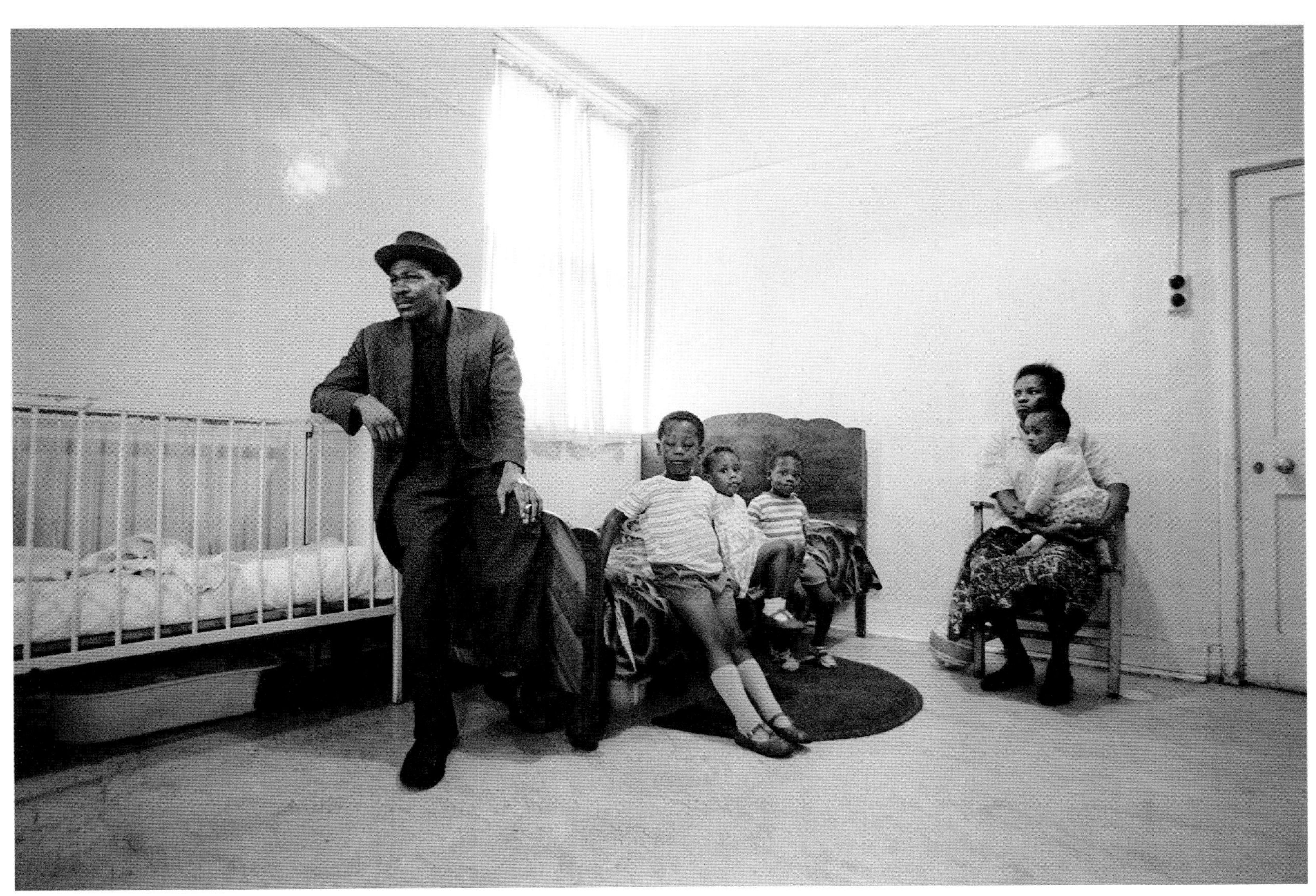

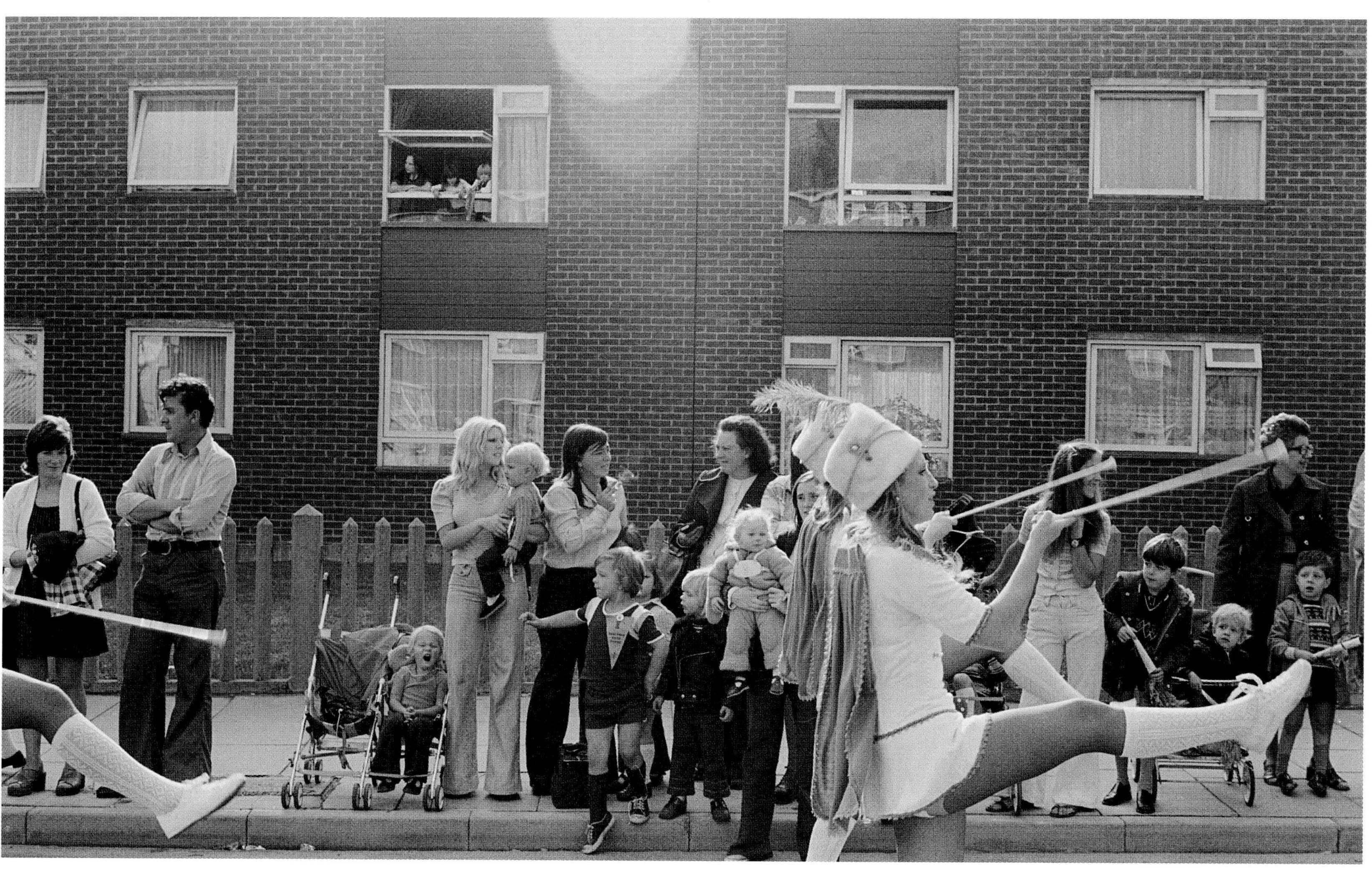

 Parade in the East End of London 1977

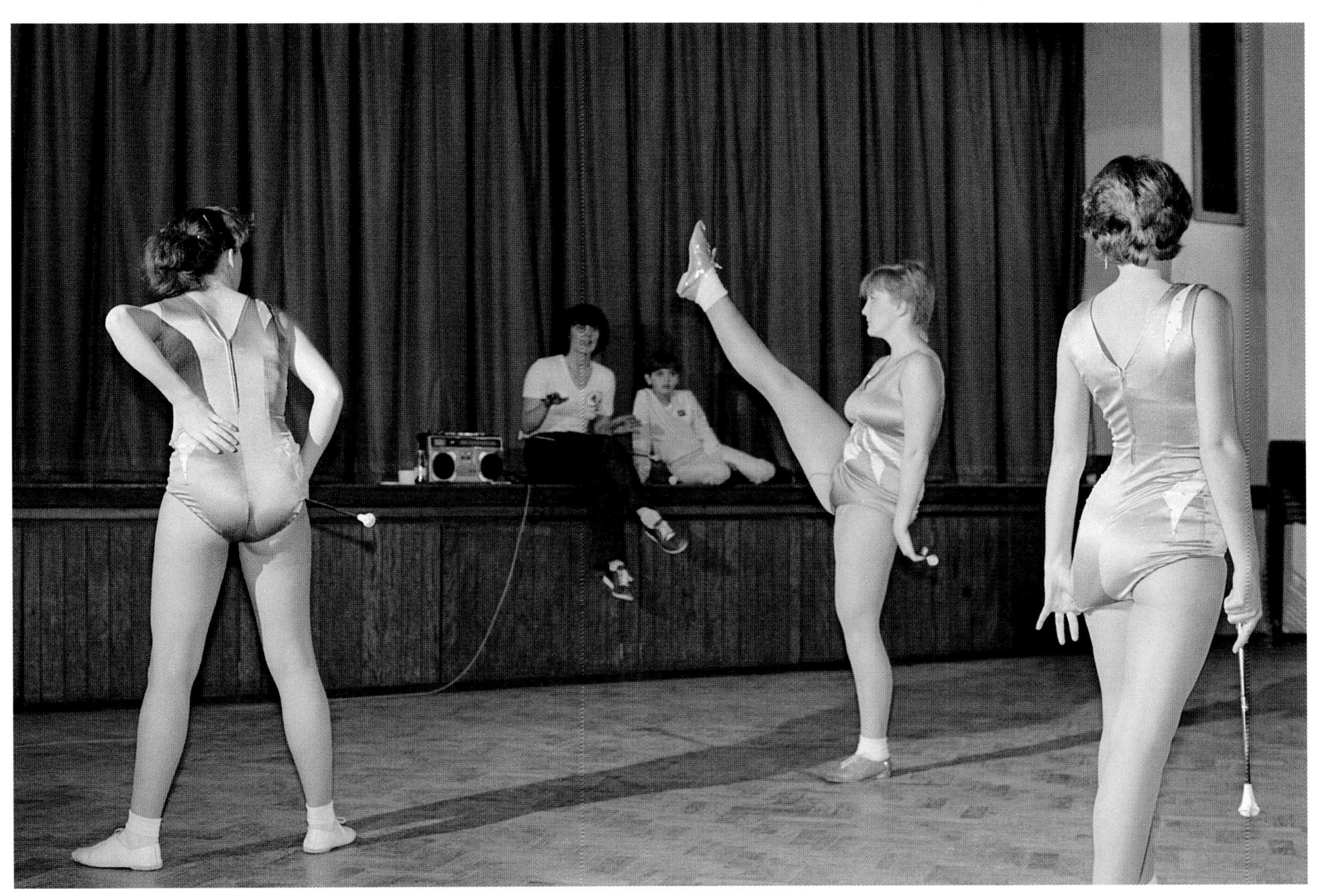

Drum majorettes rehearsing, London 1977

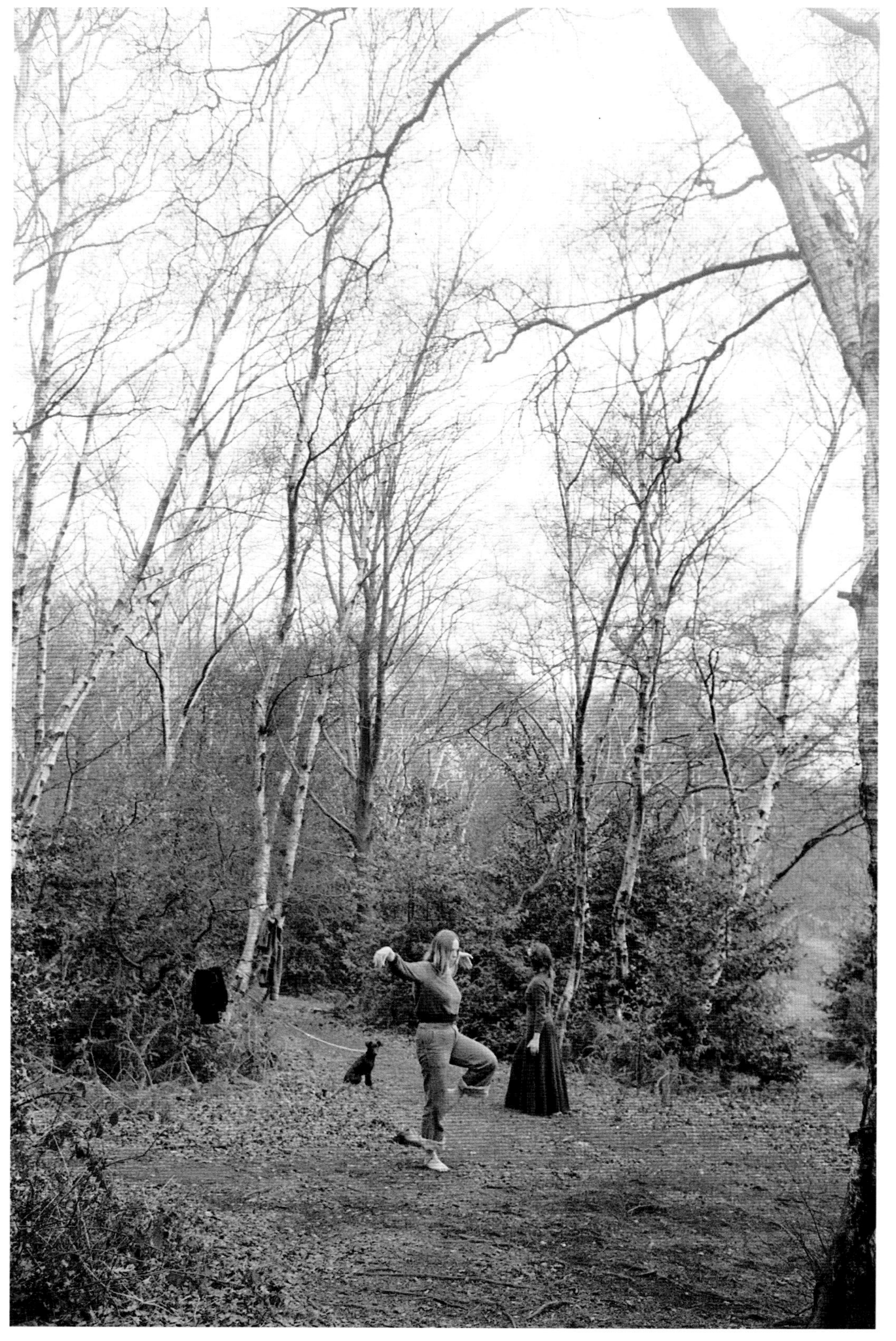

 THAI CHI ON HAMPSTEAD HEATH, LONDON 1976

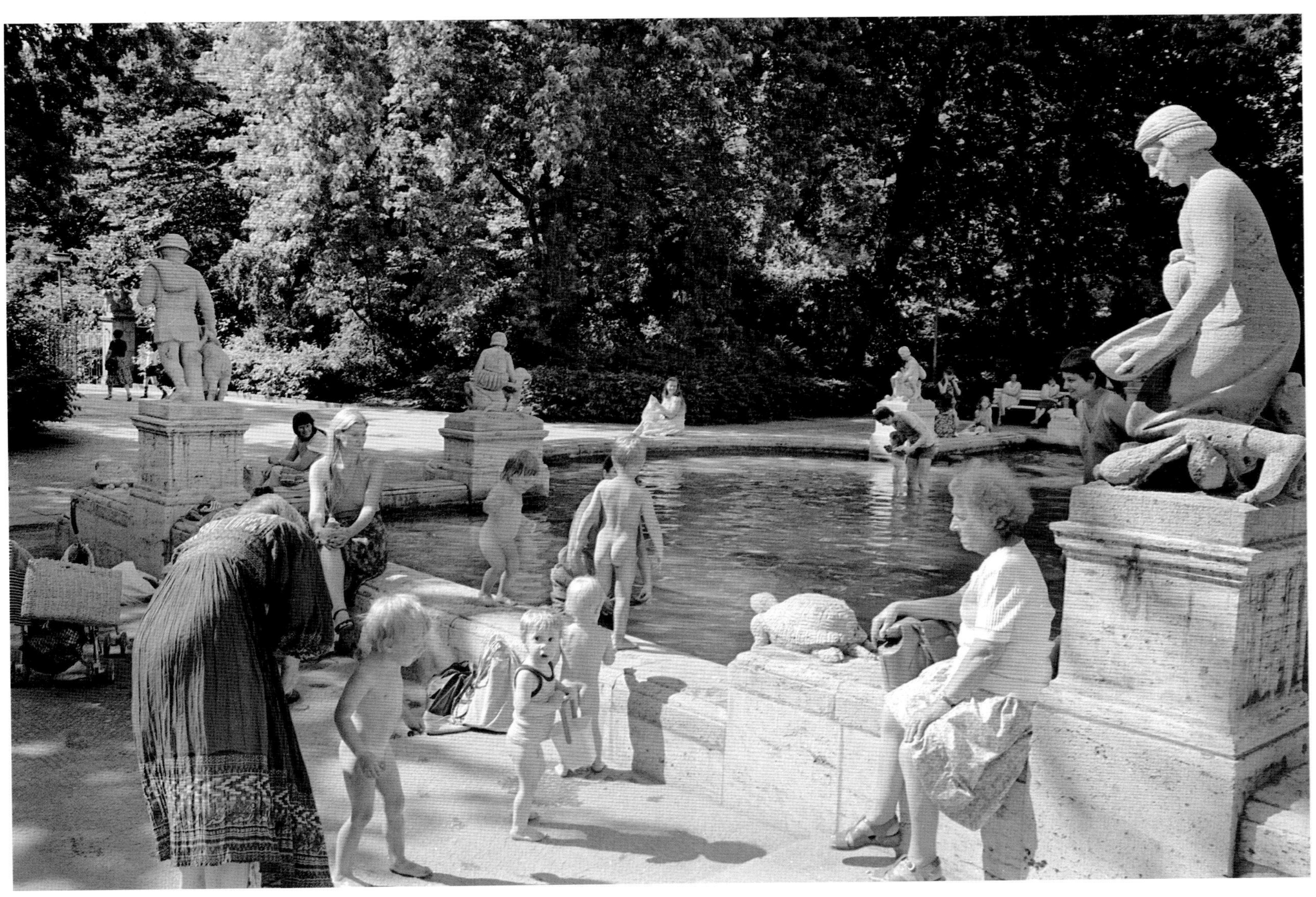

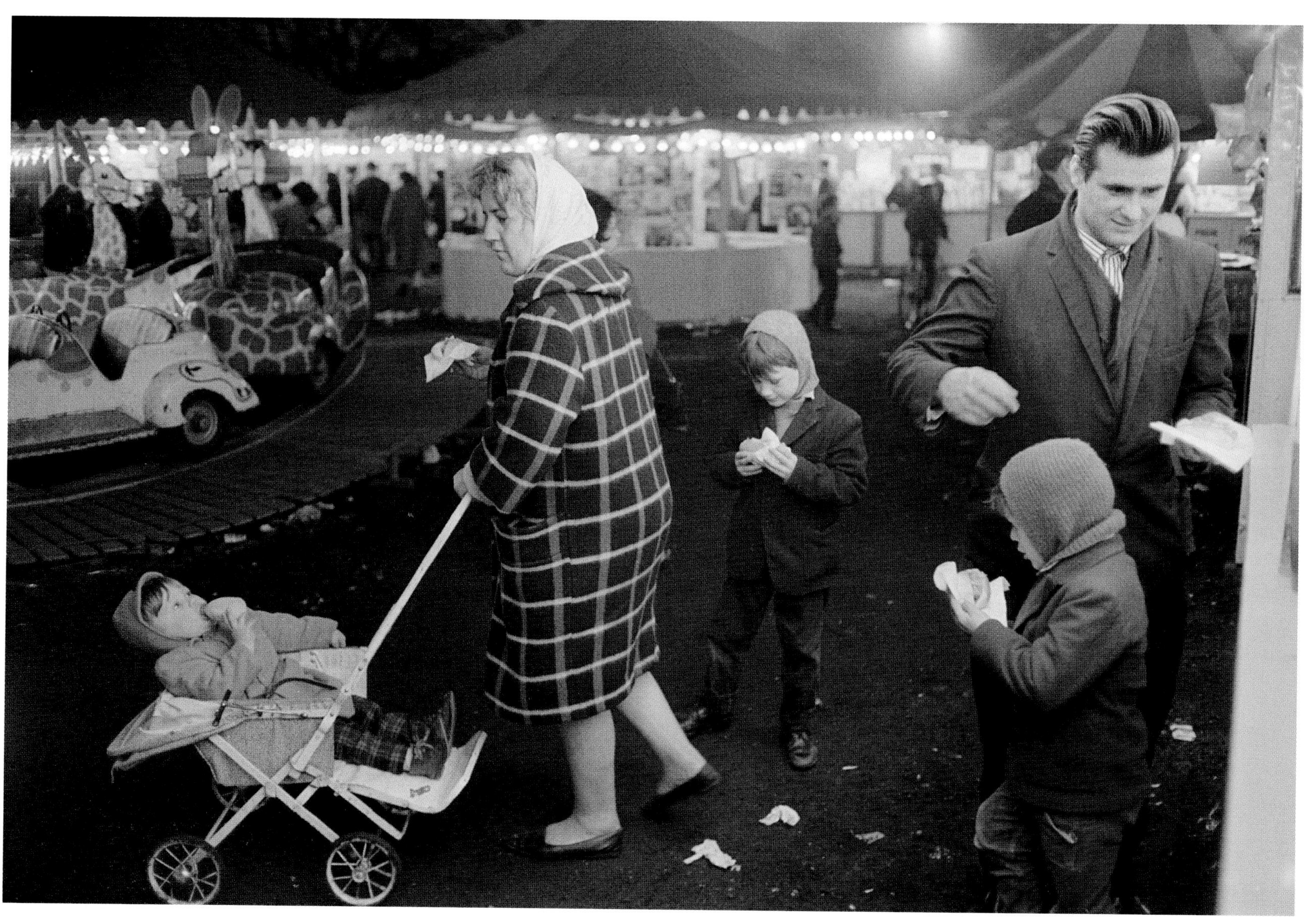

Battersea fun fair, London 1965

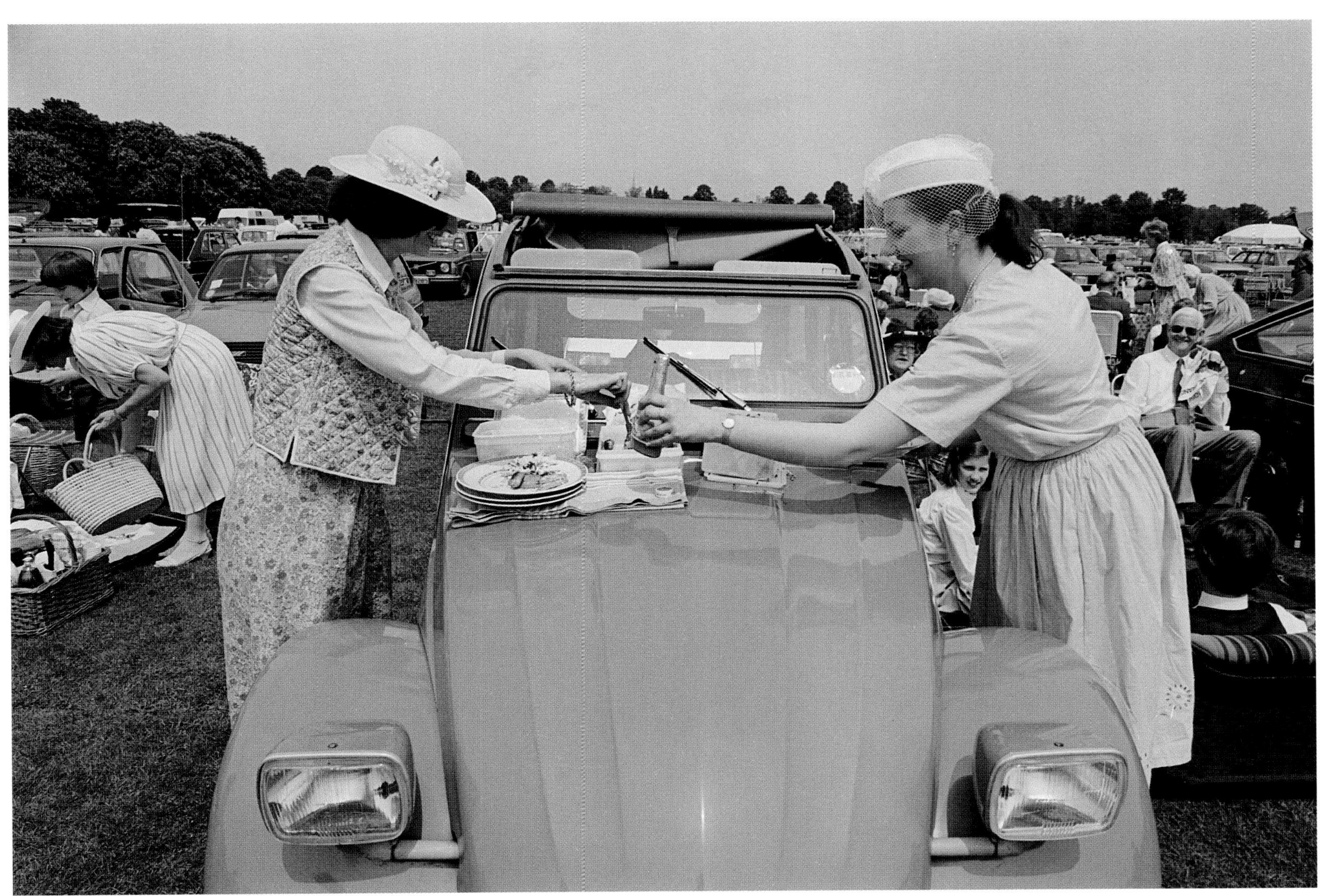

Picnic at Eaton College, England 1981

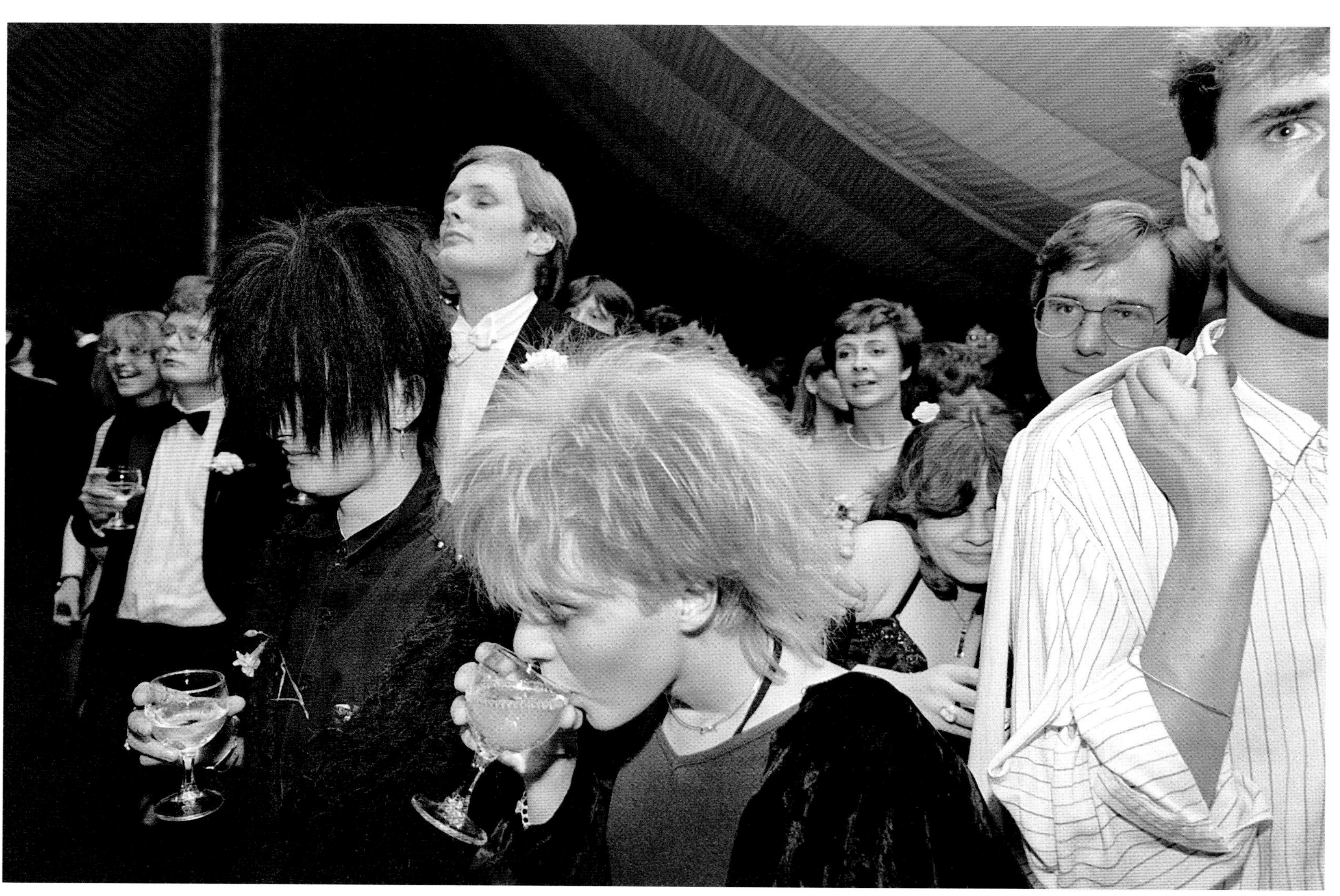

 PARTYGOERS AT CAMBRIDGE MAY BALL 1983

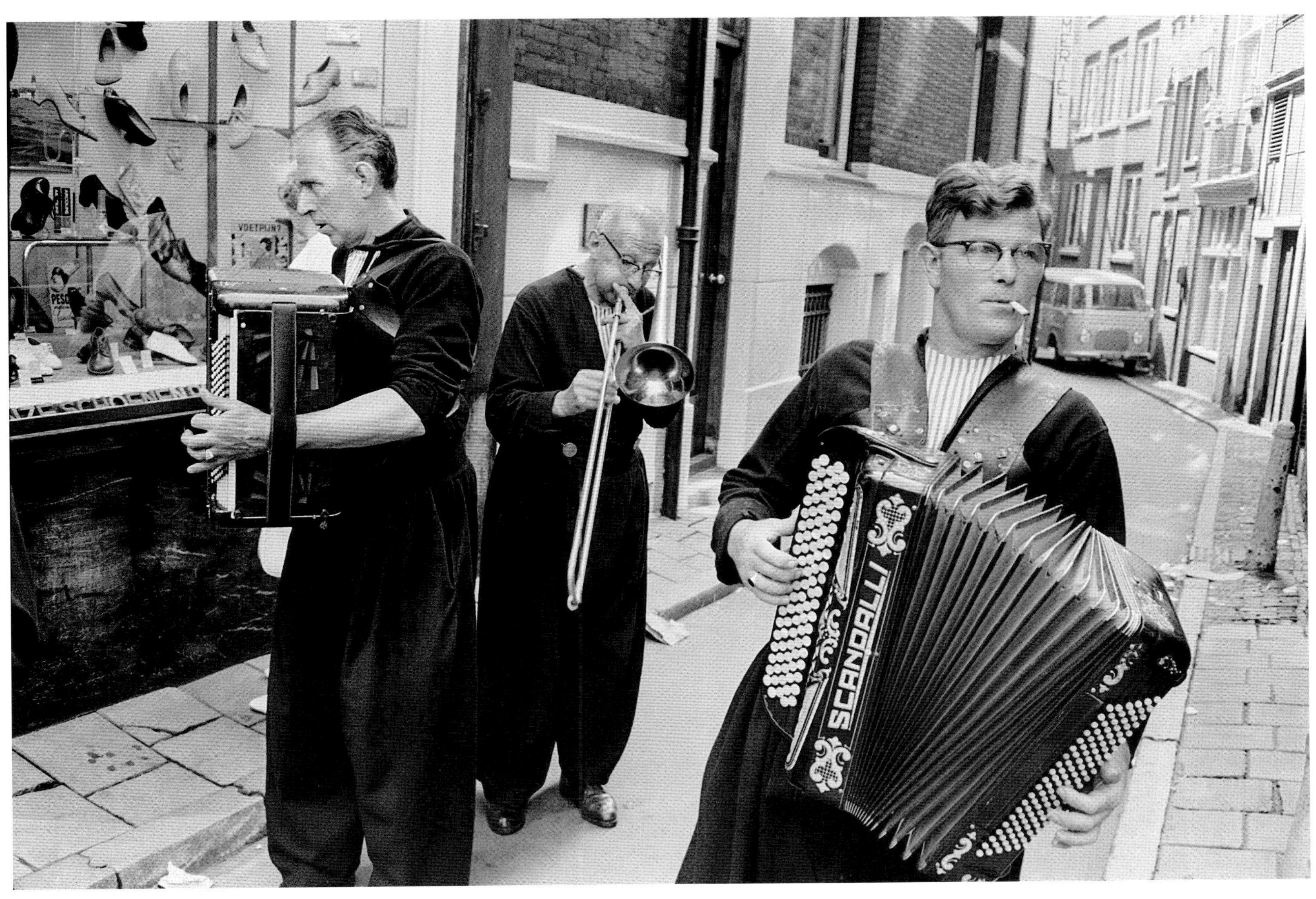

Street musicians in Holland 1981

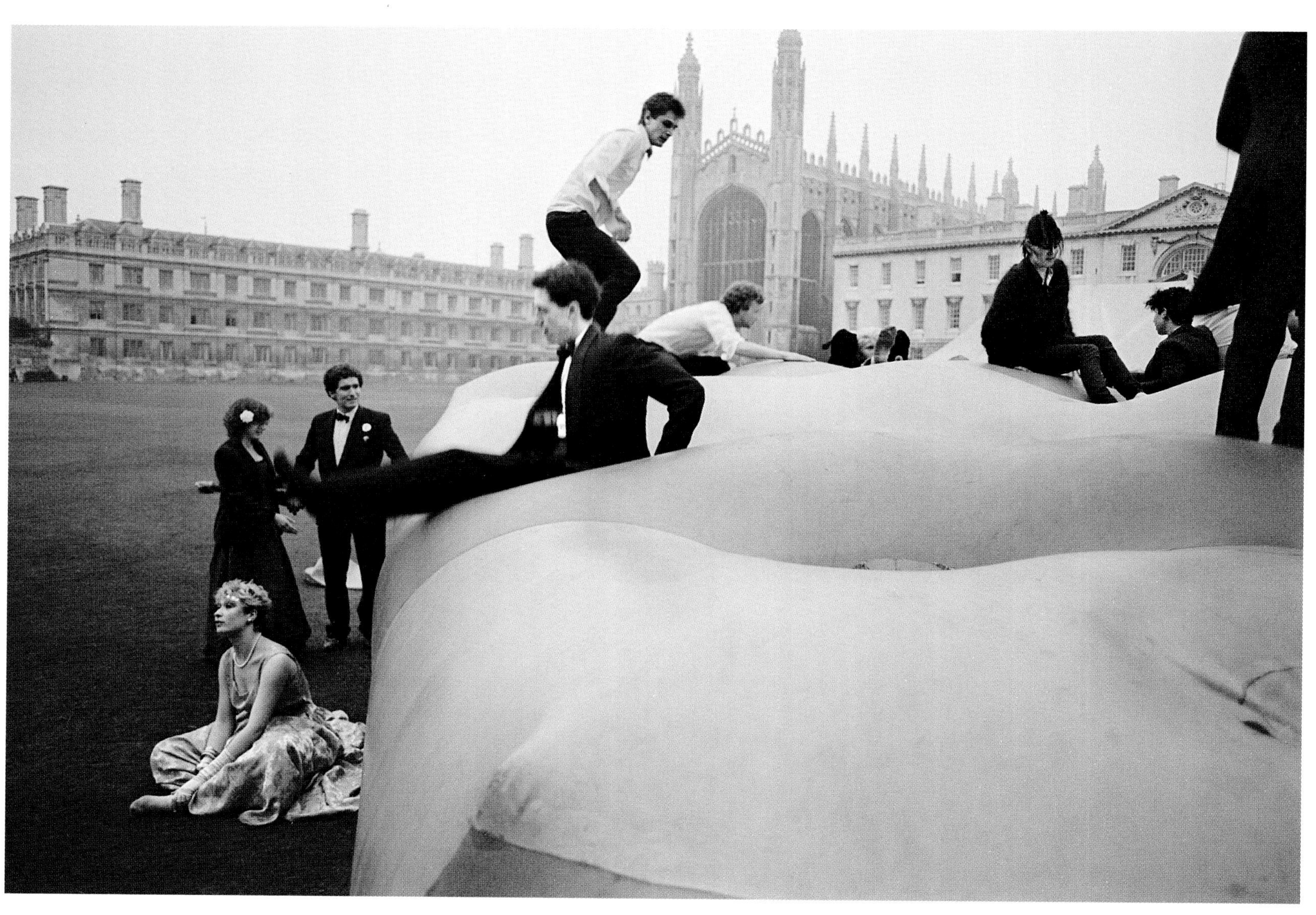

CAMBRIDGE MAY BALL 1983

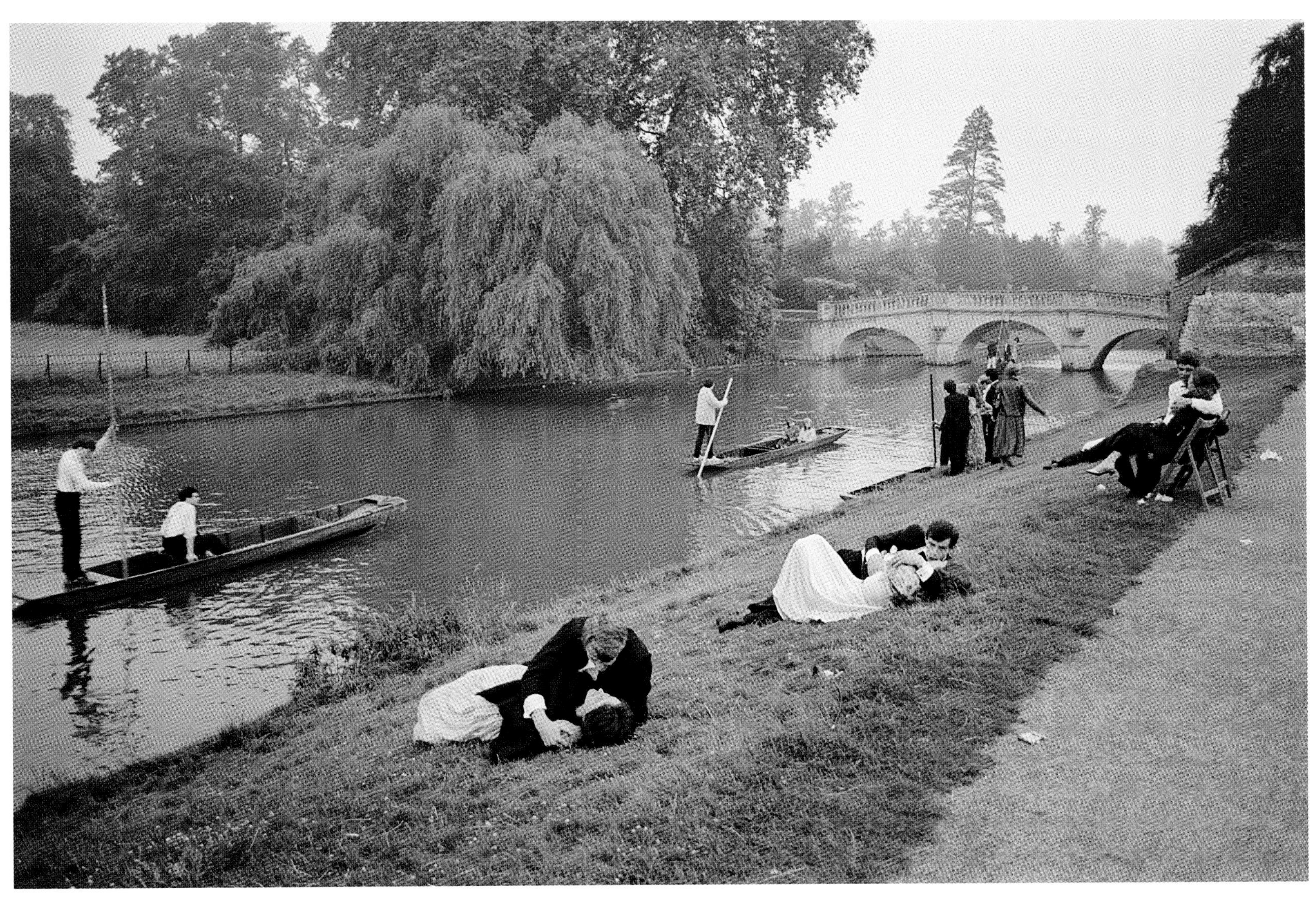

Lovers at dawn, Cambridge May Ball 1983

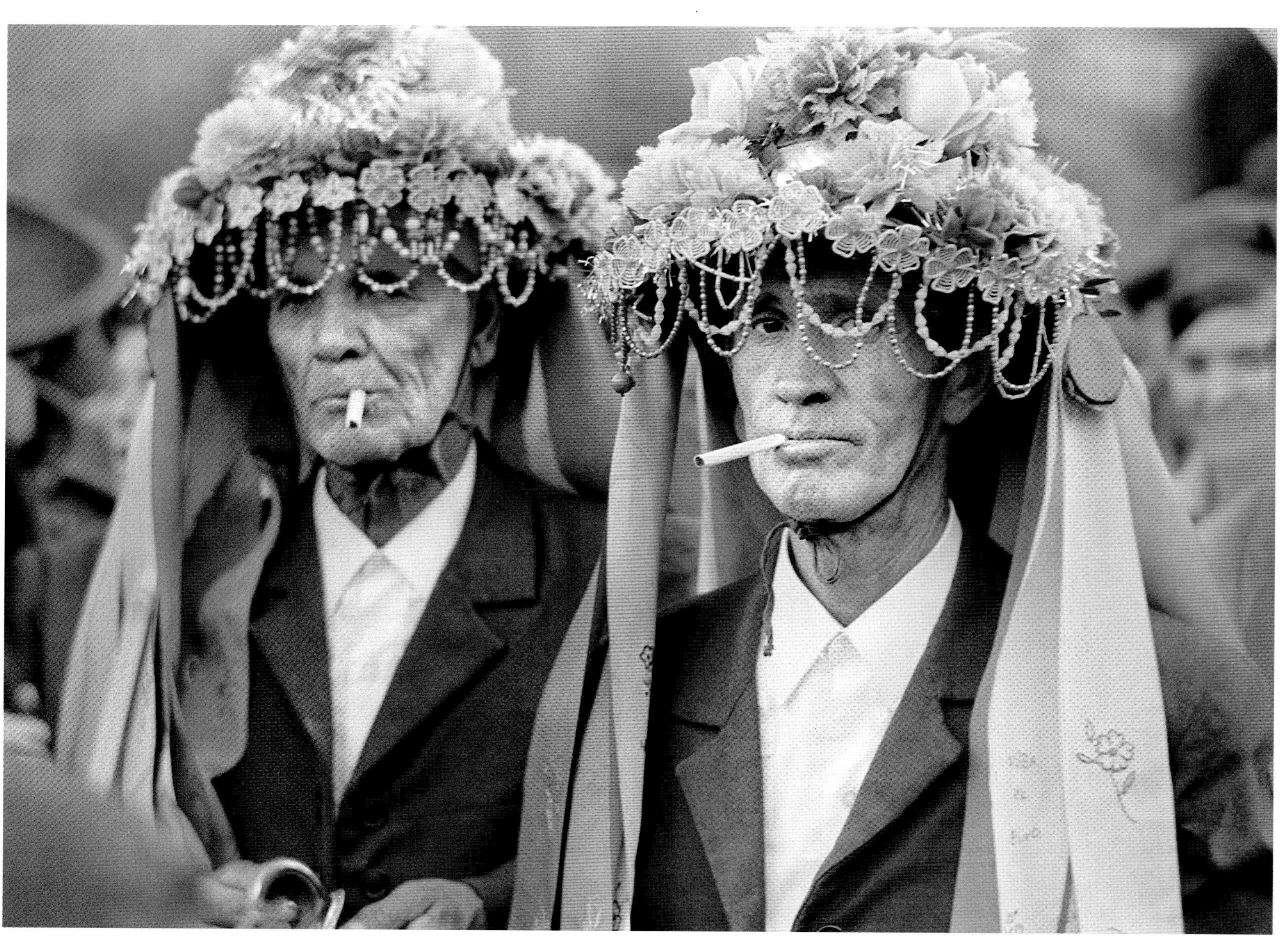

110   Smoke break, Malaga dancing festival 1969

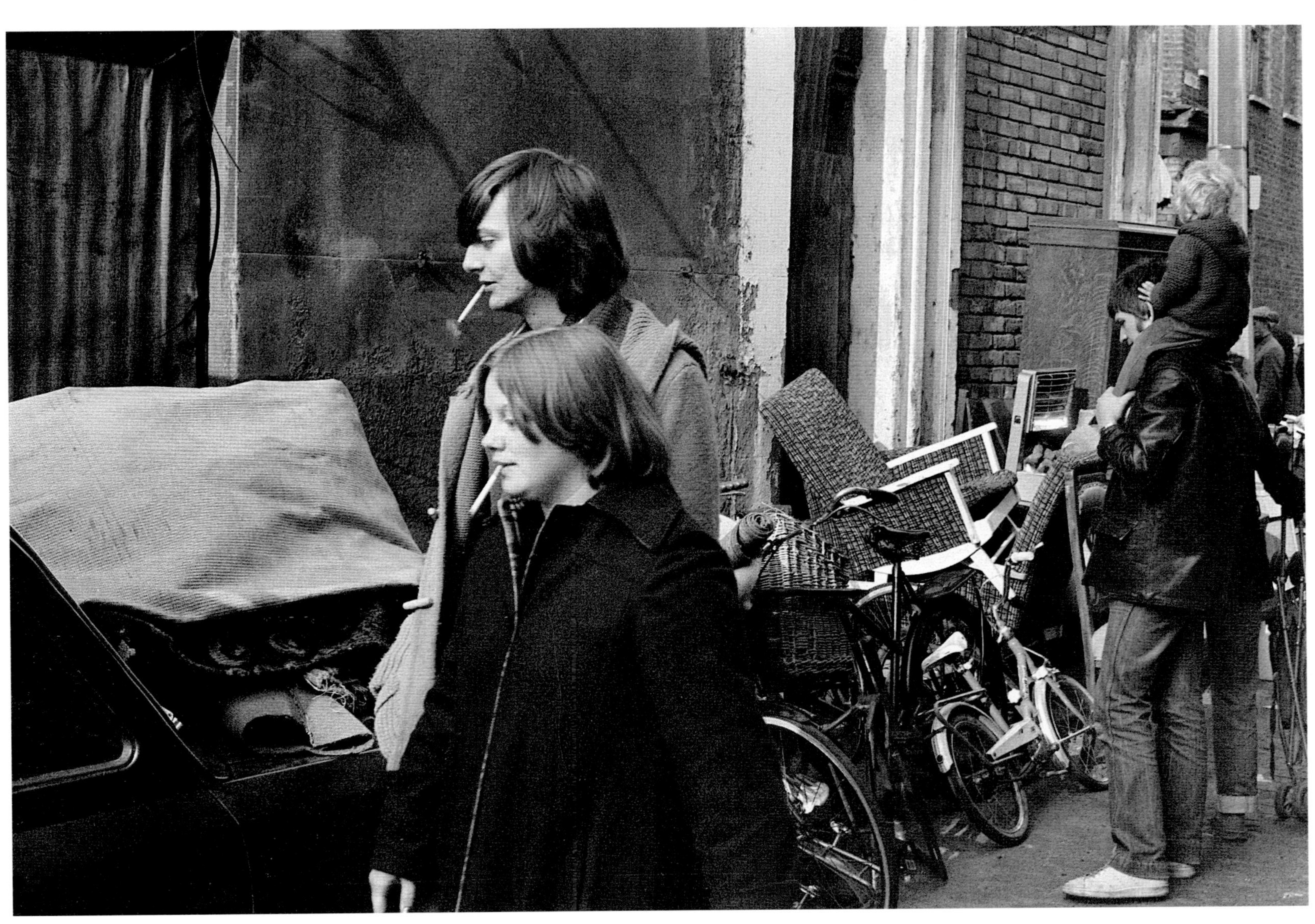

Young smokers, East End flea market, London 1978

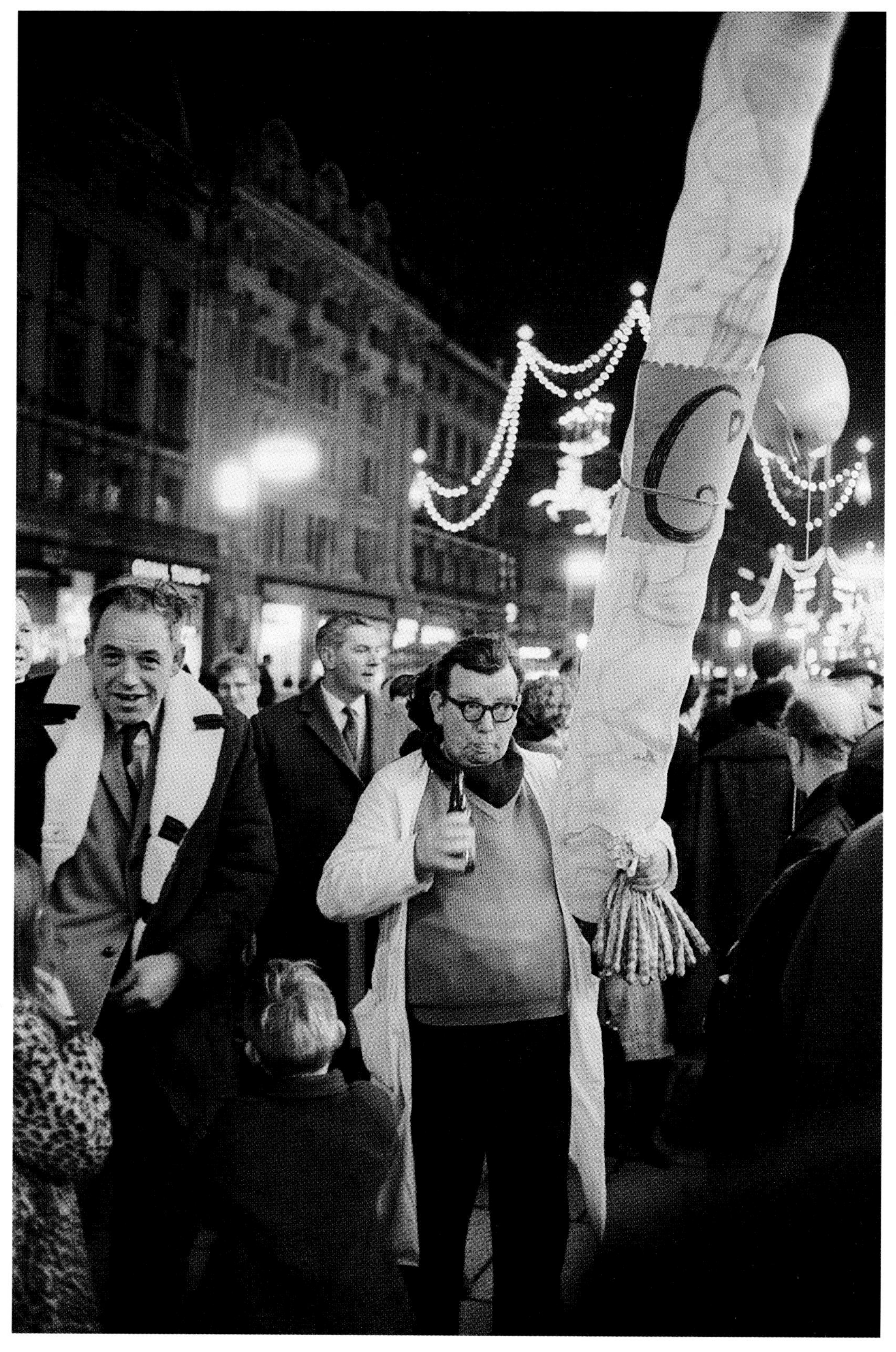

Christmas lights and balloons, Regent Street, London 1964

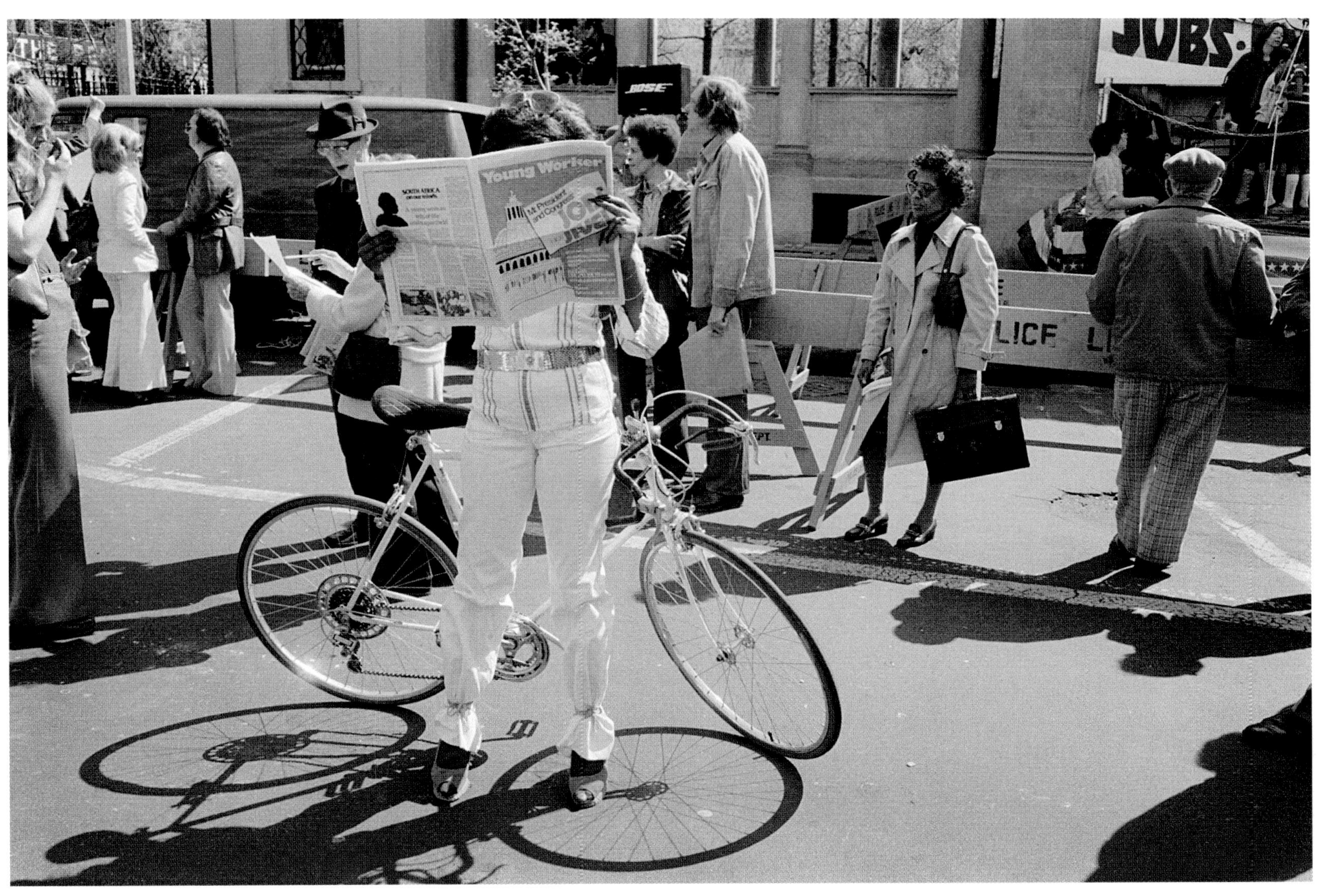

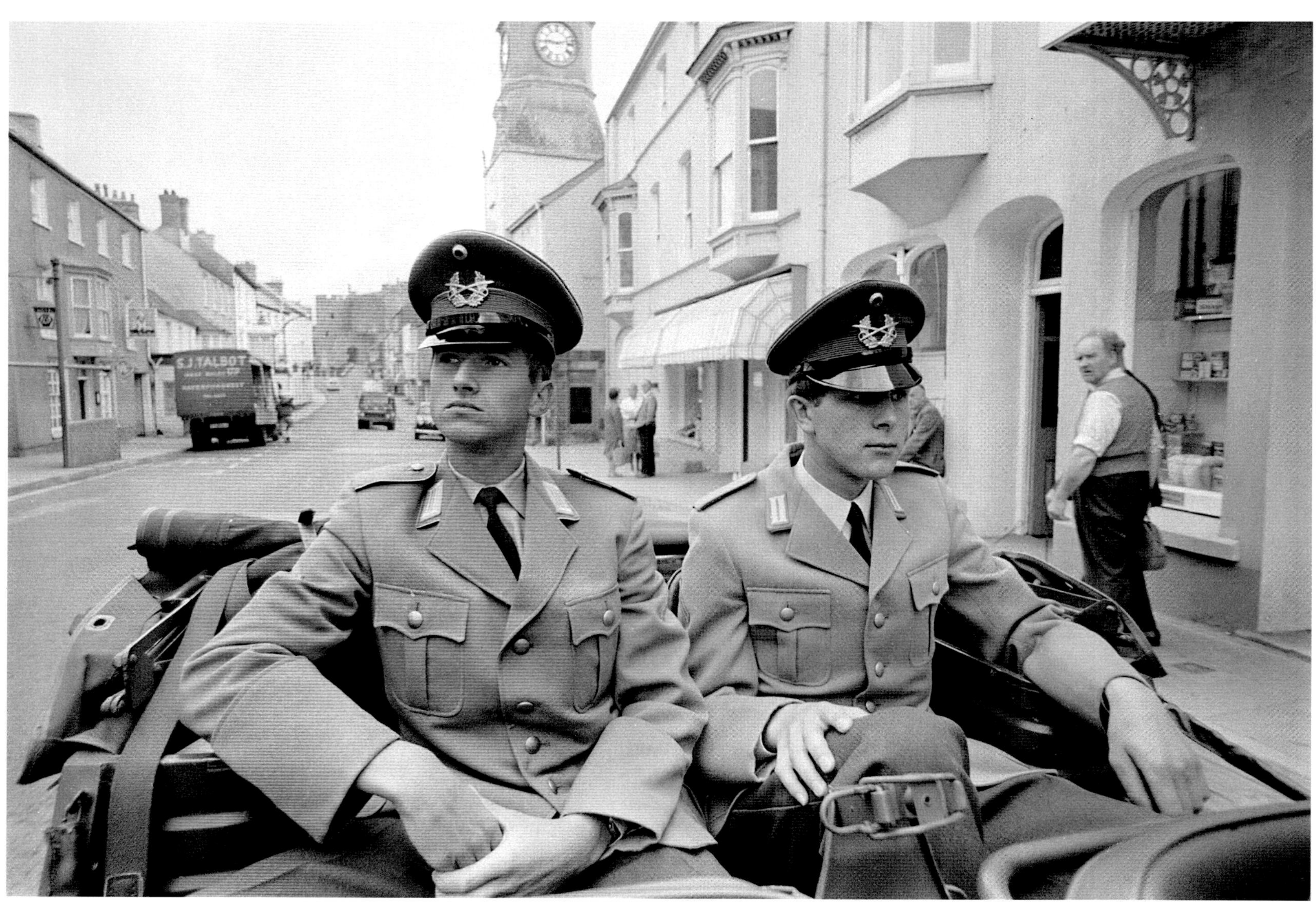

  German Panzers on manoeuvres in Pembroke, Wales 1966

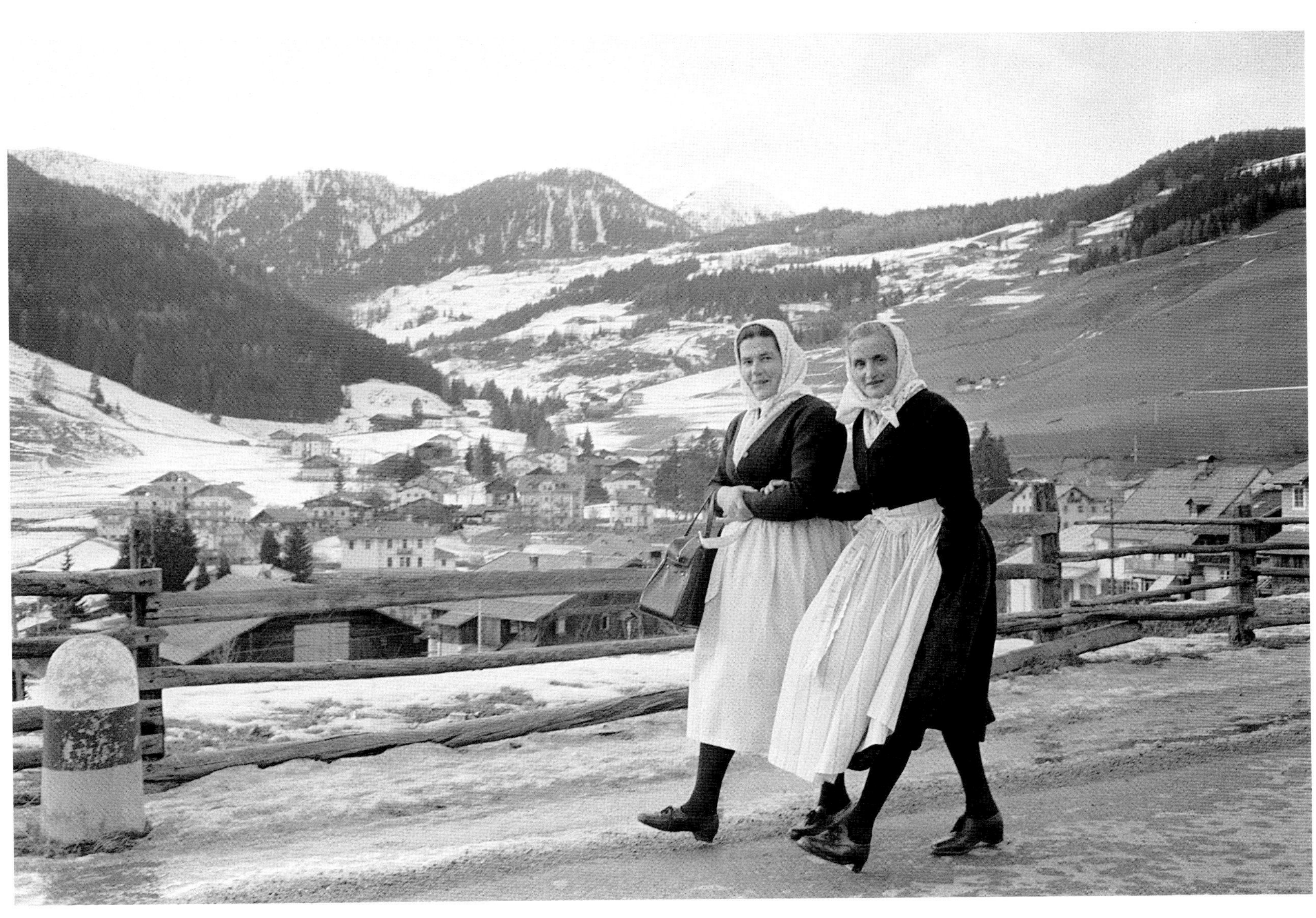

Tyrol villagers 1968

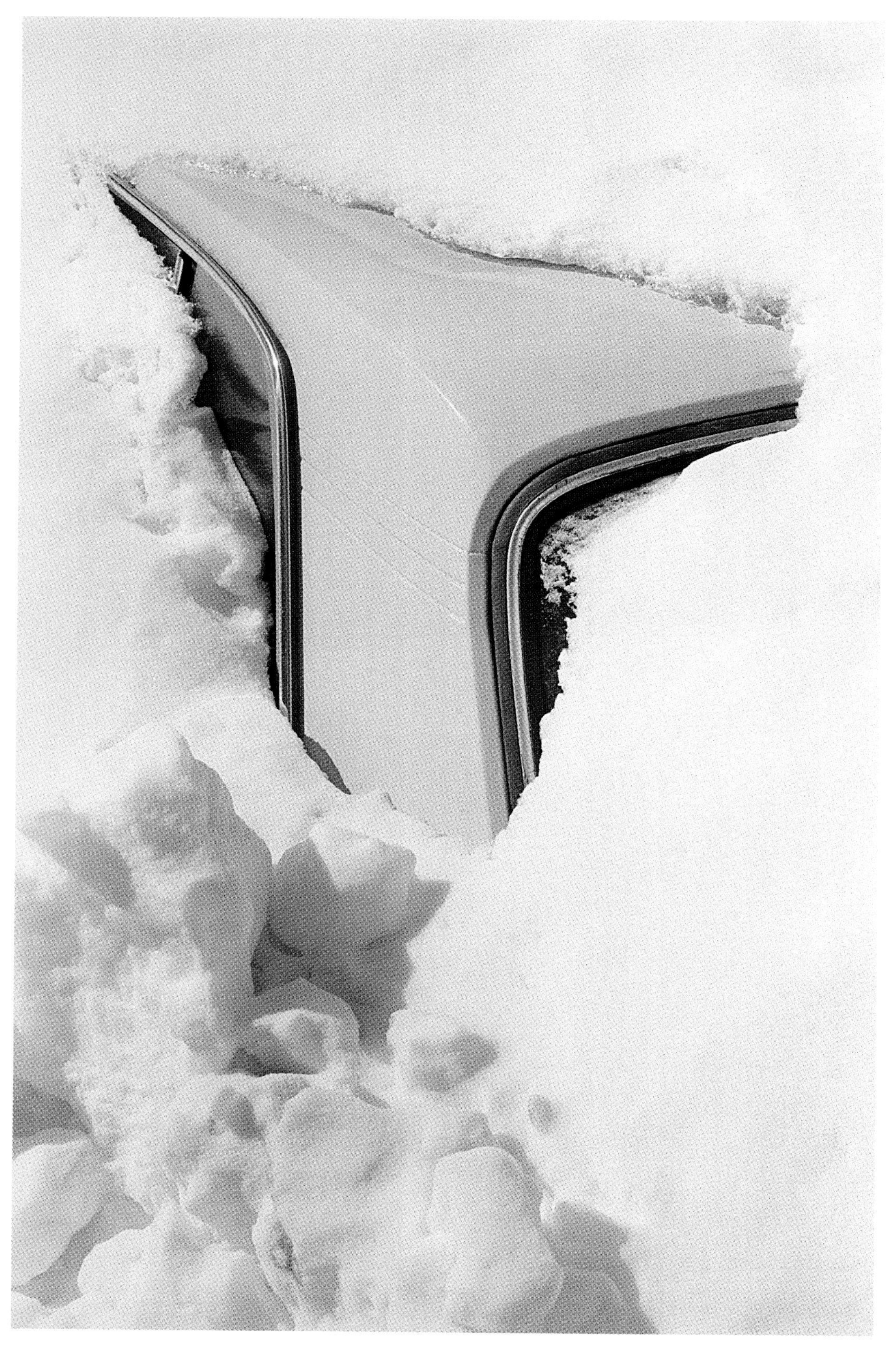

 SNOWBOUND, NEW YORK 1979

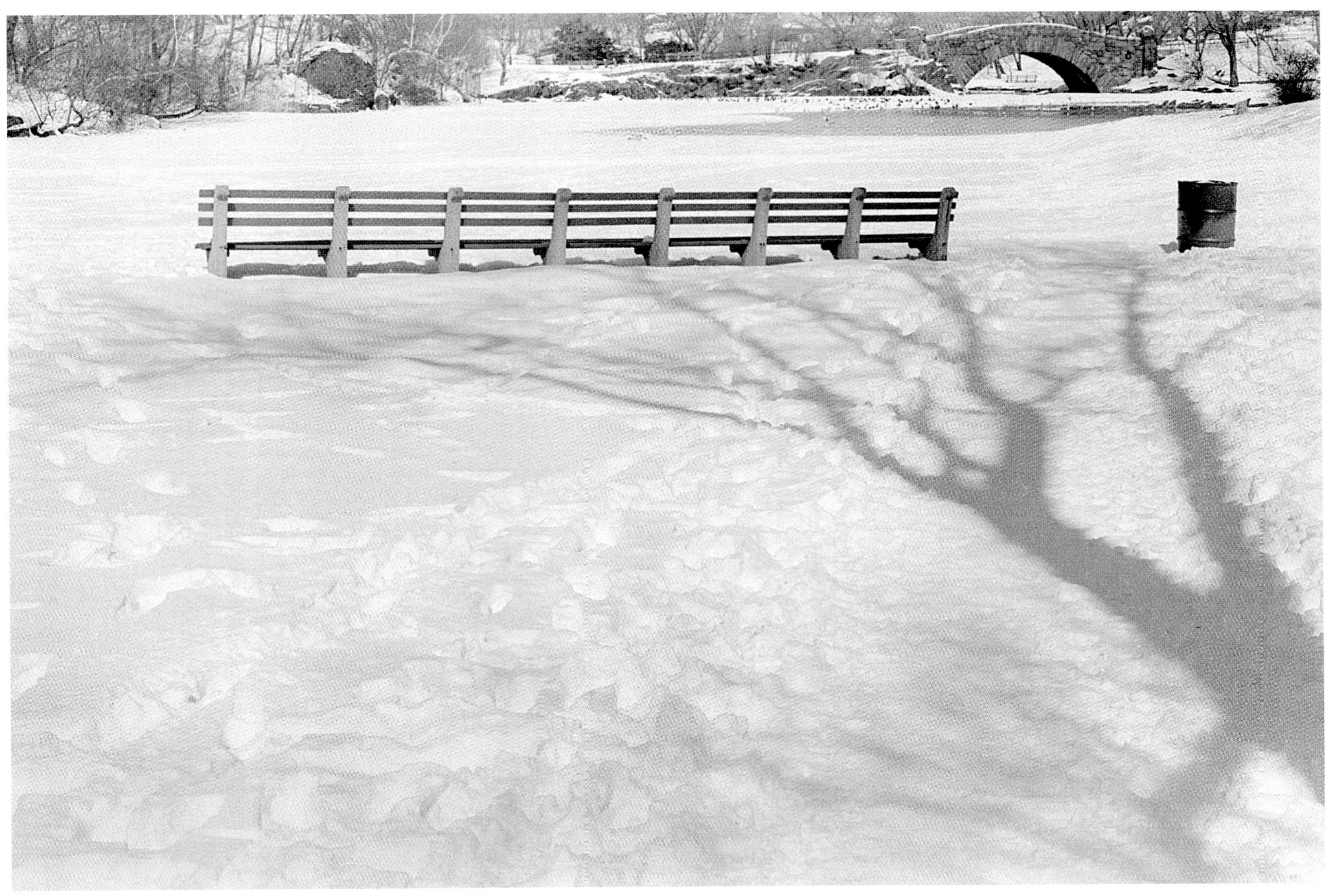

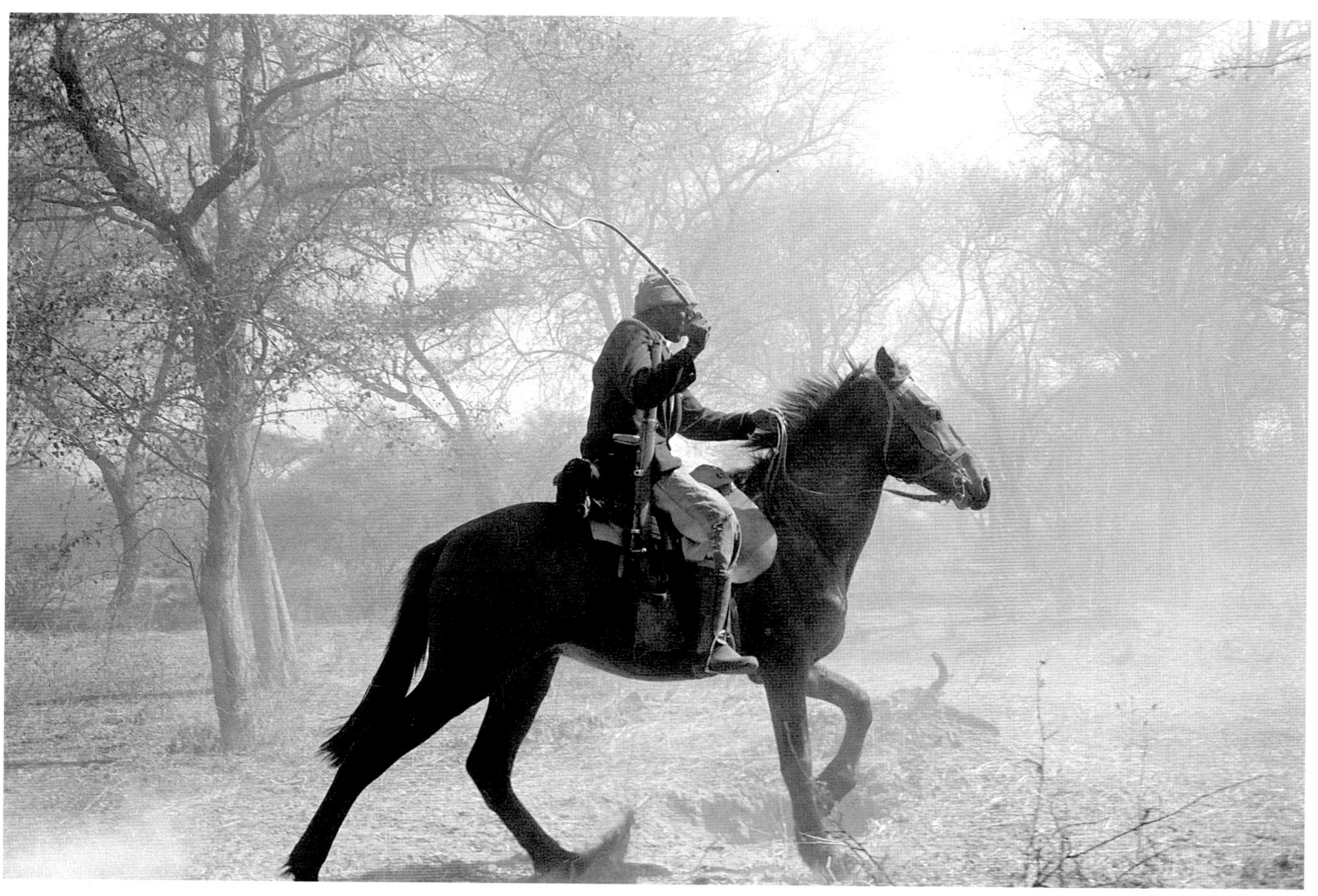

BOTSWANA COWBOY 1962

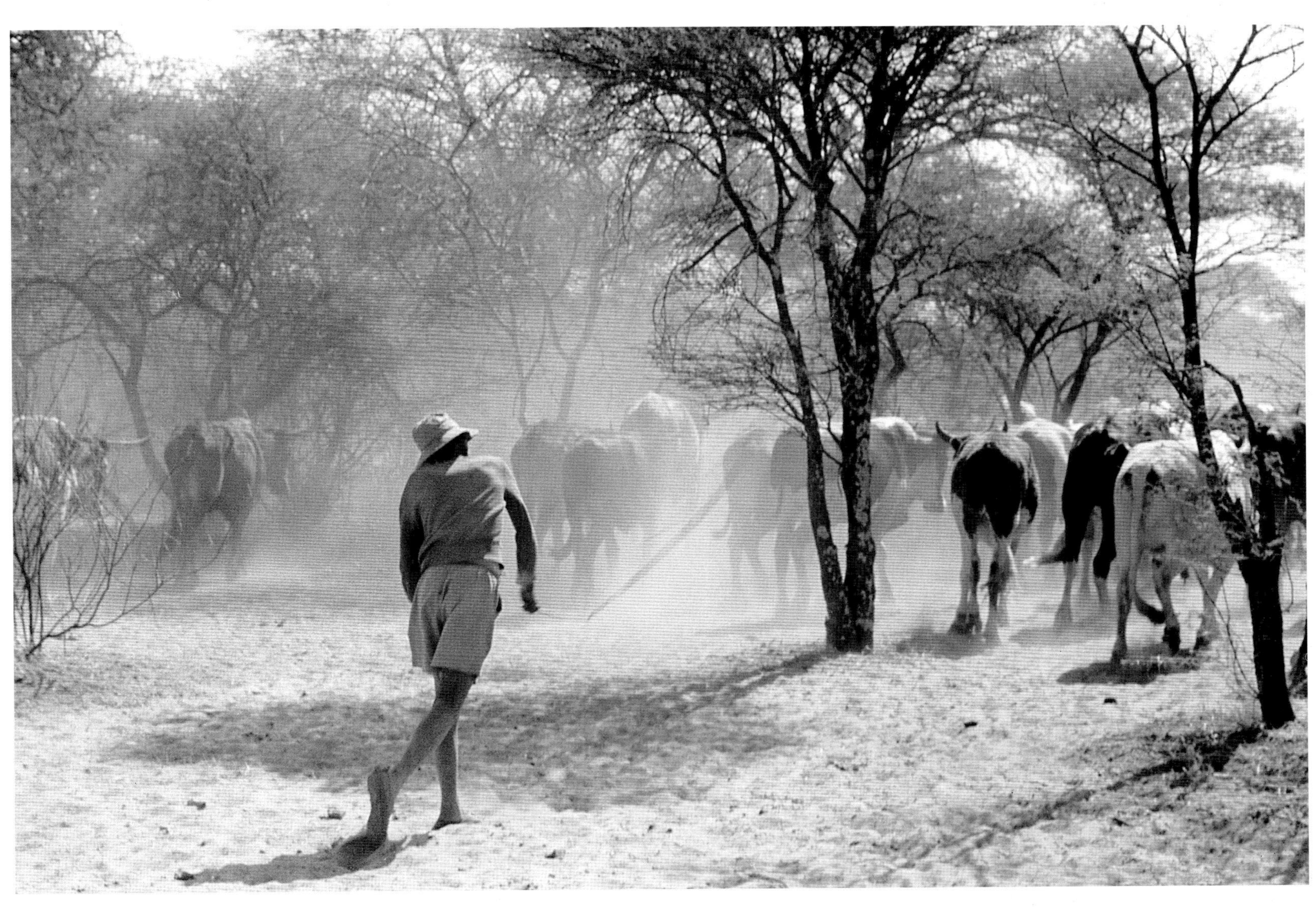

Cattle drive, Botswana 1962

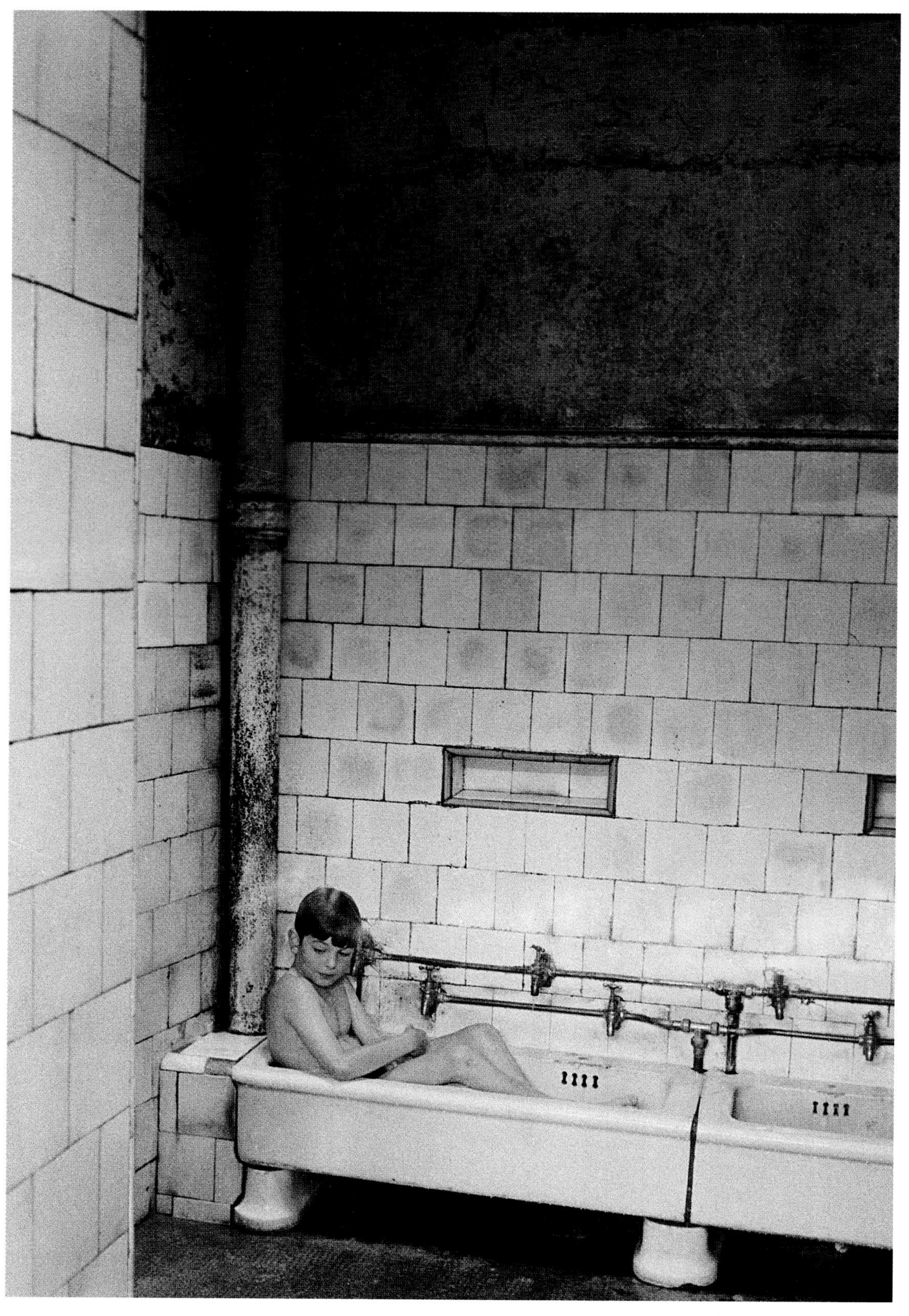

  PUBLIC BATHS, GLASGOW 1968

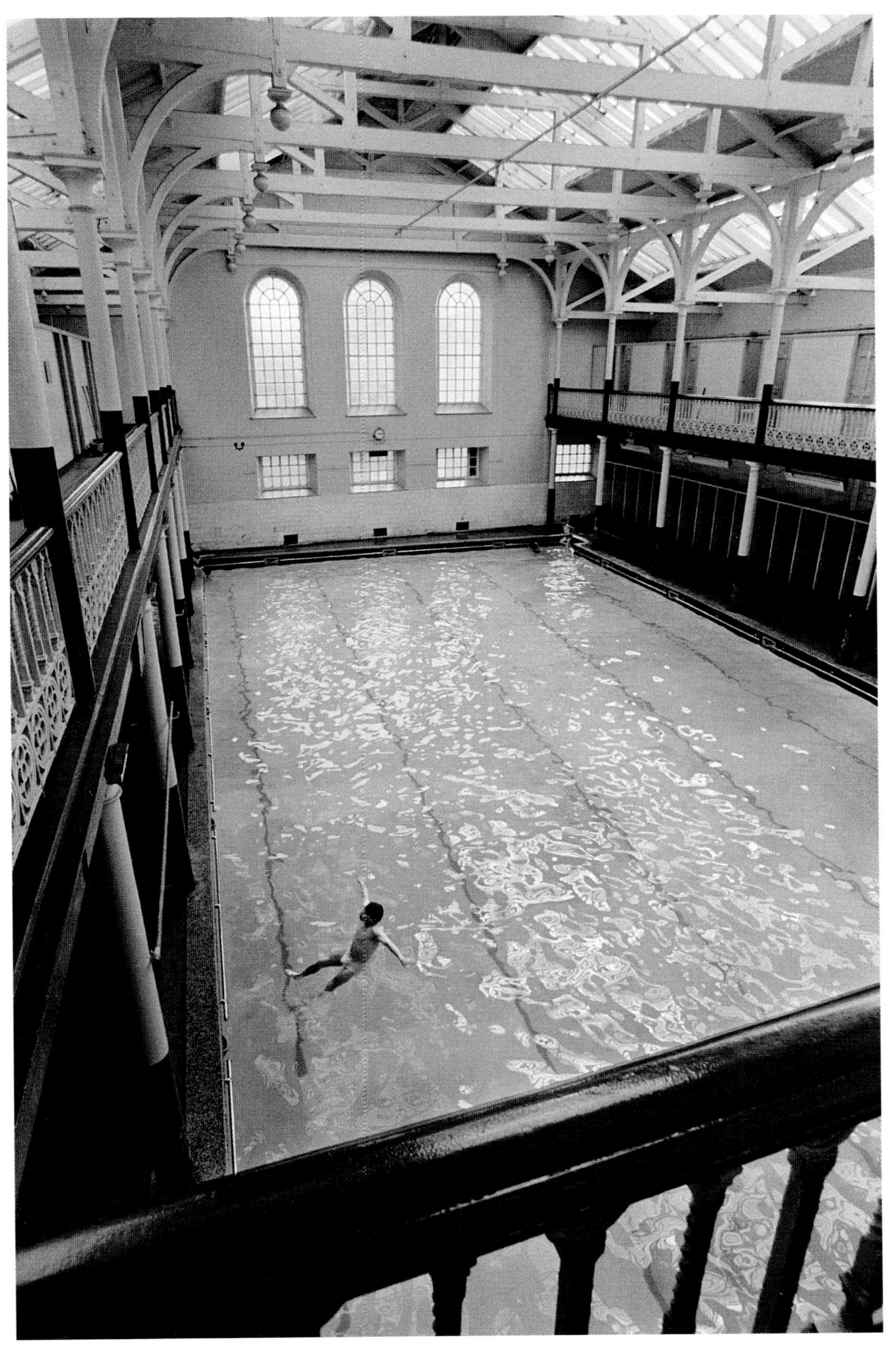

Public pool, Glasgow 1968

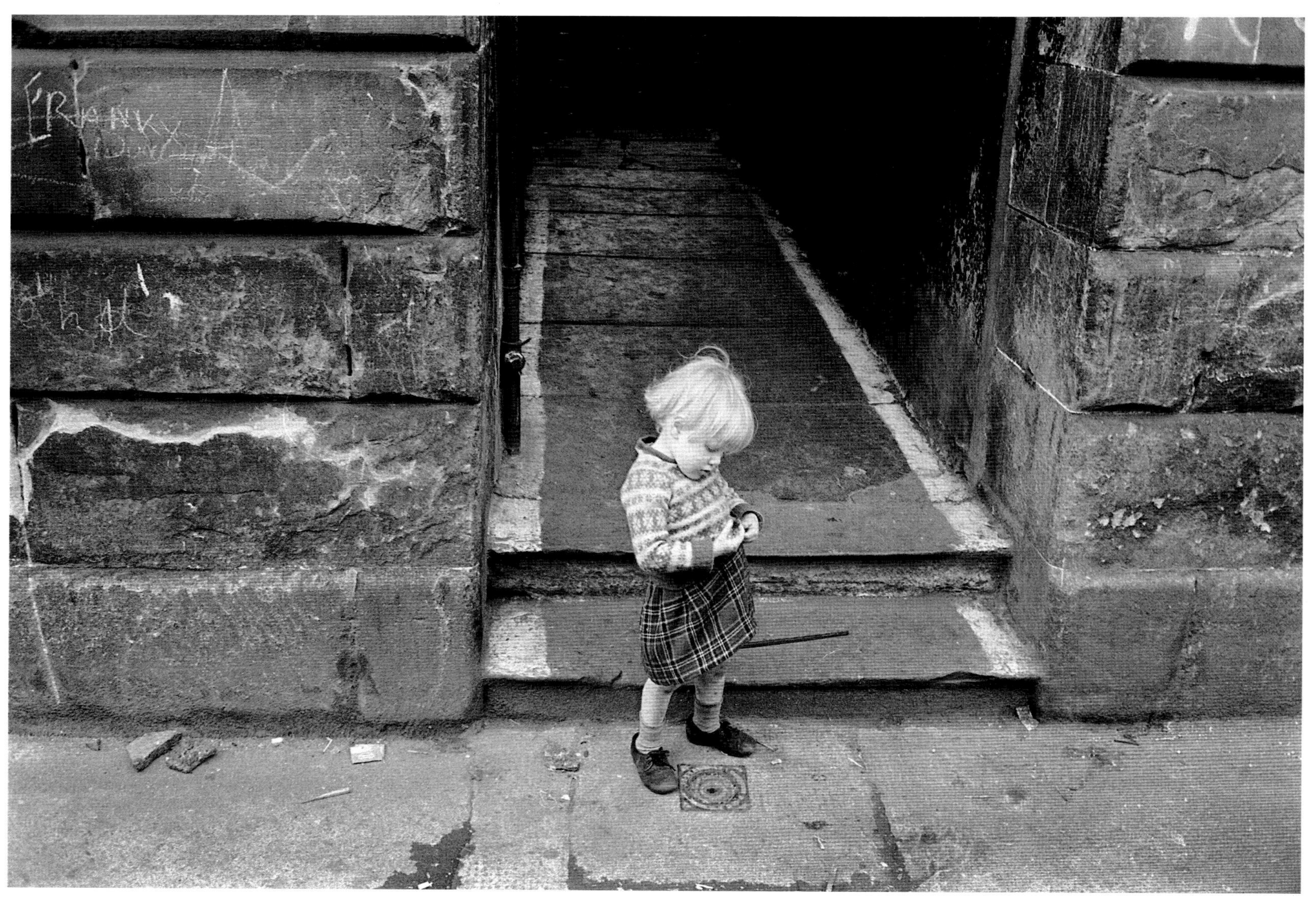

 A doorway in Gorbals, Glasgow 1968

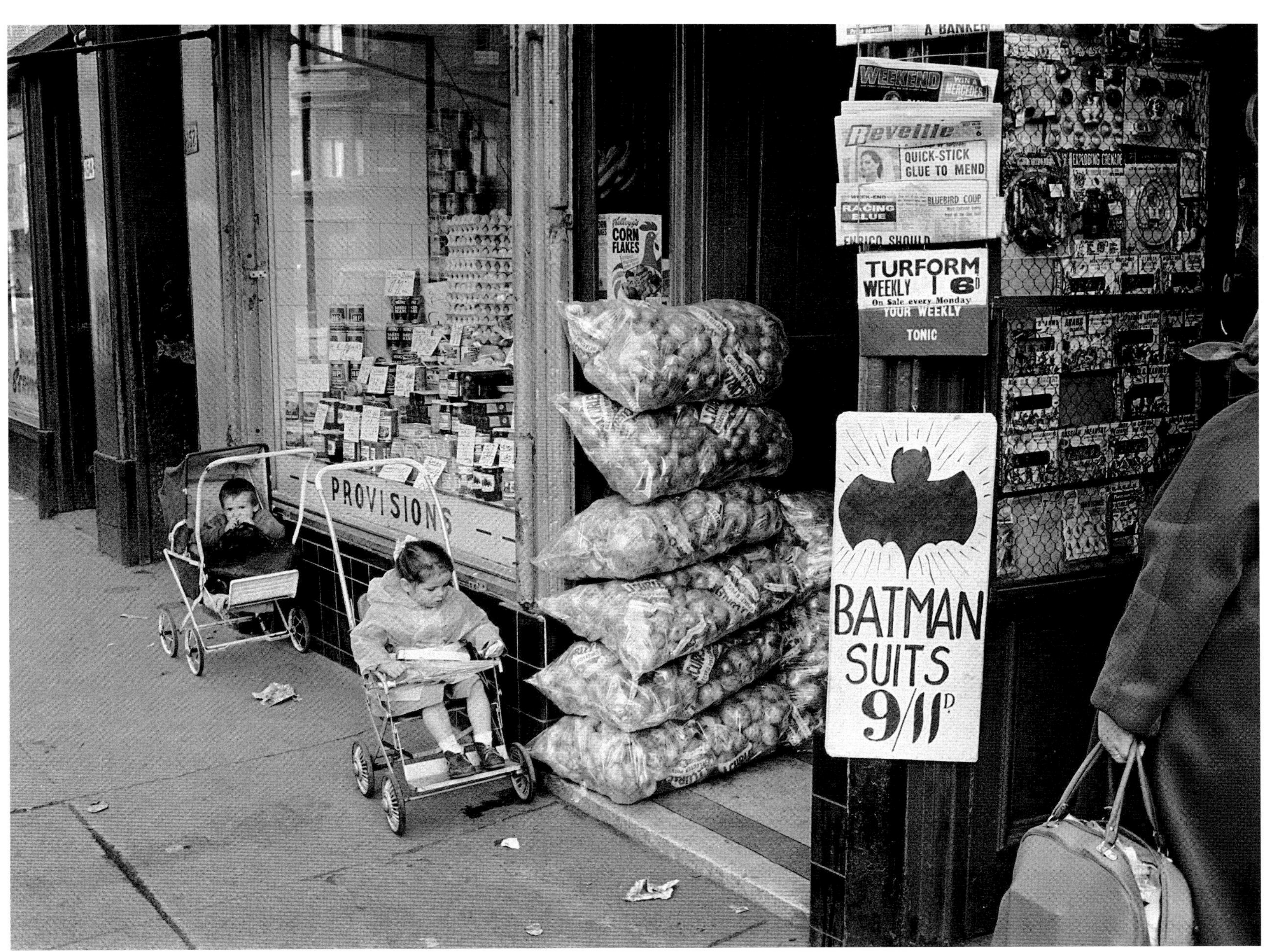
A BANKER
WEEKEND WIN A MERCEDES
Reveille
QUICK-STICK
GLUE TO MEND
WEEK-END
RACING BLUEBIRD COUP
BLUE
ENRICO SHOULD
TURFORM
WEEKLY 6D
On Sale every Monday
YOUR WEEKLY
TONIC
EXPLODING GRENADE
PROVISIONS
CORN
FLAKES
BATMAN
SUITS
9/11D

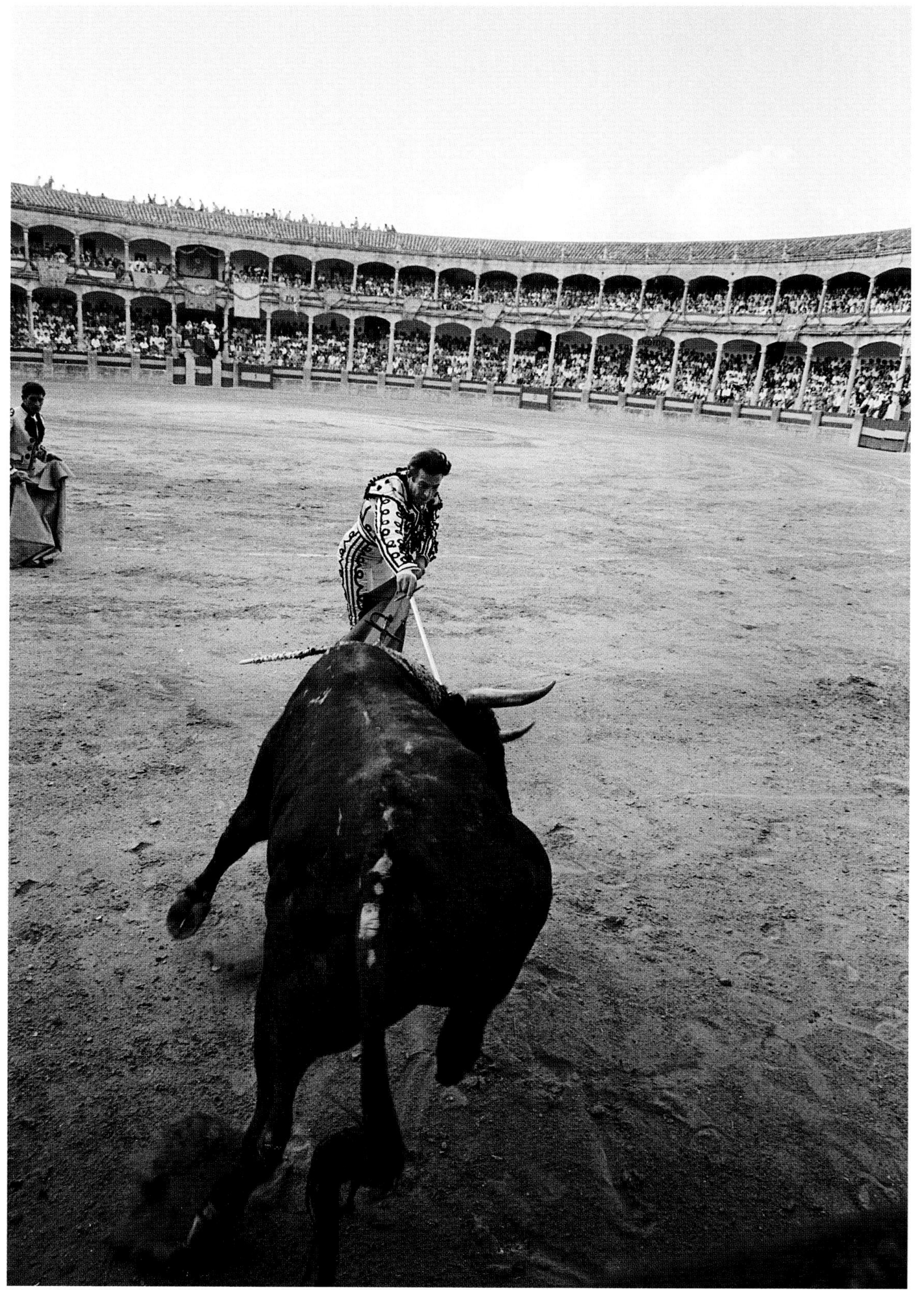

The kill, Rhonda, Spain 1969

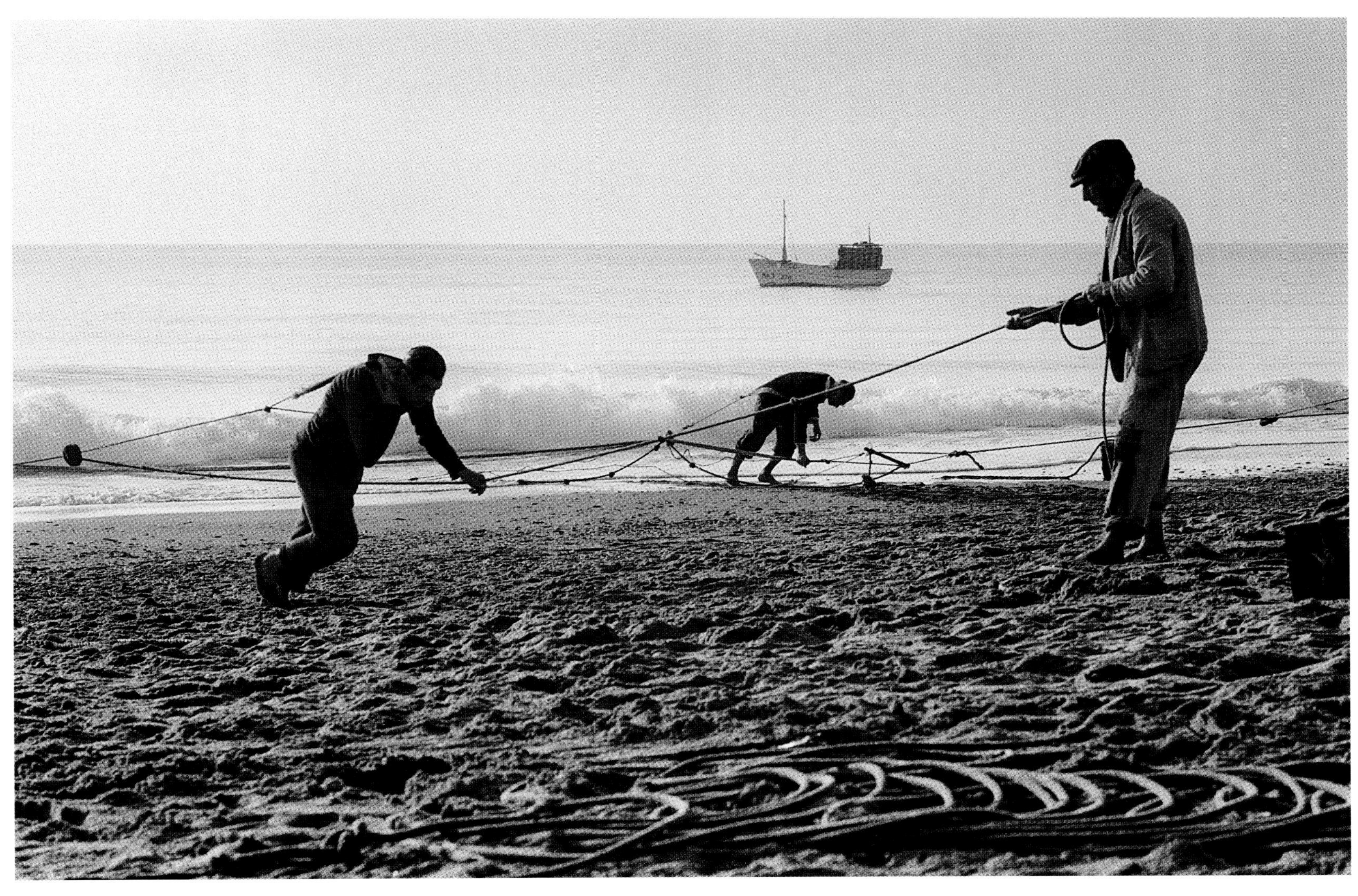

Mediterranean fishermen, Fuengirola, Spain 1970

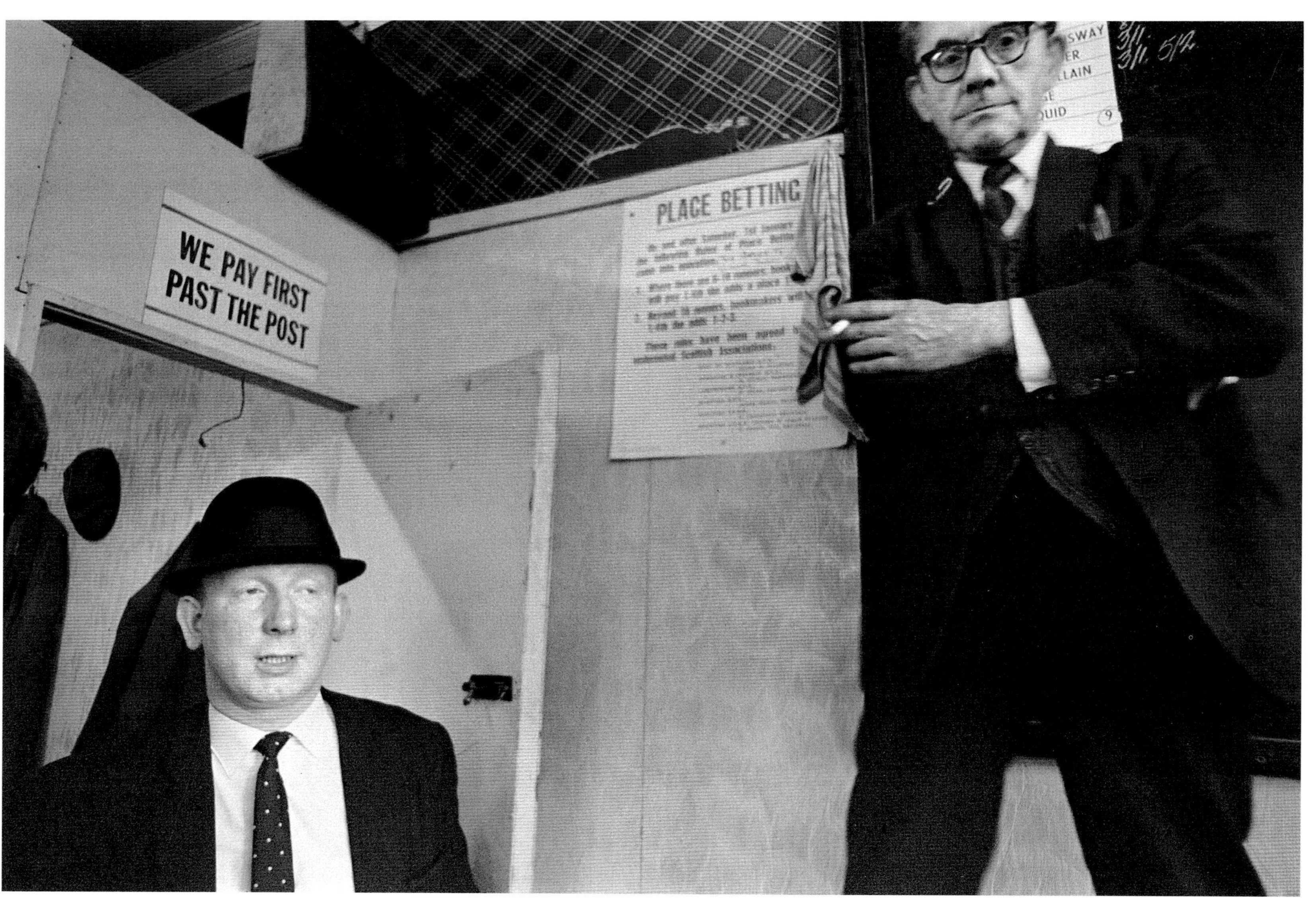

A BOOKMAKER, GLASGOW 1968

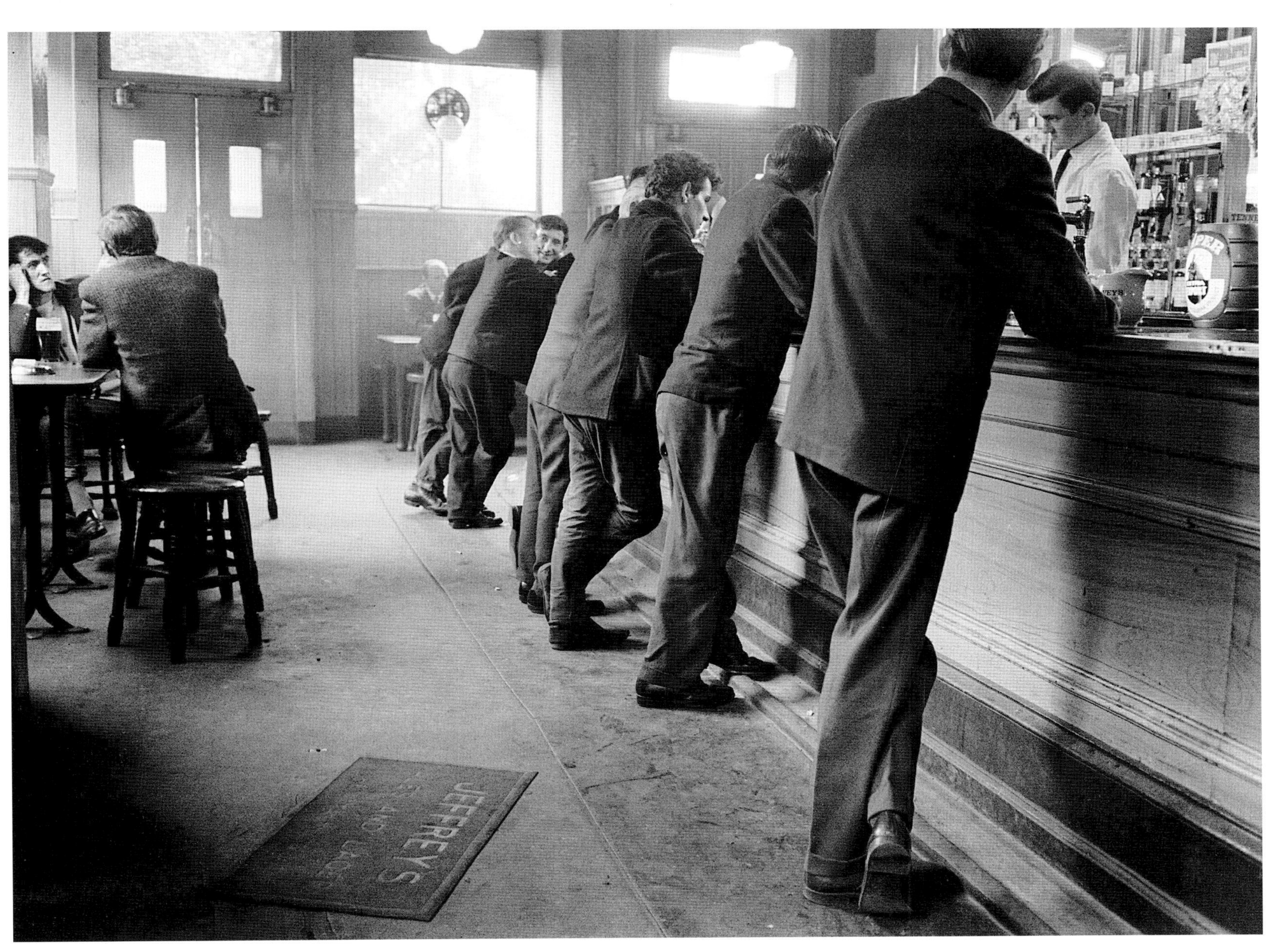

JEFFREYS

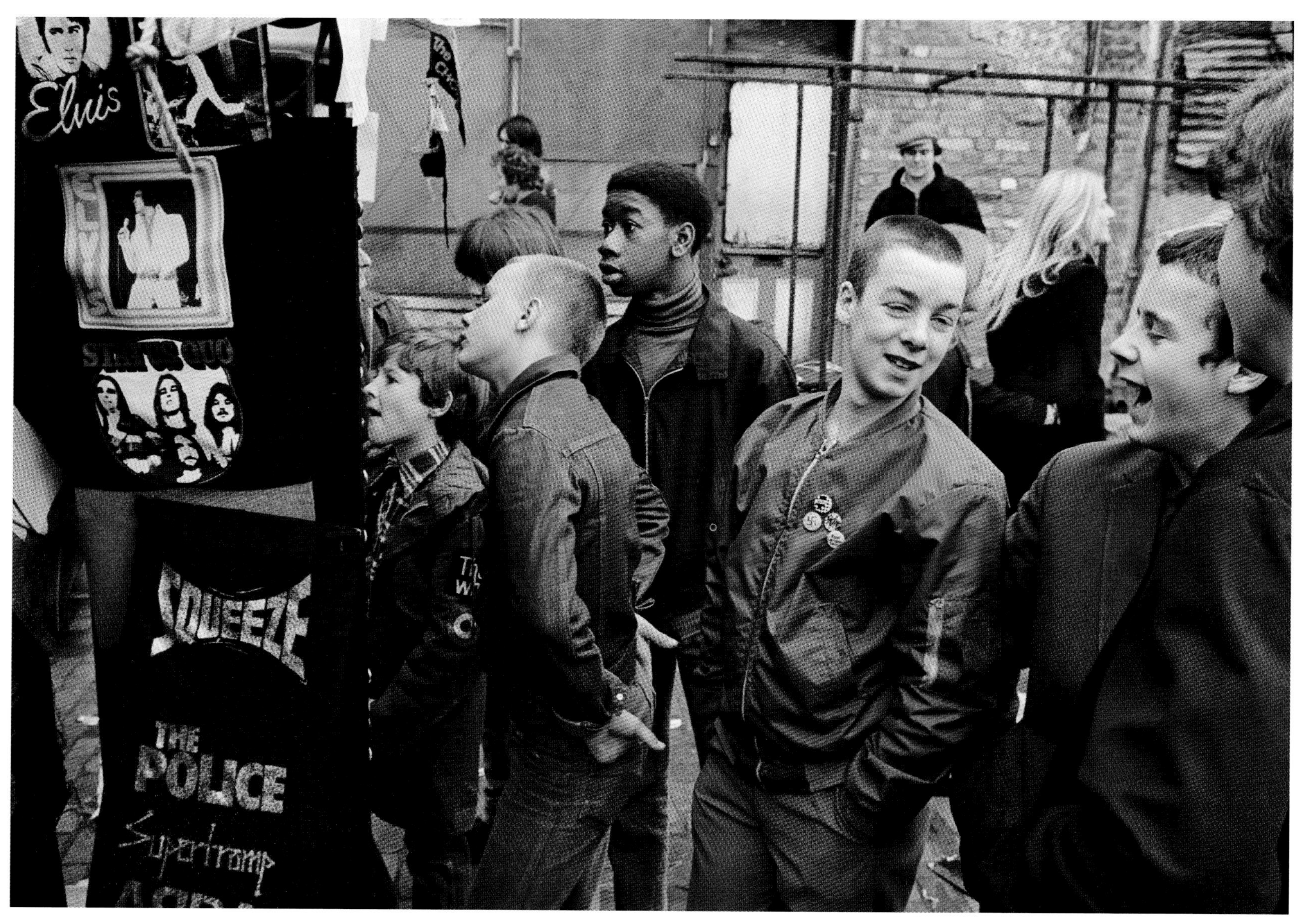

London boys at East End flea market 1977

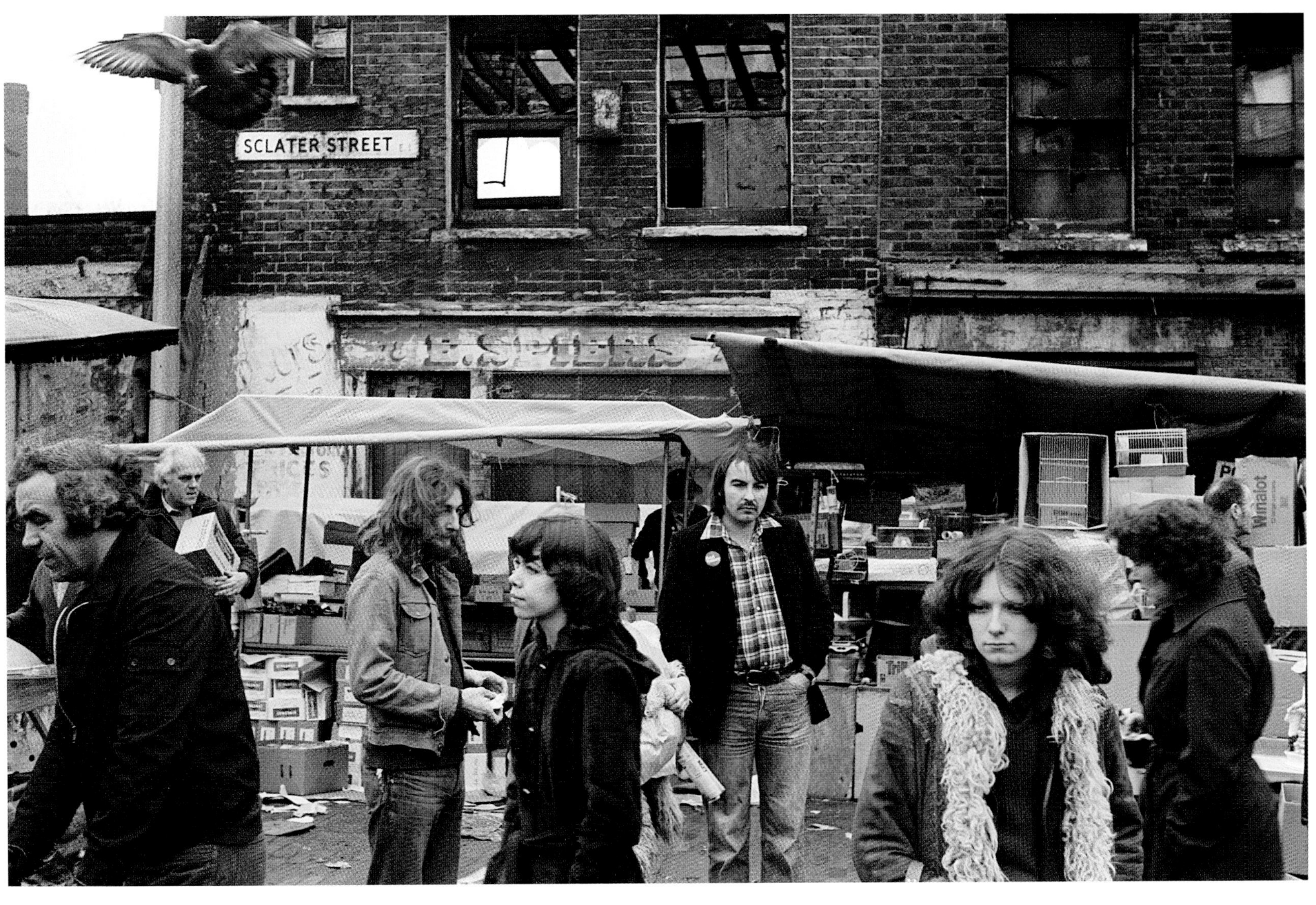

SCLATER STREET
J.E.SPIERS
Wimalot

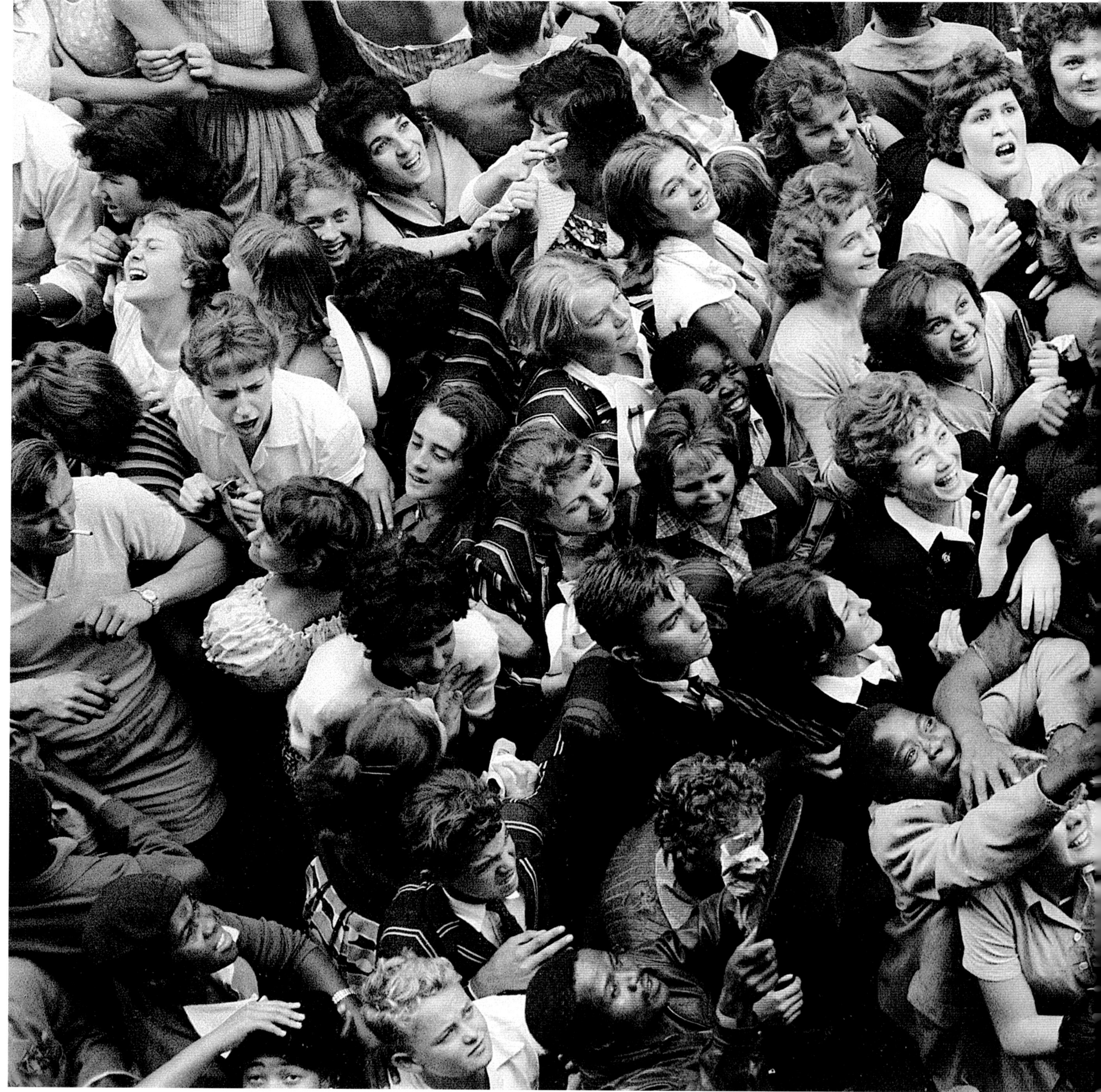

 POP FANS WELCOMING POP STAR CLIFF RICHARD, JOHANNESBURG 1960

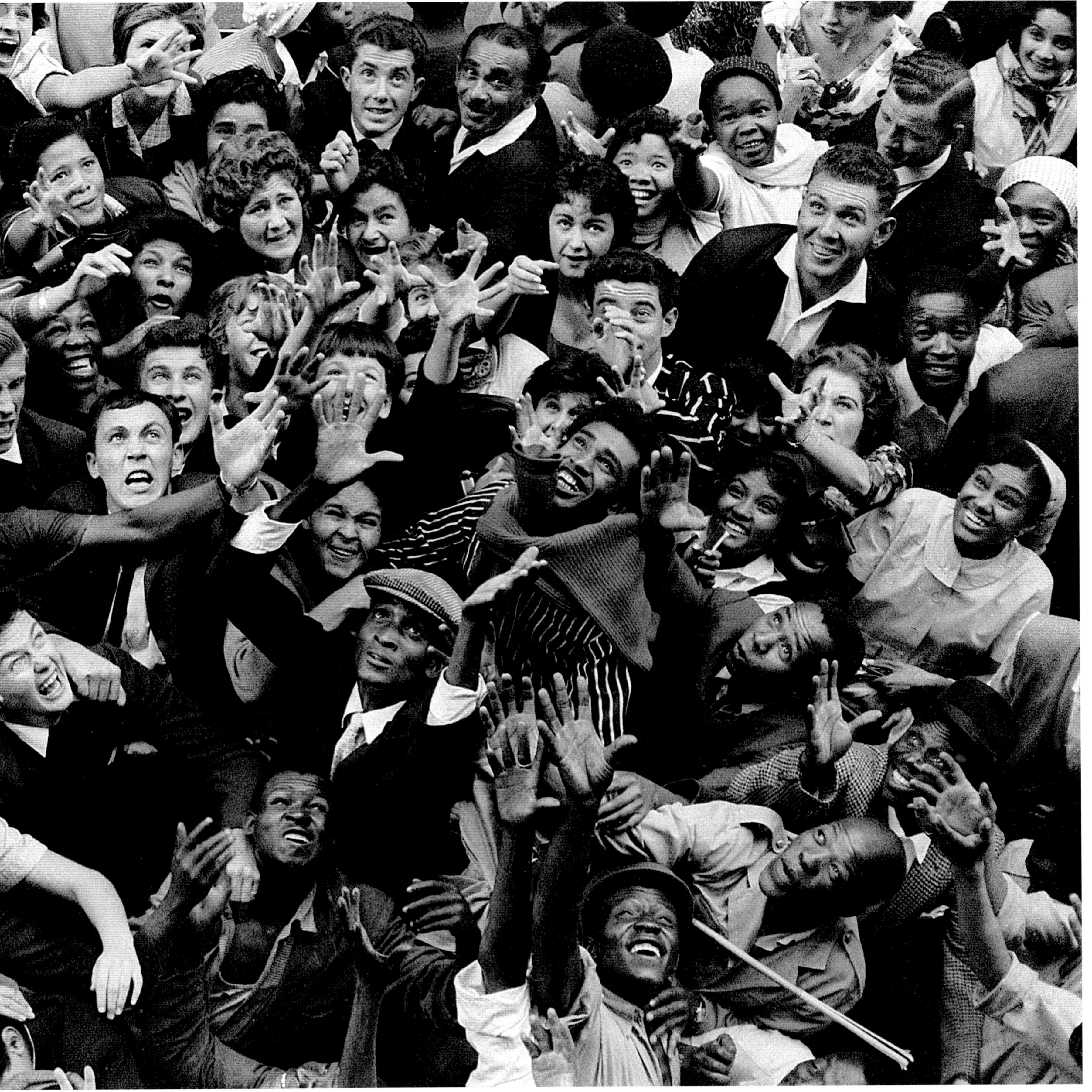

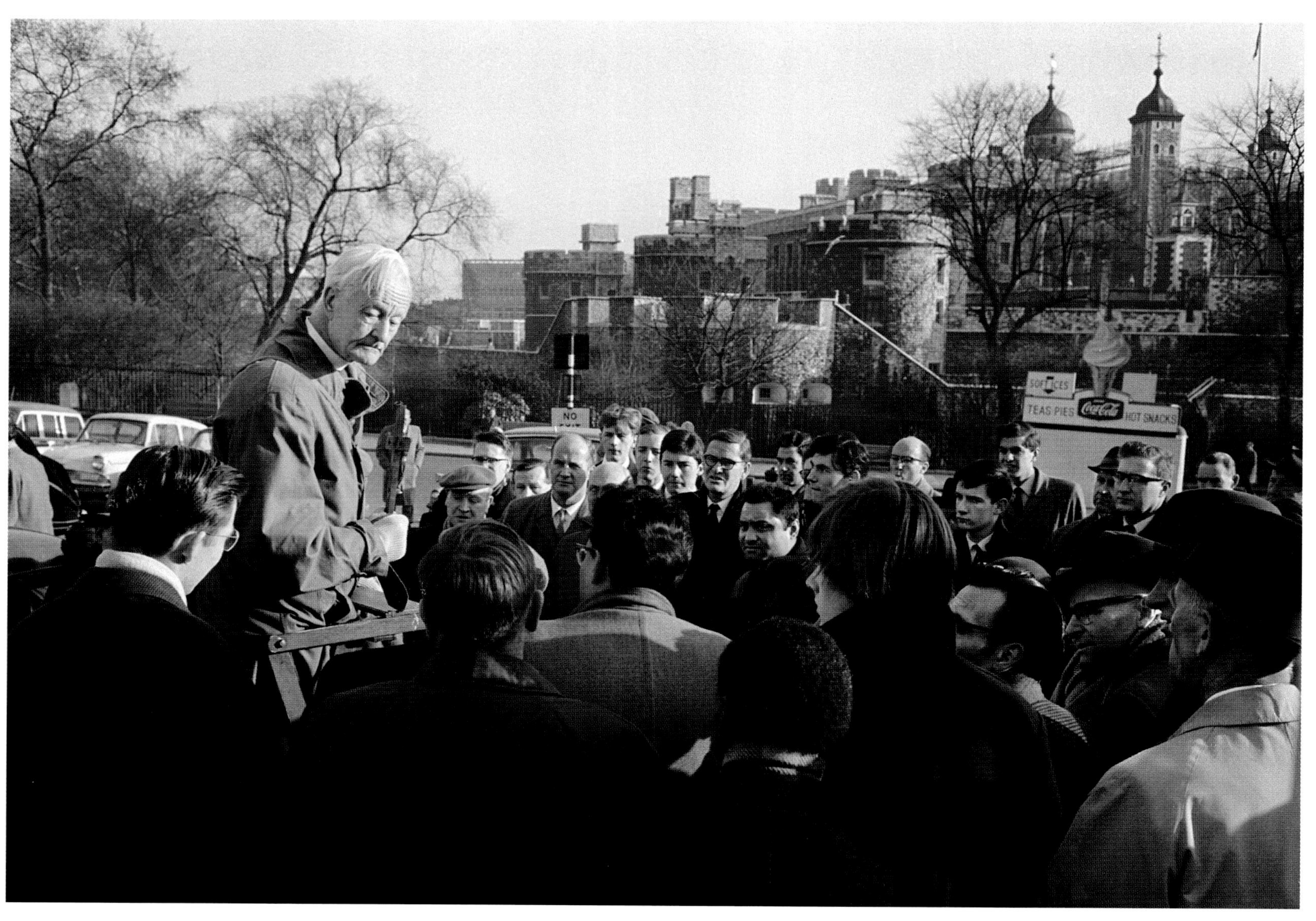

   Soap box priest, Tower of London 1964

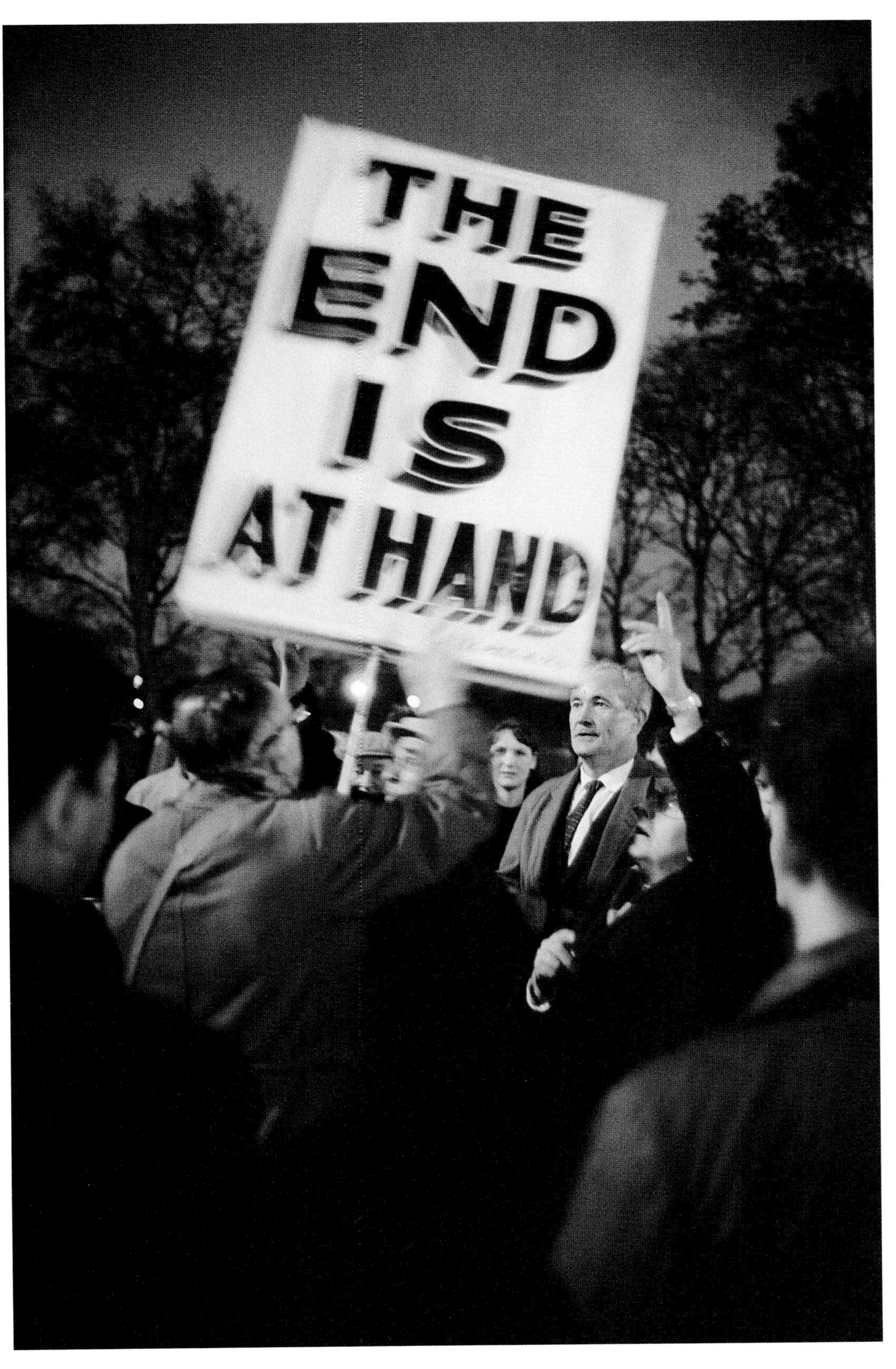

Speakers' Corner, London 1964

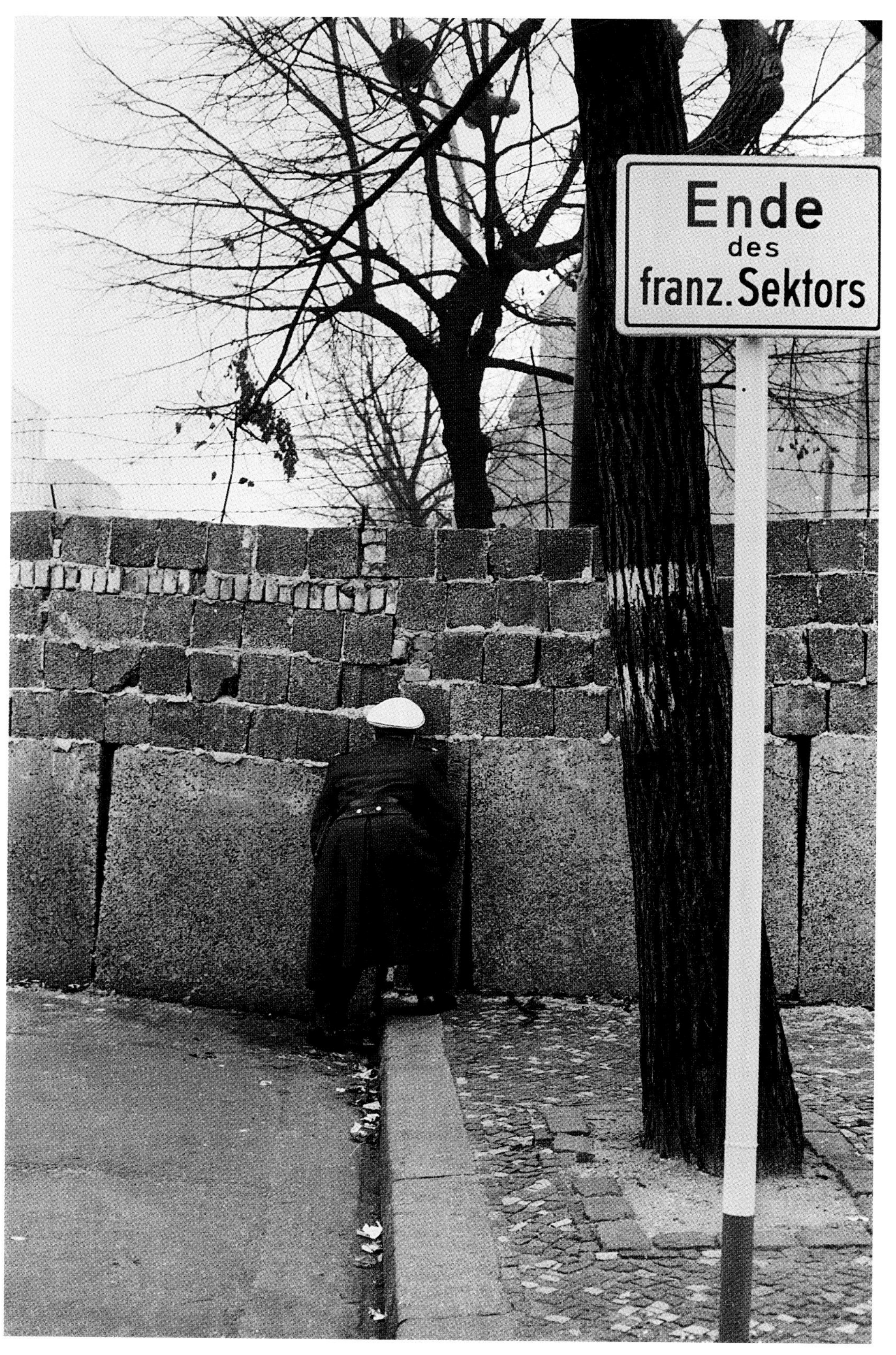

PEEPING COP, BERLIN WALL 1961

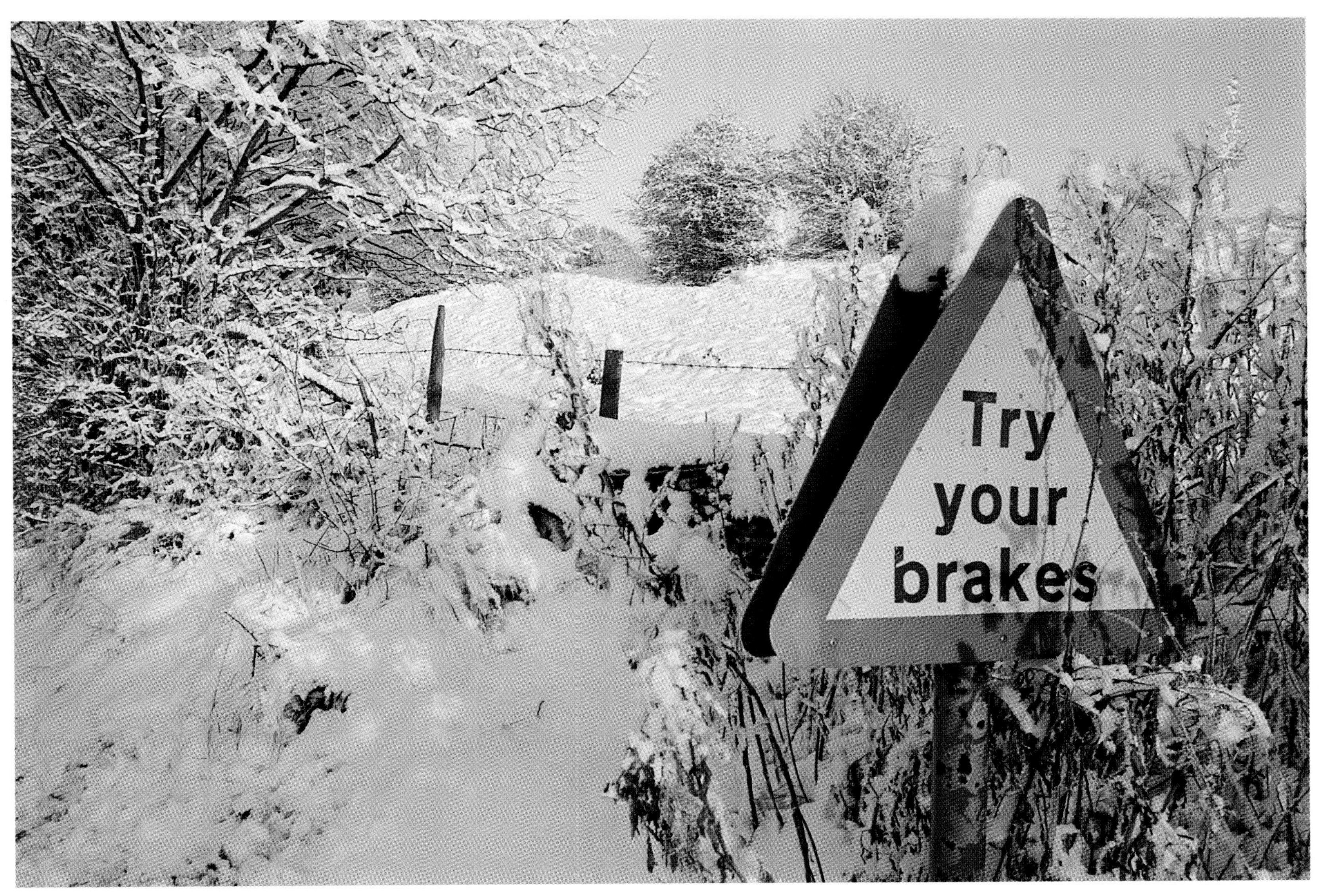

Try
your
brakes

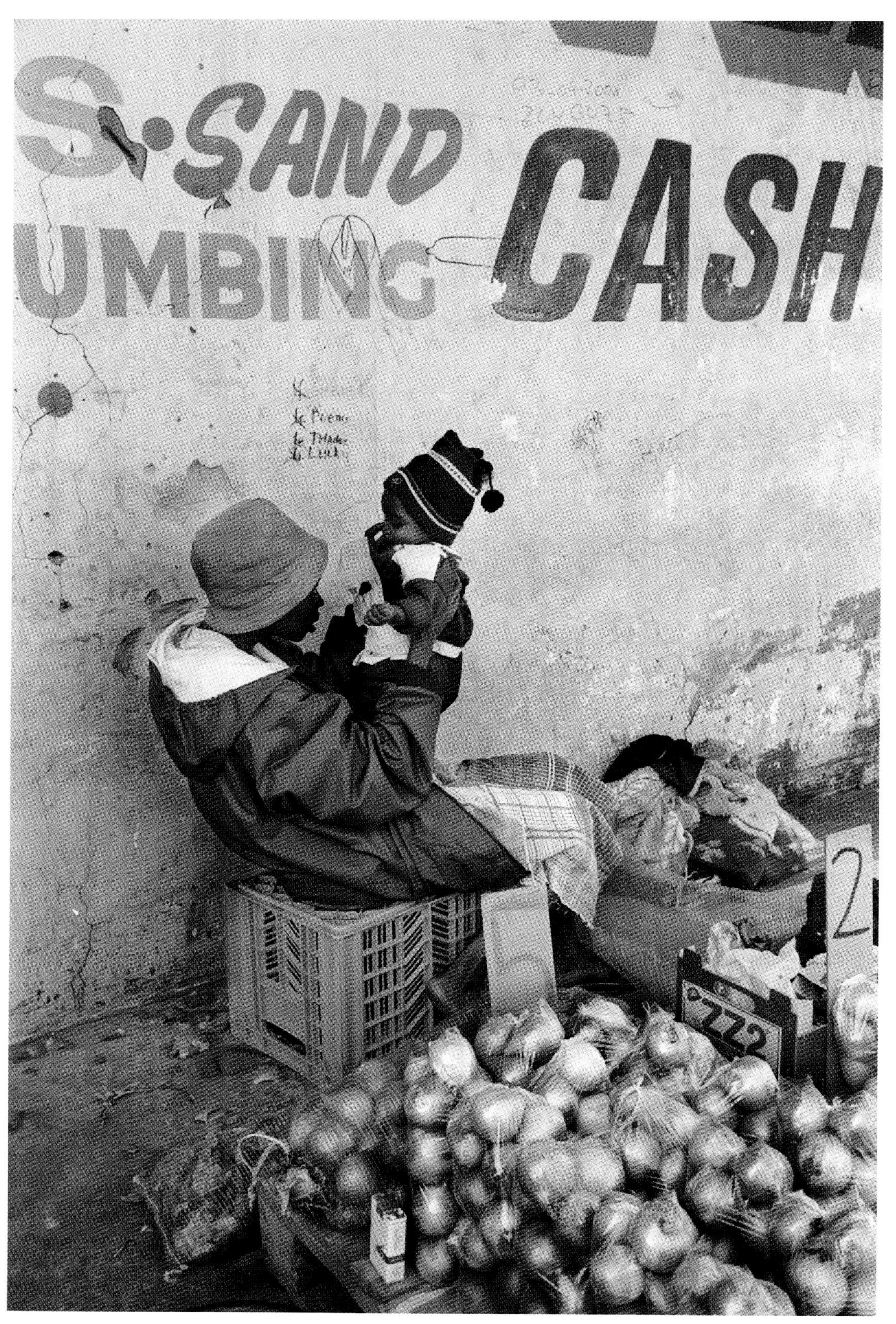

Making a living in Kliptown 2003

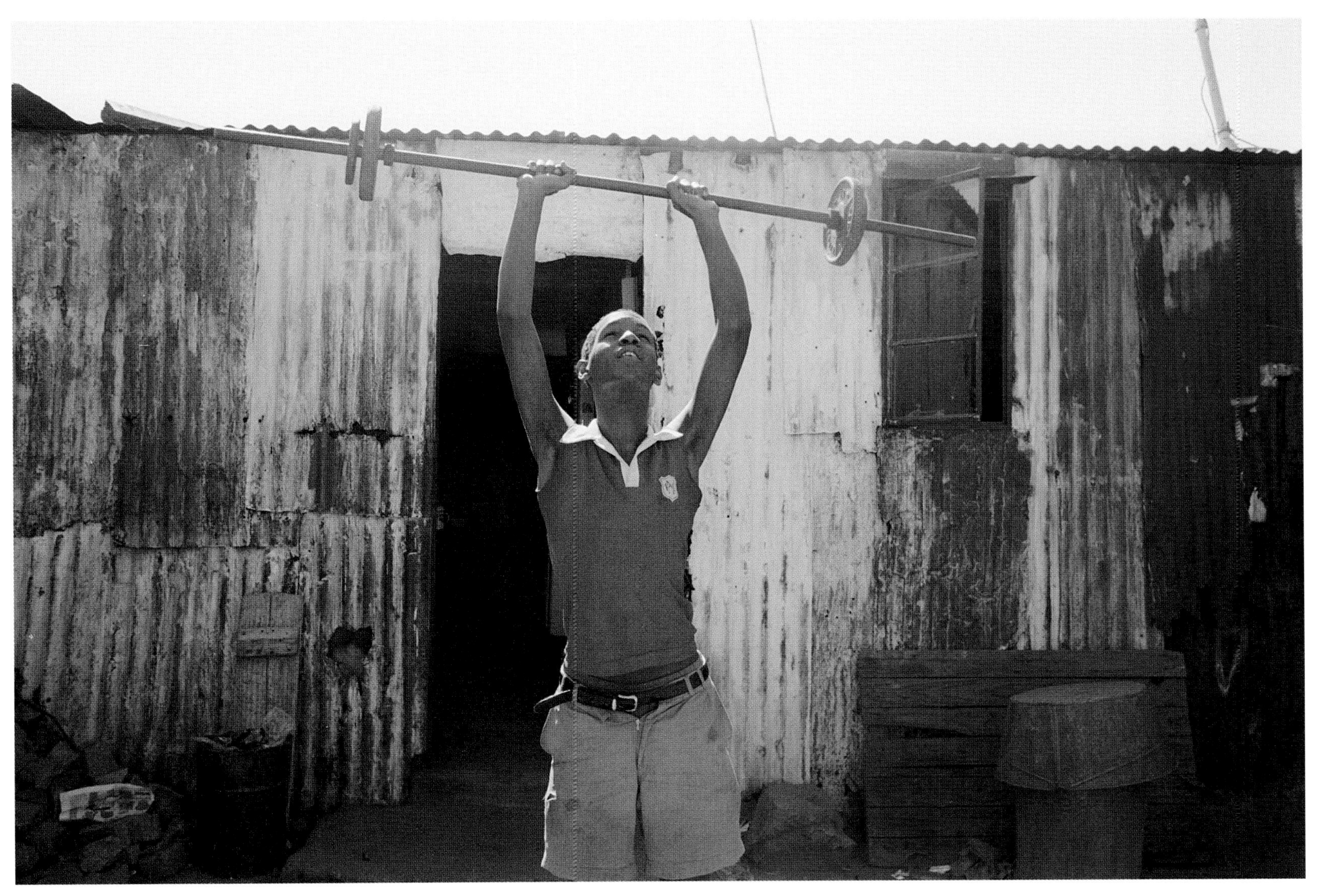

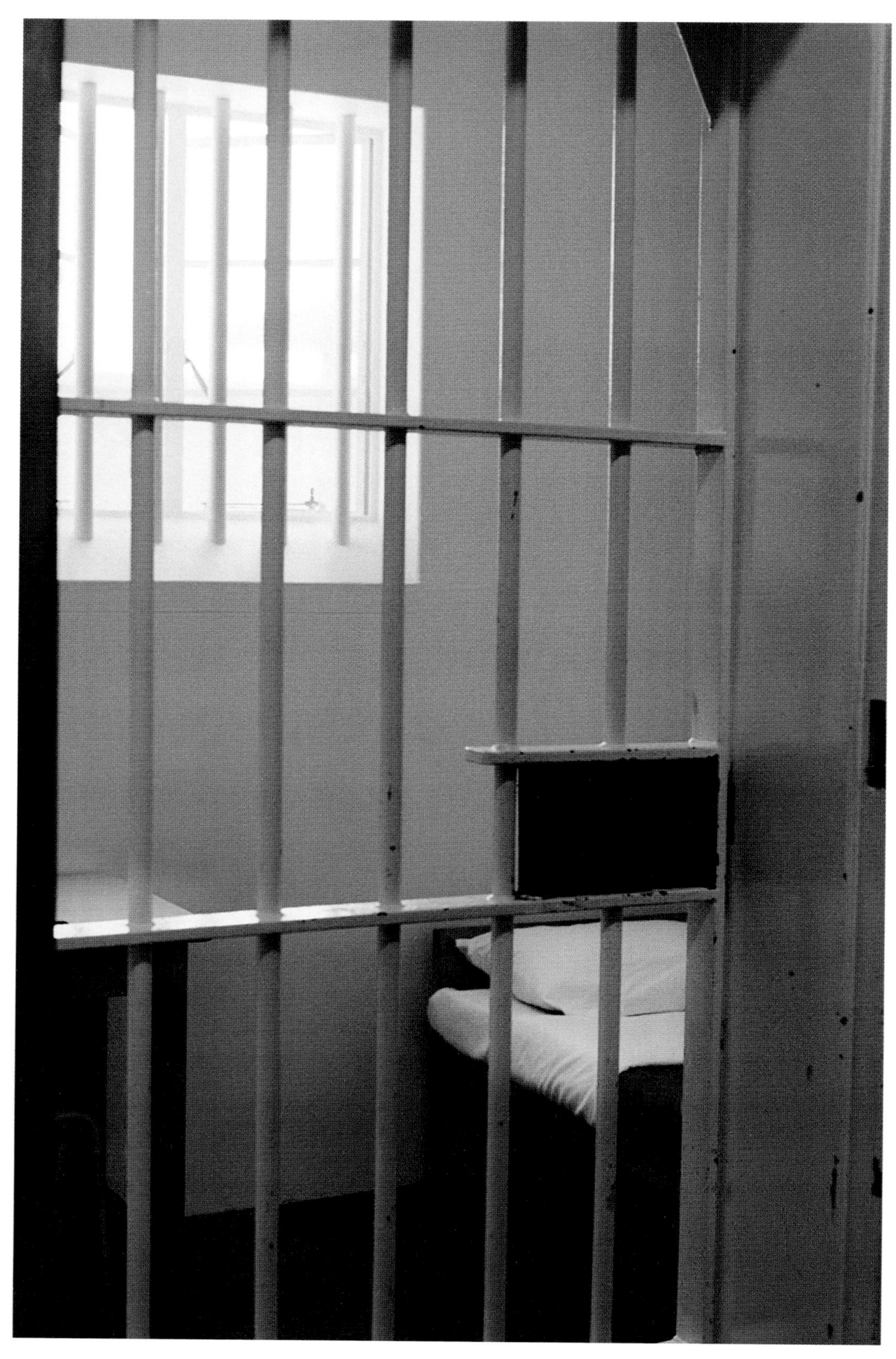

Nelson Mandela's cell on Robben Island where he spent 17 years of his 27 years of imprisonment 1994

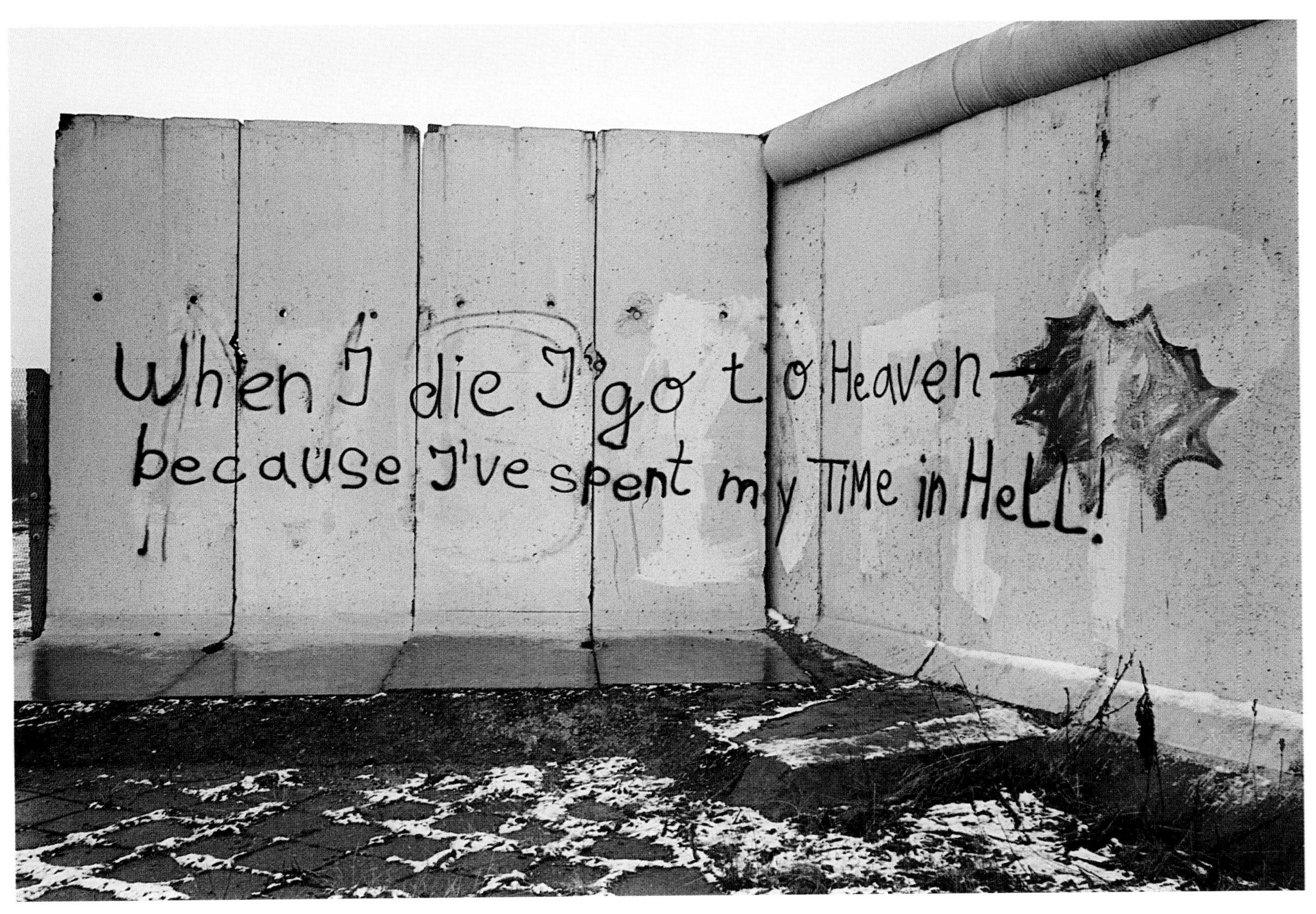

When I die I go to Heaven—
because I've spent my TiMe in HeLL!

1931	Jurgen Schadeberg born on 18 March 1931 in Berlin, Germany.
1946	Photographic apprentice with professional photographer. Studied at the School for Optic & Phototechnique in Berlin.
1947	Photographic volunteer at German Press Agency, Hamburg.
1950	Emigrated to South Africa. Freelanced as photographer. Became chief photographer, picture editor and art director at *Drum*, Johannesburg. Also freelanced for *Time Life*, *Black Star* and *Stern Magazine*.
1956–1960	Wolfgang, Martine, Frankie and Bonnie Schadeberg born to wife Etricia.
1959–1964	Freelanced and worked on staff at *Sunday Times*.
1964	Moved to London and freelanced for Fleet Street (*Weekend Telegraph*, *Observer* and *The Sunday Times Magazine*).
1965	Leon Schadeberg born to Sandra.
1964–1966	Edited photographic magazine *Camera Owner*, later renamed *Creative Camera*.
1968	Moved to Spain. Freelanced for *Lookout Magazine* and others. Studied painting.
1972	Returned to London and taught photography and film-making at Central School of Art & Design. Produced a documentary film "What do you mean by being civilised?"
1973	Hitchhiked throughout Africa on 7000-mile trip.
1974	Directed photographic exhibition for the Whitechapel Art Gallery.
1974–1976	Produced and directed group exhibition "The Quality of Life" which was shown at the opening of the National Theatre Complex at the Southbank Complex, London.
1972–1979	Continued teaching at Central School of Art & Design.
1979	Taught a three-month course at the New School, New York.
1980	Taught at the Hoch Kunst Schule in Hamburg.
1980–1984	Freelanced as photographer in London and Germany for *Die Zeit, New Society* and *The Sunday Times* and *Observer* supplements.
1984	Married television producer Claudia Horvath on 21 April.
1984–1985	Lived in southern France, freelanced and worked on film projects with Claudia.
1985	Came to South Africa to direct documentaries and dramas about black social, political and cultural life in South Africa.
1986	Produced a series of photographic books in collaboration with Claudia. Rescued the former *Drum* archives that were found in total disarray and neglect on a farm.
1986	Charlie Schadeberg born on 19 February.
1987–2004	Continues to hold several photographic exhibitions in South Africa, the United Kingdom, Germany, France and the United States.

INDIVIDUAL EXHIBITIONS

1962	Places & Faces; Adler Fielding Gallery, Johannesburg.
1963	South African Social Scenes; Gorzenich Exhibition Hall, Cologne, Germany. Together with Peter Magubane.
1970	Jurgen Schadeberg – A Retrospective; Hotel Melia, Torremolinos, Costa Del Sol, Spain.
1976	Jurgen Schadeberg – A Retrospective; Central School, London.
1977	Village Faces; Hayward Gallery, London.
1977	Face to Face; Air Gallery, London.
1980	A Portfolio; The Photographic Gallery, Southampton University, United Kingdom.
1981	London Scenes; Photographers' Gallery, London.
1988	A Retrospective; Market Gallery, Johannesburg.
1950–1994	Axis Gallery, New York.
1995	Sof'town Blues; Photographers' Gallery, London.
1996	African Women; Nantes, France. Toured France.
1996	Jurgen Schadeberg – A Retrospective Exhibition; SA National Gallery, Cape Town Oliewenhuis National Gallery, Bloemfontein. King George V National Gallery, Port Elizabeth.
1998	Fifties South Africa; Vue d'Afrique Festival, Montreal, Canada.
1998	The Berlin Wall; Goethe-Institute, Johannesburg. Toured to Namibia and other Goethe-Institutes worldwide.
1998	Selected Images; Institute for the Advancement of Journalism, Johannesburg.
1998	Selected Images; Freedom Forum, Johannesburg.
1998	Jurgen Schadeberg – A Retrospective; Gallery of Photography, Dublin, Ireland.
1999	Jurgen Schadeberg – The Fifties; The Waterfront, Belfast, Northern Ireland.
2000	The Naked Face; Sandton Civic Art Gallery, Johannesburg.
2000	Faced; Carfax Gallery, Johannesburg.
2001	Soweto 2001; Art on Paper Gallery, Johannesburg.
2001	The White Fifties; Crake Gallery, Johannesburg.
2001	The White Fifties; Bensusan Museum of Photography, Johannesburg.
2001	Jurgen Schadeberg – *Drum* Beat: South Africa 1950–1994; Axis Gallery, New York.
2001	Jurgen Schadeberg – Fine Images over 50 Years; PhotoZA, Johannesburg.
2002	The Black & White Fifties & Soweto Today; Tour of South Africa with the Alliance Française.
2002	Voices from the Past – Moving Stills over 50 years; Goethe-Institute, Johannesburg.
2002	The San of the Kalahari 1959; RAU Art Gallery, Johannesburg.
2002	The San of the Kalahari 1959; PhotoZA Gallery, Johannesburg.

2003 The San of the Kalahari 1959; Tour of South Africa to 8 venues with the Alliance Française.
2003 All that Jazz – 52 years of jazz images; Standard Bank Art Gallery, Johannesburg.
2003 A Retrospective of South African Work over 52 Years; Goethe-Institute, Berlin.
2003 Rencontrés de la Photographie Africaine; Bamako, Mali.
2003 Retrospective of South African work touring Singapore, Kuala Lumpur, Bangkok, Beijing, Shanghai, Hong Kong.
2004 Fifties Images; Dorottya Gallery, Budapest.
2004 The San of the Kalahari; Pretoria.
2004 Kliptown Today 2003; Kliptown, Soweto.

Selected group exhibitions

1987 The Finest Photos from the Old *Drum*; Durban Museum, Durban.
1987 The Finest Photos from the Old *Drum*; Market Gallery, Johannesburg.
1988 *Drum*; Impressions Gallery, York, United Kingdom.
1993 Fifties South Africa; Herten, Germany.
1995 SA Images; Foto Forum, Frankfurt, Germany.
1997 Condition Humaine; La Musée du Port, La Réunion.
1998 Under the Tropic: 25 years of SA Photojournalism; Cardiff University.
1999 Africa by Africa – A Photographic View; Barbican Art Gallery, London.
1999 Maverick; Crake Gallery, Johannesburg.
2001 Lengthening Shadows; Stephen Daiter Gallery, Chicago.
2001 Soweto – A South African Legend; German show touring 6 cities: Munich, Mannheim, Stuttgart, Frankfurt, Berlin, Hannover.
2002 Environmental Images; PhotoZA, Johannesburg.
2002 Fine Fifties Images of South Africa; La Maison Européene de la Photographie, Paris.
2004 ARCO, Madrid.
2004 Kliptown 2003; ABSA Gallery, Johannesburg.
2004 Kliptown 2003; Kliptown Centre. A project with the work of 4 students.

Exhibitions directed & produced

1970 Inside Whitechapel; Whitechapel Gallery, London.
1976 The Quality of Life; Southbank Centre, London. A 3-year project for the opening of the New National Theatre.

1969   Paintings; Raymond Duncan Gallery, Paris.
1970   Paintings, Drawing & Photographs; La Palette Bleue, Paris.
1970   Paintings, Drawings & Photographs; Don Pedro Gallery, Carihuela, Spain.

Selected works

PHOTOGRAPHIC BOOKS

1981   *Jurgen Schadeberg*; London: Photographers' Gallery.
1982   *Kalahari Bushman Dance;* London: Jurgen Schadeberg
1987   *The Finest Photos from the Old Drum*; Johannesburg: Bailey's Photo Archives.
1987   *The Fifties People of South Africa*; Johannesburg: Bailey's Photo Archives.
1990   *Nelson Mandela & the Rise of the ANC*; Johannesburg: Jonathan Ball/Ad Donker.
1991   *Drum*; Hamburg: Rogner & Bernhard.
1994   *Voices From Robben Island*; Randburg: Ravan Press.
1995   *Sof'town Blues;* Pinegowrie: Schadeberg Movie Co
1995   *South African Classics*; Randburg: Ravan Press.
2002   *The Black & White Fifties*; Pretoria: Protea Book House.
2002   *Soweto Today*; Pretoria: Protea Book House.
2002   *The San of the Kalahari 1959*; Pretoria: Protea Book House.

FILMS

1987   *Have You Seen Drum Recently? The Black Fifties in South Africa* (35 mm, 77 min.).
1989/1992   *War & Peace: A History of the ANC* (Video, 56 min.).
1992   *The Seven Ages of Music* (Video, 46 min.).
1993   *Drumbeats* (16 mm, 56 min).
1994   *Ballroom Fever* (Video, 26 min.).
1994   *Voices from Robben Island* (16 mm, 90 min.).
1994   *Dolly & The Inkspots* (Video, 26 min.).
1995   *Jo'burg Cocktail* (Video, 56 min.).
1996   *Halala Bomane!* [*Hail the Women!*] (Video, 56 min.).
1999   *Ernest Cole: 1940–1990 Photo Journalist* (Video, 52 min.).
2000   *Deadline* (Drama series, 6 x 52 min.).